The Confessions of Edward Isham

The Confessions of

EDWARD ISHAM

A Poor White Life of the Old South

Edited by Charles C. Bolton

and Scott P. Culclasure

Introduction by J. William Harris

The University of Georgia Press

Athens & London

© 1998 by the University of Georgia Press

Athens, Georgia 30602

All rights reserved

Designed by Erin Kirk New

Set in 11 on 14 Bulmer by G & S Typesetters

Printed and bound by Edwards Brothers, Inc.

The paper in this book meets the guidelines for
permanence and durability of the Committee on
Production Guidelines for Book Longevity of the
Council on Library Resources.

Printed in the United States of America

02   01   00   99   98   C   5   4   3   2   1

Library of Congress Cataloging in Publication Data

Isham, Edward, d. 1860.
   The confessions of Edward Isham : a poor White life of the
Old South / edited by Charles C. Bolton and Scott P. Culclasure ;
introduction by J. William Harris.
      p.   cm.
   Includes bibliographical references and index.
   ISBN 0-8203-2021-8 (alk. paper).
   ISBN 0-8203-2073-0 (pbk. : alk. paper)
   1. Isham, Edward, d. 1860.   2. Whites—Southern
States—Biography.   3. Poor—Southern States—Biography.
4. Murderers—Southern States—Biography.   5. Whites—
Southern States—Social conditions.   6. Southern States—
Social conditions.   I. Bolton, Charles C.   II. Culclasure,
Scott P.   III. Title.
F213.I85   1998
975′.03′092—dc21
   [b]   98-4359

British Library Cataloging in Publication Data available

Frontispiece by John McLenan (1859)

For L.B.

C.C.B.

For N.N.C.

Wife, Friend, Gentle Critic

S.P.C.

Contents

Preface

On September 3, 1902, the *Greensboro Patriot* eulogized Judge David Schenck, who died in Greensboro, North Carolina, on August 26, 1902, with these words: "In any of those characteristics which made him famous there was always recognizable the pure motive and the lofty ideal which inspired confidence on the part of others."[1] The sixty-seven-year-old judge was remembered as a county solicitor, Confederate congressman, superior court judge, and general counsel of the Richmond and Danville Railroad, a position that brought Schenck to Greensboro, where he and his family lived for the last twenty years of his life. Those aspects of Schenck's life that have most interested later historians—his postwar involvement with the Ku Klux Klan and his unsuccessful Democratic candidacy in 1876 for chief justice of the North Carolina Supreme Court—went unmentioned in his obituary. Schenck was energetic in a variety of civic affairs. The work that won him his greatest plaudits was his founding in 1887 of the Guilford Battle Ground Company, which in the years he served as its president succeeded in preserving and memorializing the site of a Revolutionary War engagement. Not surprisingly, considering the distinction of his career, no mention was made of a long-forgotten murder trial in which the young David Schenck dutifully but unsuccessfully defended a poor white laborer named Edward Isham, or Hardaway Bone, as he was known by the court.

Schenck's obituary named his widow and the six children who survived him. The bulk of his papers, including fifty years of diaries, record books of the Guilford Battle Ground Company, and several scrapbooks, passed to his son, Paul W. Schenck, who with his son, Paul W. Schenck, Jr., later gave them to the University of North Carolina's Southern Historical Collection. Somehow, perhaps as a keepsake, a miscellaneous notebook bearing some of Judge Schenck's earliest writings came into the possession of his unmarried daughter, Rebecca. Before her death in 1945, and in an era before accession records were fully documented, Miss Schenck presumably donated this unassuming notebook with a few miscellaneous papers of David Schenck to the North Carolina Division of Archives and History, as evidenced by the simple inscription penciled inside the front cover: "Presented by Miss Rebecca Schenck."[2] The notebook contains the account of Edward Isham's life that he narrated to David Schenck, his court-appointed counsel. We may wonder whether Rebecca Schenck ever read the tale with any interest; perhaps the few childlike squiggles across the end-sheets meant more as reminders of childhood scribbling in her father's old notebook.

Nothing else is known about the notebook, including why Schenck took the trouble of writing out on many pages the story he was told. Except for the fact that Schenck showed a passion for preserving records, whether they documented his state's revolutionary past or his own personal musings, there is no obvious reason for his having kept the notebook, which does not seem to have been used again after Isham's hanging in 1860. If Schenck believed that Isham's statement was potentially publishable, he did not so indicate in his diary; instead he dismissed the whole affair as an unpleasant business. That Schenck also kept for the rest of his days two sheets of notes he apparently made at Isham's trial, one of which is now little more than a scrap of paper, suggests that he felt hesitant to discard any document.

The notebook lay virtually ignored in the North Carolina Division of Archives and History until the two of us rediscovered it working independently of each other. For Charles Bolton, writing a dissertation on the experiences of laborers and tenants in central North Carolina and northeast Mississippi, Isham's story opened a window into the world of the antebellum poor whites. By contrast, Scott Culclasure serendipitously found the Isham narrative while searching for information relating to Schenck's involvement with the Guilford Battle Ground Company, and he quickly began to transcribe it and to locate other documents relating to Isham's 1859 murder of James Cornelius. We shared our research and eventually outlined a book that would bring together primary sources and interpretive essays about the life of Edward Isham. In completing this volume, we hope that the materials gathered here will allow others to glimpse the often sparsely documented but surprisingly complex world of antebellum poor whites, with the accompanying essays offering but a few examples of how one life might be understood.

In the case of the primary documents presented here—the Edward Isham narrative, the transcript of Edward Isham's murder trial, and the newspaper accounts about Isham—we have made some editorial decisions that should be explained at the outset. First, although David Schenck titled Edward Isham's statement a biography, we have chosen throughout to call the document what it actually is: an autobiography. Although this is undoubtedly not a complete account of the life of Edward Isham, and although Schenck clearly played a pivotal role in determining what information about Isham has survived, the narrative unmistakably renders the voice of Edward Isham, however incomplete and filtered through the sensibilities of David Schenck. Second, in the various sources that contain information about the life of Edward Isham, the last name "Isham" can be found spelled alternately as Icem or Isom. To avoid confusion, we have generally chosen to use Isham, the spelling employed by the census enumerators for Carroll County, Georgia, who encountered the Isham family in 1840 and 1850 while making their decennial counts. Finally, we have standardized punctuation, capitalization, and spelling in the primary documents only to the extent necessary to make them intelligible to modern readers.

As we worked to complete this project, we received advice and encouragement from a number of people. This project had its genesis in a presentation by the editors, along with David Kleit (who had also been reading the Isham account), at a session of the 1993 annual meeting of the Southern Historical Association. The small but enthusiastic group of listeners in attendance on the morning of that presentation convinced us that the Isham autobiography needed to be brought to a larger audience. Malcolm Call of the University of Georgia Press immediately recognized the value of the Isham document and has offered us assistance every step of the way.

At the press, Kelly Caudle and Jennifer Manley Rogers managed the editorial process that transformed our accumulation of documents and essays into a finished book. Marcia Brubeck improved the manuscript in numerous ways through her copyediting. The staffs at the Georgia Department of Archives and History, the North Carolina Division of Archives and History, the Southern Historical Collection at the University of North Carolina at Chapel Hill, and the Mississippi Room at the University of Southern Mississippi provided essential aid as we sought to track down information on Edward Isham and his contemporaries over five states and two decades. Marie Sykes greatly helped with typing and photocopying chores.

From the beginning the project has truly been a collaborative one. All the contributors have shared with each other information that they have uncovered about the life of Edward Isham, a fact that can be gleaned from the footnotes in the essays that follow. The editors are particularly grateful to Victoria Bynum and David Kleit for sharing details about Isham's life for inclusion in our annotations of the autobiography. We also benefited from the encouragement offered by a number of scholars, especially Robert M. Calhoon, Sydney Nathans, and Peter H. Wood.

Finally, we thank our families: Leslie Bloch, who offered constant support in innumerable ways; Laura Bloch Bolton, who always provided a diversion with her abundant enthusiasm for play; Nancy Newton Culclasure, who thought it could be done and therefore should be done; Alice Newbern Culclasure, patiently sitting through a conference presentation in Orlando, knowing that when it was over there would be other, more exciting things to do; and David Newton Culclasure, too young to understand why his father spent so much time at the computer but persistent in asking whether it was really necessary. Without their love and encouragement, our work would have been more difficult and less meaningful.

Acknowledgments

The editors are grateful to the North Carolina State Archives, custodian of the David Schenck Papers, for permission to publish the autobiography of Edward Isham. The editors are also grateful for permission to reprint chapter 5, which appeared in slightly different form in the *Journal of Southern Legal History* 3 (1994): 71–96. Chapter 4 was previously published, in slightly different form, in the *North Carolina Historical Review* 70 (January 1993).

Introduction

J. WILLIAM HARRIS

The leather-bound notebook is one of the type often found in the papers of well-to-do nineteenth-century lawyers. Turning the pages in the archives, one finds the commonplace jottings of David Schenck, a young man of serious intention and ambition: quotations from Shakespeare, Longfellow, and other authors to remind him of the qualities of beauty and the ways to wisdom, a list of precedents in assault and battery cases. And then, suddenly, like the famous movie moment when Dorothy steps from the drab black and white of her Kansas farmhouse into the brilliant colors of the Land of Oz, one encounters the "Biography of Edward Icem Alias 'Hardaway Bone.'" And what a story it is—a first-person account, apparently dictated to Schenck and taking up over twenty-five pages, of almost nonstop mayhem, occasionally interrupted with stories of gambling, sexual encounters, or general carousing, a narrative in some ways unlike any other we have from the antebellum South.

The story is not unique in the sense that we have no other images of antebellum poor white men available to us. Indeed, the phrase "poor white trash" conjures up an image that has endured in southern history and popular literature since antebellum times.[1] The image fit in neatly with the antislavery critique of the South, which argued that slavery produced, among other things, a backward and brutal society that condemned most whites to a life that fell considerably short of civilized standards. No one summarized the indictment more succinctly than the British antislavery writer J. E. Cairnes, who wrote that southern society, like all slave societies, fell naturally into "three classes broadly distinguished from each other and connected by no common interest—the slaves on whom devolves all the regular industry, the slaveholders who reap all its fruits, and an idle and lawless rabble who live dispersed over vast plains little removed from absolute barbarism."[2]

A good deal of historical writing has been devoted to the worlds of the nonslaveholding whites in recent years, and it is fair to say that most of it has, implicitly or explicitly, sought to contradict Cairnes's view of poorer southern whites. As long ago as Frank Owsley's *Plain Folk of the Old South,* published in 1949, we learned that the South's nonslaveholders were likely to be respectable yeomen. Subsequent writers have often disputed Owsley's particulars (and each others'), but almost all of them have tended to picture the Old South's nonslaveholders as much closer to "yeomen" than to "trash." These nonslaveholders typically owned land. They worked hard, went to church, and read their Bibles. Their families were as important as anything in their lives, and they hoped to pass along a farm, if not more, to their sons and to marry off their daughters to folk at least equally respectable. They took their politics seriously, and they shared many values with their wealthier planter neighbors and with white Americans outside the South.[3]

This description fits "Hardaway Bone" not one bit. Indeed, Bone, or Icem, as David Schenck called him, or Isham, as his family name should probably be spelled, fits the image of the poor white trash, "little removed from absolute barbarism," as a hand fits a glove. Isham was a bigamist who recounted sexual affairs with a dozen women; a man who, while usually supporting himself by unskilled labor as a miner and in numerous other jobs, preferred to earn his living as a gambler; whose brief membership in a church ended when the congregation expelled him for fighting; and who narrated his life as a passage from one violent conflict to another, beginning as a child and not finally ending until he was arrested, and ultimately hanged, for the murder of his North Carolina employer.[4]

The resemblance of Edward Isham's narrative to the tall-tale traditions made familiar by several antebellum authors alerts us to the problem of its authenticity. Historians' traditional concerns with the validity of their evidence have been sharpened of late by some of the tools of literary critics, who remind us that autobiographies share characteristics with other kinds of accounts usually classified as "fiction." An autobiographical account is, we need to remember, a representation of reality rather than reality itself, and it is subject to some of the same kinds of shaping—by virtue of plot, of inclusion and exclusion, and of considerations for the audience—as more obviously fictional ones. This statement is particularly true for confessional tales that appear under the auspices of the legal system, where one might well expect the tale to be shaped by the hopes of the teller for justice or at least mercy.[5]

Fortunately, evidence both internal and external gives us good reason to think that Edward Isham's autobiography is (with caveats to be mentioned below) both essentially honest and largely true to the events it recounts. The internal evidence is straightforward: the contents of the story are very far from what we might expect from someone hoping to put his actions in the most favorable light possible and, in particular, to exonerate himself from a charge of murder. The autobiography is an almost unbroken record of violence meted out to other people by just about every weapon that might have been available to Isham, from fists to rocks to knives and guns. At one point Isham describes, literally, getting away with an earlier murder. Only toward the end, in Isham's description of the killing of James Cornelius, for which he was eventually hanged, does the reader clearly sense a shading of the truth. Here Isham tries, none too successfully, to portray himself as the more aggrieved party in the fatal encounter. As one of Scott Culclasure's essays here shows, evidence from other witnesses contradicts Isham in important details.

As for the external evidence, here we are indebted both to Isham himself and to the diligent editors and other contributors to this volume. Isham was illiterate, but he seems to have had a sharp native intelligence and a notable memory for details. He names both people and places in his many encounters. Scott Culclasure and Charles Bolton, to whom we owe the "discovery" of Isham's life story, and Victoria Bynum and David Kleit, have tracked down many of these people through surviving census records and other sources. While, understandably, not all details can be checked out, many can, and from these it is apparent that Isham was quite faithful to the facts. We can be pretty sure when and where he was born, we can trace his kin and some of the people he fought, and we can follow his sexual partners; we can confirm, in short, the essentials of his life account. This editorial work suggests many ways of exploring the meanings of this remarkable document. In the essays collected here, several writers have demonstrated how far such exploration can take us into the hard-to-document world of the old South's poor whites.

If Isham seems to have lived largely *for* violence, like most men of his day he had to live *by* work. Charles Bolton's essay explores this world of work. As a propertyless white man, Isham, like tens of thousands of other white men, had to do whatever he could to survive.[6] He was almost constantly on the move, going from one form of manual labor to another. At times he was engaged in more or less simple exploitation of the physical environment, mining or gathering wood. At other times he "worked" on the margins of criminality, gambling (and cheating when he could get away with it) or stealing. Often, though, he had to work for others as a wage laborer. The work was hard and low paid—at various times he drove cattle, split rails, dug ditches, and worked in a lumber mill. His employers included relatives, individual farmers (even a free black man), and big companies like railroads. He could supplement his income with hunting and fishing, but he relied primarily on such opportunities for unskilled work as could be found in the niches of a slave society. As Professor Bolton has already shown us in an earlier book, this dependence on the market was common for truly poor whites in the Old South.[7] Such dependence fits poorly with the common picture of whites in areas peripheral to the plantation regions as largely relying on a "family" or "household" economy relatively independent of market pressures.[8] Of course, only a man with a family can engage in a family economy, and as Bolton notes, Isham was temperamentally unsuited to the kind of rootedness that usually comes with a wife and children.

And yet, despite his unusual aversion to settled family life, Isham was still in his own way embedded in a world of kinship.[9] These kin, as David Kleit emphasizes, were important resources in many ways. At one point Isham worked with his brothers in lumbering, at another for his brother-in-law as a herdsman. Kin were important also in protecting Isham from what generally proved to be the short arm of the law. At various times he fled from the sheriff to his mother, brother-in-law, or aunts and uncles (it was no doubt a matter of considerable convenience, from the legal point of view, that some kin lived across county or state borders). Of course, with a man like Isham, kinship did not necessarily entail friendly relations; in one of the scrapes he describes, his brother John broke a chair over his head. Still, Kleit's essay, which places Isham's narrative in counterpoint with the story of the much wealthier George Swain, shows how vitally important kinship relations were even in a rough frontier area like Georgia's northwest.

When Edward Isham was arrested and tried for murder in 1860, he was in North Carolina, far away from his network of kin and friends. As Kleit and Scott Culclasure observe, this remoteness may have been one reason that the law finally, and decisively, caught up with him. After he killed James Cornelius, Isham had no one to run to, no one to rally to his defense, no one to appeal to the governor for clemency. In two essays here, Culclasure explores the murder case in detail and places it in the context of other murder and manslaughter cases in North Carolina in the 1850s. Remarkably enough, Isham seems to have received an able and conscientious defense from young lawyer David Schenck (to whom we owe his autobiography). This circumstance suggests that poor white men in the antebellum South at least sometimes had access to a relatively even-handed justice. The point is amplified in the light of Culclasure's examination of memorials and petitions to the governor concerning thirty cases of convictions for murder or manslaughter in the decade before the Civil War. As Culclasure demonstrates, when a man could show some evidence of support from at least a portion of the local community in which he lived, he had a fair chance of receiving a pardon, as half the perpetrators did in these cases. While richer and more respectable folk had some advantage in these appeals—a reputation of consorting with free blacks was a serious impediment to clemency—local communities sometimes appealed in behalf of poor perpetrators, poor victims of crime, and even a "poor but hardworking stranger" from Ireland. Such concern for legal equality may have helped to blunt, in perception at least, the otherwise sharp distinctions of status and wealth among white men in the South. If so, the disabilities under which black men and all women labored served only to heighten the relative status of even the poorest of white men.

Victoria Bynum's essay here on the women in Isham's narrative teaches us a good deal about the disabilities as well as about some of the ways in which white women could subvert them. Bynum has already done more than any other historian to uncover from court records and other documents the world of poor white women in the Old South.[10] Bynum's subtle reading of Isham's autobiography alerts us to one of the suspicious silences of the text. Women appear in many roles, as lovers, wives, and fighters, sometimes appreciated and sometimes abandoned but never as victims of Isham's violence. Is it possible that a man who lashed out at almost anyone who thwarted him, or even happened to be in the vicinity during his rages, did not do so as well against the women in his life? Both our contemporary experience and the often melancholy stories that have left their traces in southern court records suggest that the opposite may have been true. Moreover, while attorney Schenck seems to have recorded most of Isham's account verbatim, evidence of selective editing points to what Bynum calls his apparent "distaste for overtly sexual language." There may have been, in other words, even more sex and violence in Isham's life than his own story reveals.

Bynum's attention to the literary tradition of the "tall tale" is most helpful in understanding the roles of the women in Isham's narrative. As she notes, the tall tale and the literature that evolved from it depicted a relentlessly masculine world. Women, when they appeared, were often the kind of "wild" women portrayed by Isham—rough and tough, sexually active, prone to drink, ready to pick up an ax and attack an enemy. Yet in addition, the women in Isham's life—or at any rate in his life story—provide most of the few moments of peace and respite from violence. One of them, his wife Rachel, is truly exceptional in the narrative as one who "never quarrelled" with him and even managed to keep him sober for six months.

With few legal rights and little formal power, poor women in particular often had to rely on men for protection in a difficult world. At times, they found themselves in consequence obliged to abandon one man for another despite the bounds of respectability and of the law, as pretty Mary Brown abandoned Isham himself. Despite all their disadvantages, the women of Isham's narrative seem notable for their spirited independence and their determination to make the best of what was often not a good lot in life.

Finally, Joseph Reidy brings together several of these themes in his essay on Isham. Like Bolton, Reidy stresses Isham's class position and the ways in which that position constricted the possibilities for a man with so few material resources, especially land. Reidy also explores the ways in which the culture of lower-class whites in the Old South both resembled and differed from that of the solid yeomen. On the one hand, much of Isham's fighting was, beneath the violence, structured around notions of male honor that appeared most dramatically in the duels involving individuals with more aristocratic pretensions. At the same time, his relationships with women were sharply at variance with public morality in the South, and his frequent mingling with people of color in relatively egalitarian contexts signified what was, in the eyes of slaveholders, perhaps the most dangerous tendency of poor whites. The relationship between poor whites and slaves is certainly one that deserves more attention from future historians.

Just as Bynum uses the southern tall-tale tradition to illuminate Isham's autobiography, Reidy places it in the context of the popular literature of what might be called the "Murderer's Confession." Here Reidy has noted numerous parallels, even though Isham's story was never (until now) published. Most of the confessions recount similar childhoods of poverty and deprivation and similar stories of early corruption leading inevitably to later catastrophe. Yet even against this background, Isham's story stands out, not least in its utter lack of remorse and its tone of feisty defiance.

All these essays teach us a great deal about the world of poor whites in the South, a world that remains quite elusive. Indeed, after three decades of immensely productive research, we know far more about life and culture among slaves than among these poor whites. Edward Isham's autobiography is a very rare case of one poor, illiterate man's story told in his own words. We can be grateful to the editors for making it available to us and to the contributors here for showing how much even a single such document can tell us. Together they do us an invaluable service, helping us "read" Isham's narrative by tracking down verifying details and by providing the multiple contexts in which the narrative must be understood—from the Old South's economy to its courts and its systems of kinship, gender and race relations, and slavery.

And yet readers should not be content to read *about* Isham and his world; they should read his story in his own words. His narrative, with its directness and vitality, vivifies a world that has almost disappeared intos legend and folklore. Edward Isham seems to embody in his person what one historian, writing in a very different context, called "a restlessness and a capacity for violence at the center of the human spirit that can never be contained."[11] Certainly, neither the restlessness nor violence in Isham's life were contained until that day in May 1860 when the state of North Carolina hanged him.

1

Autobiography of
Edward Isham,
Alias "Hardaway Bone"

Was born in Jackson County Georgia[1] was 5 years old at the time of the cold Friday and Saturday. My father[2] was dissipated and spent what property he had and moved first to Biles Mills, then to Carroll County Georgia and went to digging gold. Every one dug where he liked and could get a location. I lived with my father in the suburbs of a little town called Pine Mountain town.[3] I went to school five days to a man named Scroggins and never went again. I recollect when 10 years old fighting a boy named Jake Blakenship, and hurting him with a rock. I went home scared and told my father and he told me I was a fool for being scared. I then fought a boy called Wm Garthard[4] and bit him severely and then hit him with a rock. I also fought with William Compton. I had long hair and he held me by it, and beat me severely. I went home to my father and he cut off my hair so I could have a fair chance and I went back and whipped him. The next difficulty I had was at Hickstown town with two boys named McQuister and I whipped them both. I was then growing up and began to work for myself in the mines and made money. Tom Godfrey and I quarreled about water for washing gold and he came to cut down a dam I had made and we fought. He struck me with his shovel and I threw rocks. His friends came and I ran off to my fathers and got his rifle and fired on Godfrey but some one knocked up the gun and I missed him. He then struck me with a shovel and we were parted.

McCurdy one of his friends went to town for a warrant to Squire Ruffin and I pursued him. I found him at the Squires and fell on him with a hickory stick but was arrested by the Squire and sent to Carrollton to jail—was put in at midnight. On the next day, I broke out by prying up the floor and creeping out under the house. I went home by dusk, ate my supper and fled. I went to *DeKalb* County to my uncle Charles Icems,[5] a farmer and remained there some time. I went up to Nance's creek[6] and joined the Methodist Church at Centrals meeting house. John M. Smith was the preacher. I got into a difficulty with a negro about a fishing pole and tried to cut him but was prevented, for this they turned me out of the church.

I went with my Uncle and a party swimming in Nances creek. We all got drunk and I had a fight with Wash Smith, a free negro, who choked me very severely. We went on towards home and stopped at Henry Islys Grocery. There the free negro got drunk, and I drank no more and got sober and watching my chance I fell on him with a rock and beat him very severely but we afterwards made friends. I left next morning and went to Forsythe County Georgia to my Uncle Hardin Millers[7] and dug gold. There while working on the road,[8] a man accused me of stealing milk from his spring house and I tried to kill him with my axe but was prevented. I went then to a little cross road town called "Shake rag town" and got to gambling with one Rogers, who tried to cheat me and we had a fight but neither was hurt. I then went back to John Millers and then started for Carroll. On the way I stopped at a muster at Howells Mills[9] in Cocke County.[10] There two men were quarreling and one refused to fight because he was sick, the other pressed on him and I volunteered to be his second, so they went to fighting and during the fight one Gus. Wood, a great bully, attempted foul play and I struck him with a heavy hickory stick and hurt him badly. The men were then parted and the other party gathered in force to mob us and we fled. I was not yet grown at that time. I went back to the mines in Carroll County and in a short time I was at a Grocery in Pinetown and got into a difficulty with Thomas Wallace and hit him with a glass tumbler. I then took a stick from my bro in law and beat him severely. I was not arrested. About this time I used to visit a girl named Jane Mobley and we were intimate. A young man named Thompson was courting her and one night he eavesdropped me and next day told Jane what I had said to her. I was half drunk and went down to the Grocery and Thompson and I fought about it and were parted but got at it again and fought til he hollered. I then made him go with me to Jane and acknowledge he told her a lie. While fighting Thompson one of my friends struck at Thompson a rock and hit me and hurt me badly. I continued to dig for gold and made money. I went up to "Cross Ankles" to a horse race and heard my brother had a difficulty with one Maxdale and there was a warrant out for him. My brother lived in Macon county Alabama, so I went back with him. A fellow named Jim Cordry went along and got into trouble and we started back. On the way at "Silver Hill" Tallapoosa [11] a county I got into a difficulty with one Bratch Ward and we fought desperately, his sons and nephews joined him, and Jeff Chambers [12] a friend of mine joined me. We fought at a grocery, and we finally whipped them and they shut themselves up in the grocery. In the fight I accidently struck Chambers, with a heavy stick and nearly killed him. I helped him home. The other party gathered a crowd to kill us and we fled to the woods. I then came back to Carroll County and commenced mining. I got into a difficulty about water again and had a fight with rocks with a party who tried to brake my dam and I whipped them off.

They went for a warrant for me and while they were gone I broke up their rockers and shovels and fled to DeKalb county again to my Uncle James Icems. I stayed a month or so and returned. Everybody was afraid of me and no officer would attempt to take me. I continued to visit Jane Mobley in Pinetown, and at a frolic there Jim Fletcher and I fell out about her but Jim was afraid of me but Jims father [13] who had just got out of the penitentiary for killing a man sent me word, he intended to kill me at sight. I replied I was tired fighting and did not wish any difficulty. I was afraid of old Fletcher and thought he would kill me.

In the meantime while mining a man named Porterfield and I fell out about a spike and in a fight he stabbed me on the shoulder. I followed him to Hargroves [14] store to kill him but was prevented. In a few days I went to Hickstown town to sell my gold and on my return near home I met old Fletcher in his wagon. He stopped and said now was the time to settle our "fuss." I told him I did not want to fight, but he commenced to get down and seeing a pistol in his bosom I ran up and struck him over the head with a 4-lb bowie knife and then ran. He rose and snapped his pistol. I then turned and threw my knife at him but missed. I went then to my brothers and got a double barreled gun and went up to see Jane Mobley. While there my brother came running and told me that Fletcher and a crowd were after me, so I escaped to the woods. I then went to Cocke county [15] and from there to DeKalb, stayed 3 months and returned to the mines and went to work. Everybody was afraid of me. They took out warrants for me and I fled to Walker county on the Tennessee line but returned shortly again. I went with my Brother to whip one Adams intending to kill him with a rifle if he resisted but he was not at home. We then went to Macon county Alabama to one Hutchinsons [16] and remained a short time. While in Alabama before, I was engaged to [a] girl who married Peter Windley after I went away. I saw her and she and I agreed to run off and we did so. Her name was Mary,[17] she was 20 yrs old and very pretty. We came to Carroll county, to my mothers in Pinetown. My father had taken up with another woman and left my mother alone. I went up to Walker county to hunt a house, and split rails for James Fulcher [18] at 25 cts pr hundred, til I got money enough to bring my mother and Mary up there. Here I raised one crop but getting into several fights, at a logrolling and at Gordons Grocery, I sold out and went up to Chattanooga to work on the Rail Road. While working there I got into a difficulty with some Irishmen boat hands about some lewd women and left the Road and went aboard the "Sam Markin" [19] on the Tennessee river as fireman.

I worked there sometime, and was on the boat when the volunteers from Mexico returned.[20] We were anxious to get to Chattanooga soon and I made a bet with Charlie Harris engineer about when we would get there. I won. Next day we quarreled about it and he struck me with a board and I stabbed him under the collar bone with my pocket knife. The boat hands took Harris part and I fled. They swore vengeance on me and whenever the boat came to town I would leave to avoid them. I took to gambling for a living and lost all I had even to my pistol and knife.

I then took up with a man named Napper, a wild fellow who lived over the line in Walker county, who had a farm and some negroes. He gave me a pistol and knife to fight Harris. Harris never attacked me. While riding one of Nappers horse[s] to water one day I saw him and one Jake Floor[21] fighting and I ran up and hit Floor with a brick bat and ended the fight. I then took Nappers horse and fled to Georgia but in a short time returned and found there was something wrong with Mary, she did not treat me kindly and I became jealous. I pretended to leave home one day, but rode up to "Bald Hill" where I could see my cabin and watched. I saw my wife start for water but stopped in a cabin on the way—so I slipped up there, it was about dusk, and I saw a fellow named Noah Vineyard sitting on a bed with her and his arms around her. I went round to the door and spoke and Mary ran out and went off. Vineyard denied anything wrong but I told him he must fight. He said he would fight me in town, so we started for town and while riding along, he threw suddenly two rocks at me and struck my hat. I drew my revolver and fired three times at him but never hit him. I then jumped off and pursued him with my bowie knife. In the race he fell and commenced begging and said he was badly shot so I left him and went over to Nappers and sent a man to see about it and found out he was not shot at all. I stayed at Nappers til Christmas and we were all invited to a "Treat" at Gordons Mills[22] in Walker County. We played Chuck Luck[23] all day and all got drunk. I fought one Scott Victory and got soundly beaten. Napper and Tracy fought and I interfered. Tracy struck me and I struck at him with my bowie knife and scabbard, forgetting in the excitement to unsheathe it. This saved his life and all made friends. I stayed with Napper a few months drinking, hunting and gambling. I then went to Chattanooga and stayed with my mother. She sold cakes and whiskey and boarded work hands for a living. I had but little to do with Mary. There were warrants out for me and I fled to Ringgold Georgia[24] stayed 3 or 4 months drinking & gambling, then returned. On Sunday while drunk I went to a [ ][25] House and got into a difficulty and a fellow named Bernice slipped up behind me and knocked me down with a rock. It knocked me senseless and next morning I came to at my mothers, not knowing who did it. I was hurt badly and it scared me very much. I reflected on my course and for awhile was disposed to do better, but warrants issued for me and I fled to Ringgold and became very intimate with a gambler named Riese [?]. We went to a House and got into a fuss and a warrant issued and I was tied and carried to jail but Napper sent over in five or six days and bailed me. I stood my trial and had to pay the cash. I then moved my mother down to Ringgold.[26] She sold cakes for a living and I gambled. Mary (Windley wife) had married Hiram Brown[27] and they had moved to Ringgold too. We never had anything to do with one another. I went up on the first train of cars to Tunnel hill.[28] Got drunk at a grocery. A friend of mine named James got into a difficulty with a man named Parrigan and being too drunk to fight, I took his place and fought Parrigan. I then went back to Carroll Co. to Pinetown. At Cross Ankles I was playing marbles for money and a fellow from North Carolina was drunk and kicked out the marbles. I was going to fight him but he drew a bowie knife and I left him and went back to Pinetown and came back to the grocery where he was. He was dancing and swearing he could whip any one. Jef. Chambers my old friend was there and told me to watch him knock that fellow down but I told him to hold on, he had imposed on me and I intended to whip him. Just then he danced on my toes and said are you the man that was playing marbles. I said Yes, and immediately struck him with a rock I had in my pocket and knocked him down; but he was too much for me. I couldnt hurt him any more; but Chambers and my friends kicked him and hurt him badly and he hollered. I then left him and went back to the mountain to work. I worked four or five months and made a considerable amount of gold. I gambled every night and fought chickens on Sundays. We had a regular cockpit made for the purpose.

One day two men named Morgan and Gray came from Hickstown town to Pinetown and swore they could whip any Democrat in Pinetown and they intended to whip the Icems before they left. I was eating supper and some one told me the news. I got a piece of a shovel handle which I had sawed off for a bludgeon and went up to the grocery—Warner Lyon's—and asked Morgan if he had said what I heard. He said he did and I knocked him down with the shovel handle. Gray then jumped on me, and a friend of mine named

Murphrey joined in the fight. The candles were knocked down and we fought for a long time in the dark.

Grays eye was knocked out by a weight thrown by some of us, and he ran and we pursued him with rocks and he left town very badly hurt. Morgan ran out the back door in the meantime and escaped. I was then boarding with a man named Price and was keeping his daughter. A warrant was issued for me but the officer was afraid to take me. I concluded to leave and a brother in law of mine named Wm Bivings[29] and I started to Cobb Co to dig gold. Near to Powder Springs[30] while traveling in the wagon we met "Gray" and being afraid he would get a crowd and kill me, I jumped on my bro in laws horse and ran. I went to Marietta and from there to my Uncle John Everetts[31] in Cobb Co Georgia. I got there early in the morning. Soon after eating I discovered 8 or 10 men with guns coming after me and I slipped out and ran. I came to Vickerys creek[32] and swam it, which chilled me and stiffened me. I went on til I came to Chattahooche[33] and tried to swim it but couldnt and came out, and went down to Govins ferry and crossed over to an Aunt of mine and waited til Bivings came. He went to work in the mines but I concluded to leave and went up to Lumpkin Co[34] and stayed four or five months. While there I took up with a woman named Thirs. Murphy[35] and had a severe fight with a man who had been keeping her. I became intimate with two men named Ball Gilbert and Jim Gilbert. They had a feud with a grocery keeper named Thomas Ball. We went up to his grocery one day and broke up everything he had decanters, glasses and barrels and his fiddle. He went down to Deloneger[36] and got a warrant for us. They caught Ball Gilbert and put him in jail. I was going down next day to hear about it and overheard some officers who were after us and hurried back and told Jim Gilbert and we went off to the woods. Ball Gilbert broke jail but he and Thom. Ball compromised, and Gilbert worked, to pay the damage, for Ball. I was there a few days after and while Ball was away from home, made his wife sell me a pair of shoes and paid her a bill on a broken bank. I never counterfeited any and knew nothing about it. I then left went to my Uncles in DeKalb and he bought me tools and I went to Cobb Co to dig gold. We had to cook for ourselves and, while at my Aunts one day, I met a pretty girl named Mary Dagget and hired her to cook for me, and we took up together. I made very little gold and concluded to leave. I took this girl with me to DeKalb to Isleys old grocery and there left her and went back to Pinetown in Carroll and went to work.

My Bro in law bought up a drove of beeves and hired me and Bill Clemmens to drive them to Montgomery Alabama. We drove them there but found them due sale (I had three brothers John lived in Macon Co Ala, James and William, my name is Edward). From Montgomery Bill Clemmens and I went down to Macon to my Brothers, built a little shantie on the river and rafted lightwood to Montgomery.

While there I took up with Mandy Hatch, (a sister to Mary Windley, whom I took from her husband Peter Windley and a sister in law of my brother John). We used to meet at a spring of nights. Bill Clemmens and Bivings watched me one night and we came near fighting about it. Shortly after this, I shot a mans hog that used to eat our things at the shantie and he took out a warrant for me and I left and went over to my brothers; but John was very angry because I had taken up with his sister in law and we got into a quarrel. He struck me with a chair and cut my head badly. I went over to Franklin [37] and got Dr. Wilburn to sew it up. He put seven stitches in it. I then went down to the shantie and Bivings gave me some money and I took the cars [38] and made my way back to DeKalb Georgia. I then took my sister, Bivings wife, and we went back to Pinetown. My father was living there with another woman. Shortly after that I had a difficulty at Hickstown town with a circus company but had no fight. Also with Allen Fletcher who had the bowie knife I struck his father with [   ] [39] but we did not fight, friends interfered. I was then in my prime, about 24 years old, was a great wrestler and could not be thrown down. My thumb was then off. It was blowed off one Christmas morning, before breakfast by the busting of a gun when I was only 10 years old. [40] I next got into a difficulty with Dick Fenley, [41] a great bully and we agreed to have a set fight. My old friend Jef. Chambers was my second.

Fenley bit my finger very badly, the prints are there now and tore my flesh off my bosom with his long nails. I bit him too and gouched one eye nearly out; but they parted us before either hollered, though Dick got the best of the fight. When we were done I jumped on Fenleys son, who had shown some foul play, and beat him til he hollered but he gouched one of my eyes very badly. The bite on the finger got very bad and I could not work for a long time.

After some months I went to my mothers at Ringgold, and continued to gamble and drink. I was at Brown's grocery one day and an Irishman wanted to bet five dollars he could whip any man in town. His name was Clark. I took him up and we fought. He was too drunk and I whipped him and got the money. I then helped a friend named James Gordon in a fight at the same grocery and was arrested and Gordon paid the fine and got me off. I took up with Caroline Brown a sister of Hiram's (Mary's husband) and she became pregnant. I then quit her and married Rachel Webb,[42] the daughter of a widow in Ringgold. I drank very hard and got completely out of money and concluded to go back to the mines in Carroll. I worked made some money and sent for my wife, and we went to housekeeping in Pinetown. A man named New[43] claimed the place I was working but I made him leave and we became mortal enemies, but nothing passed between us for some months. I could hear of his threatening to kill me. One Saturday evening I went up to Biving's grocery, and when Biving was shutting up, I was closing the shutters and heard "New" say "stand aside." I looked round and saw him coming with his gun and cocked it but just then my father ran up and caught the gun and the crowd interfered. I then made at "New." I had a rock in my pocket and I took it out and struck him a severe blow. We then parted but afterwards stripped off and took a fair fight and I whipped him. We were both arrested next morning but compromised and "New" paid all costs, and we made friends.

I then went to work, and continued sober and civil for some months and made a good deal of money in the "diggings" but I then got too intimate with a free girl and took her to "Warner Lyons" grocery one night and there got into a difficulty with Betsy Wedding a girl Lyons was keeping. This made a feud between us, and I went back one night to get some liquor and they wouldnt let me in. I saw her on one side of the door with a double barreled gun and Lyons on the other and heard Lyons tell her not to be afraid but to shoot as "he passes back up town." This enraged me and I went to Bill Williams and borrowed his rifle and watched for three hours by moonlight to shoot "Lyons" but couldnt get a chance. I then went to his door and told him I would see him in the morning. In the morning, I took an axe helve and went up street to Lyons grocery and pushed off his hat and cussed him but he wouldnt fight and I left him. (No preacher could ever live or preach in Pinetown, one lived there once and they tore down his fences and run him off. There never was any school there.) I then went to work, kept sober and made some money and was peaceable for six months. While sitting in my house one Saturday evening I heard a noise up at the grocery and went up. I found two Smiths and a hired hand of mine named Hendricks[44] quarreling. I started to take Hendricks off and Smith threw a rock at me. I returned another and hit on the burr of the ear and every body thought he was dead. I ran down home got my money and left but came back and found out about midnight that he had come to. A warrant was issued for me and I went off to DeKalb Co. I then concluded, I would slip back and get my wife but "New" my old enemy discovered me at my bro in laws and told it. While asleep that night, the house was surrounded by about 30 men and the bailiff one "Slaughter" took me prisoner. They took me that night to Hickstown. I tried to get an opportunity to escape but failed. Next morning, I told the guard I wished to step aside and I watched my opportunity and fled. They fired three pistol shots at me without effect. I went to Marietta, took the cars and came to Ringgold and sent down for my wife. My mother had moved back to Chattanooga and we went over there.[45] I gambled and drank very hard and spent all my gold. I there took up with one "Ann Baldwin" and finding out she had some money, I concluded I would get it. I won a little money rolling ten pins and sent my wife to her mothers, who was then living in Walker County Georgia. I went with this girl to walk one day and met a man who had been her old beau. He tried to take her away and I struck him with a rock and hurt him severely. "Anne" and I then went on to her fathers and as we came up he came to the door and cursed me for being with his "gal" and fired a horse pistol at me but missed. I then threw a rock at him but struck the door, then put at him with a knife but he shut the door on me. In a few days "Anne" and I ran off and went down to Pinetown—and from there to Atlanta Georgia. I had a quarrel with her in a few days, and with some money I got from her, I took the cars and went to [my] wife on Hiwassie Rail Road.[46] I found her sick, but when she recovered we moved 5 miles above Chattanooga on the Nashville Rail Road[47] and went to work.

I was civil and worked hard for about six months, until one day I met an old enemy named McAustin at a grocery and we had a fight. I was very drunk and he got my head between two bars of iron and would have killed me but I hollered and they took him off. I then borrowed Joe Dobbins rifle and watched on the RRoad for three or four days to shoot him. He found it out and one of his friends came to me and begged me off from it as McAustin had a wife and three children. I got into a fight with a Runnels about that time and hit him over the head with the rifle and hurt him very badly but did not kill him. About this time my wife had a child, which was born dead. She was an easy good tempered woman and never quarreled with me. I quit work on the Rail Road and went to gambling. I met a fellow named Jim Waters and he beat me and we then made a bargain to go "halves in cards and in our fighting." So we followed up and down the Rail Road between the river and Chattanooga, playing cards with the hands or any one we met. I dressed well, had plenty of money, and supplied my wife with all necessaries; but took up with a woman named "Beck Caldwell" with whom I stayed more than my wife, but she never complained. I got into a fight one night about her with a fellow named Moore, he had a revolver and rock and I had a little pocket pistol. He hit me with a rock, and I snapped the pistol. We then fought on. I snapped the pistol three times on his side but it would not fire. I then took the muzzle in my hand and beat him severely. It was a desperate fight and we were both hurt. The Marshall while trying to arrest us had his arm broken by a rock from the crowd but the police finally took us. Moore was fined twenty dollars but I got off.

Waters and I continued to play cards on the Rail Road and won a great deal of money. We once had a "big game" with a gambler named Smith and won $100 and came near getting into a big row. Waters and Smith played with a bowie knife beside them. I finally became tired of this and went down to Pinetown to see Jane Mobley but she had moved. I followed her to Campbell county and we agreed to run off; but she found out I had a wife and we parted. I came back to Chattanooga and Tate Miller a grocery keeper and Waters and I cheated a fellow named "Napper" out of $250 by packing cards, and we fell out about dividing the money. Waters and I finally concluded to move to Arkansas. I bought a gun and went off without paying for it but the fellow pursued me and took it back. We then went on with our wives to Johnston County Arkansas.[48] I worked here splitting rails, hunting deer and bees and enjoyed myself better than ever before in my life. I stayed there six months and got along very well.

Waters had a "set fight" with a fellow named "Steve Thompson" the greatest bully in the county and I was his second. "Waters" whipped him and it created a feud between their friends. The Blacks were on Thompsons side and hated me very badly. I moved down on the river and followed the business of getting lightwood for the boats, so did the Blacks and it made us worse enemies. One day while sitting in my cabin Pete Daily and another fellow of Black's crowd came by and my dog barked at them and Daily said he could whip the dog and me both and we had a fight. The other fellow hit me with a stick while we were fighting and my wife ran him off with the axe. I then went down to Jim Iverys and while there old Black and three others came in pursuit of me. We went out to fight Ivery promising to help me but he backed out. Old Black threw a tomahawk at me and as I dodged it cut my coat. I drew a pistol and shot him in the back as he ran but never killed him. I then pursued him with a knife around the house and overtook him but the other three hit me with rocks and sticks and got me down and took my knife and I had to holler or be killed. So I hollered and they let me off. My wife came up with my rifle, hearing the noise but the Blacks went off before I could recover and use it. Waters and I then left and went up to Fort Smith.[49] I followed gambling there for some time, made money and had no fights; but after awhile I got intimate with Ben Harmand a half breed indian (in the mean time my wife came, she then had one son whom we called James). Ben Harmand had a feud with a man named "Reeder" and we went to "Fort Smith" one day to fight it out.

They met at a grocery where we were all drinking. I had two pistols and two bowie knives. They fought and I kept the crowd off with my knife. Harmands pistol wouldnt fire and he then drew a bowie knife and cut Reeder very badly. Reeder then broke loose and ran and as he went I fired my pistol at him but missed him. We pursued him to the grocery but were shut out. Reeders friends came and we fled. We went out to John Borrows and got money and horses and went down to my old home in Johnston county leaving my wife. From there we went to Napoleon and then to Memphis, there to Paducah, being afraid we would be taken, then to Smithland. Here I fell in with "Jim Ingles" whom I knew in Chattanooga and we gambled together for awhile but lost all our money. I had but a half dollar left, and went to chopping to get some; but meeting a wagoner I went with him to "Nashville." There I got on the hind steps at the back of the cars and rode down 80 miles until the conductor discovered me and made me get off. I sent word by the brakeman to my mother to send me money to come home. She sent a girl by whom I had a child in Atlanta for me and she met me up the Road, had the child with her but I did not know her. We came on down to Chattanooga. I was very ragged and my brother who had just come from "Ducktown" with a good deal of money he had won gambling gave me some clothes and some money and hearing of "Reeders" death at Fort Smith I left on the cars and went to my Brothers in Macon Co Ala. There I made shingles & cut lumber and rafted to Montgomery awhile, and there three of us formed a company to fish and gamble.

We had a grocery on the river and used to have great crowds there fishing and playing cards—until some fellows came from Opalachee[50] to play cards and one drew a pistol on me at the table. I was afraid to get up, but watching my chance I sprang to my double barreled gun jumped out of his way, and as I ran around to the other door cocked it and fired at him just as he was coming out. The whole load struck the door jam and missed him. He ran and the other barrel was not loaded. We afterwards made friends. A few days after this I went up to "Franklins" grocery on the Rail Road and had a serious affray with one Blake Edwards, in which he tried to shoot me but was prevented by my Brother, who drew a sword over him. I continued fishing and gambling at my shantie on the river for some time, and finally took a raft and went down to Montgomery and stayed five or six days gambling and drinking. My brother and I went into a house there before we left to get breakfast. It was kept by an old negro woman and she was drunk. While we were in there, I saw a pocketbook on her table which I stole and then left. It had about $25.00 in it. We then came on to the shantie and continued our former course of living.

Until at one Proctors, at a frolic there was a general feud created by "Rushing" a partner of mine. We went from there to "Franklins" grocery again and I gambled with a negro there from whom I won some money.

I then went on home with Proctor that night and a man named "Jim Runnels" with whom I had an old feud followed me there, having his cousin with him. While in bed in the night heard them talking about jerking me out and stamping me but concluded to wait til morning. In the morning he came up to me but I avoided him and left with Susan Proctor, with whom I had agreed to run off but after talking with her an hour some distance from the house, we went back to get a drink of liquor. When I came up Mrs Proctor told me that "Runnels" had loaded his pistol and said he intended to kill me. I then said "this fuss had been going on long enough and I would end it." I then went about a quarter of a mile to my brothers and got his double-barreled gun and went back to the house.

When I got in the yard I called to Runnels and told him we must end this fuss now. He came to the door and as he slipped on the ground, I shot him with the whole load of small shot in the breast. He exclaimed "Oh Lord" and reeled off behind the house (and as I afterwards learned died soon after). I then fled to the Coosa river.

(Runnels had hit me across the back with a rifle gun and hurt me badly and I had often avoided him because I thought he was armed to kill me.)

I left Proctors next day, intending to get onto an island in Coosa river but had no boat. I slept on the cane that night, until my brother came and took me across the river to *"Harland* Bones." I stayed there all night and then made my way on foot to "Hickstown" to my brother-in-law Edwards, who then went on with me to Cartersville, avoiding all public notice, went on to Gilmore county [51] and on to Ducktown. At Gilmore county I first assumed the name of *"Harland Bone."*

I stayed at Ducktown all night sold my double barreled gun and played cards for money. From Ducktown [52] I went down to the Rabun gap Rail Road [53] and worked for a man named "Alexander." Here I took chills and was unable to do anything more and went to playing cards for a living, and at a Grocery near by, one Saturday had a difficulty with a man named "Ripley" who afterwards pursued me to the Road to whip me but the hands kept us apart. We both had weapons. I then went to Luckaseage river [54] and worked for Thompson, then over to the Tennessee river and worked for a free negro named "Fax." [55] Then from there I came to "Brindle town" N. C.[56] stayed all night, saw them fighting chickens and gambling. I left there next day and went to Morganton,[57] then to Statesville,[58] then started for the Rail Road [59] to work, but stopped on the way at "James Lesleys" [60] for whom I dug a well and did some other work and finally married his daughter *"Mandy Lesley."* [61]

I then bought 10 acres of ground from Charlie Carlton,[62] cleared some and raised a crop. At the election I had a fight with one "Clarke" who returned me to the Grand jury.[63] One "Beavers" then told some lies about me and my mother in law and I threatened to kill him, intending to do so if he didnt retract and he swore the peace against me.[64] To avoid the officers I went up near Taylorsville [65] and remain[ed] a week or more, gambling with some white men and free negroes and won some money. I then came on back and moved into *Lincoln County* [66] and lost all my crop. I ditched for various people and made money. My wife had one child and died. *"James*

Cornelius" [67] then hired me to clean out some old ditching while he was gone to market. When he came back we went down to look at the work and he expressed himself satisfied but said the price was too high, it was more than the law would allow me. I told him "I would see about that" and I sued him for $7.00 but got judgement only for $5.00.[68] I expected to get this money to redeem my gun which I had pawned to Dr Motte[69] but Cornelius stayed it. I went home that night to Reed's where my child was and got pretty drunk.[70] I told Reed I was going to the fishery and started with that intention, and came by Wash. Sherrils[71] and exchanged knives with him til I came back. As I went through the bottom, I cut a small sweet-gum stick. I then came on to the house of James Cornelius[72] and stopped in one of his negro houses and inquired if I could get across the ferry and they said I might if the bateau was on this side.[73] I went on to the river but there was no bateau. I then hollered there for a long time but no one came. I was then on my way to the fishery, and had never premeditated "*Cornelius*'s" death.

I then started on back to go down to another canoe landing, but as I came up to Cornelius's house again, he was sitting just[74] inside the door washing his feet in a bowl. We both said good morning. It was Sunday.[75] And he then asked me if I would come in and I did so. I walked and stood leaning against a table in the middle of the floor. I then told him I had come by to get that little money he owed me. He replied that he had stayed it. I told him I would take $4.00 and let the other dollar go to the cost if he would pay it, and he said "I have but 25 cts in the house." I replied "You can get that amount anytime if you want it" and he then pointed to his gun over the door and said it would be settled if that would settle it. I replied "You need not talk that way to me, I am not afraid of you or your gun." He then stepped to the porch with the washpan in his hand and threw out the water. I stepped to the porch too and asked him if he intended to pay me and he said he did not. I then struck him with the stick, and he jumped off the porch and hollered for the negroes and picked up a piece of plank or a shingle, and we both struck at one another about the same time. We struck about two licks apiece, one lick hit me over the left eyebrow. He then ran off a few yards towards the kitchen and called for "Jim" a negro of Littles,[76] and "Jim" came running with a rail in his hand. Cornelius and I were together again and when I saw the negro I dropped my stick and drew my knife and as "*Cornelius*" came at me, I cut him two or three times. We ceased a moment and I gathered a rock to throw at "Jim" but when I looked up, the negro women were holding "Jim" and Cornelius was running towards his horse and I threw the rock at Cornelius as he galloped off on his horse. (To this statement he added some very strong and solemn appeals as to its truth and correctness.)[77] My thumb was cut pretty badly in the fight; when it was over I left very quickly. I passed by "Bill Sherrill"[78] in the bottom and told him not to tell anyone he had seen me. I went on to Reeds, got a gun and some powder and lead and told them I was going to Beattus ford,[79] but I crossed the river and took right up the bank 5 miles and then took the big road, avoiding houses on the way by taking the woods. At sundown I came to Daniel Finks[80] and got supper but became uneasy and left and traveled on when the moon went down. I laid down by the road and went to sleep. I had been drinking since my wife died and was sick and was very tired. This was in 5 or 6 miles of Taylorsville. In the night I heard horses crossing a bridge and I thought then they were in pursuit of me. Before day I got up to go and was so tired and sore I could hardly walk. I stopped outside of the road a while and Charlie Carson[81] and another passed nearby me, looking for my tracks in the road. I was in full view but they were looking down and did not see me. I then took off the road, went through the woods around Taylorsville and waded a stream above a factory and took into the mountains.

An old man whose house I came to gave me some breakfast but I was too sick to eat. I traveled on taking mountain roads, got my supper at a house and went on. Slept under a tree. It rained all night on me. Tuesday traveled in same way over the mountains, got some dinner at a widow's. It rained all day. Left "Boone"[82] 6 miles to [unreadable]. Wednesday got to Taylorsville Tenn[83]—passed around it—met Waugh[84] in the road, had a little talk. That day the hand bills with $200 reward came on by stage and Waugh overtook me as he said in the mountains. I suspected him from the first but couldnt get away. As he came up, I gave the road and as he jumped off his horse I wheeled to strike him but my foot slipped and I fell. He then tied me. We stayed at Jones that night. They kept me tied, but I watched my chance and got off and took the river but they pursued and took me again and brought me on to Newton[85] jail.

Hanged 25 May 1860[86]

2

Edward Isham
and Poor White Labor
in the Old South

CHARLES C. BOLTON

"He is a ditcher," the Salisbury *Carolina Watchman* announced in a May 1859 advertisement describing for Piedmont residents a white laborer who had murdered his employer, the slaveowner James Cornelius of Catawba County, North Carolina, over a disputed wage. The Charlotte *Western Democrat* added to its announcement of the same day that the accused murderer, Edward Isham, had worked in the gold mines of Georgia and had "been speaking of going to Gold Hill for a week or two," a mining region in nearby Rowan County.[1]

Most people in North Carolina's Piedmont undoubtedly knew individuals like Edward Isham, white men who owned little or no property and lived and worked on the margins of the local economy, eking out an existence by laboring for other whites. In fact, despite proslavery rhetoric that stressed how black slavery eliminated the need for a white laboring class in the antebellum South, such people were a common sight throughout the southern states. In 1850 perhaps as many as 100,000 adult white males throughout the region worked for wages as day laborers or farm laborers.[2] During the 1850s this segment of the Old South's nonslaveholding white population swelled as the fortunes of the region's poorest white citizens generally declined during the cotton economy's boom years preceding the Civil War.[3]

Few records survive that detail the lives of the Old South's white laborers. In fact, the autobiography that Edward Isham left behind stands as one of the few extant life histories of the antebellum South's poor white class. As such, the document offers an invaluable though imperfect source for understanding the poor white experience in the antebellum South.[4] More than a catalog of his frequent brawling and his scrapes with the criminal justice system, Isham's autobiography also provides a detailed look at how a poor white laboring man made a living in the antebellum South. What does Edward Isham's autobiography, viewed alongside evidence from the lives of other white laborers, reveal about the nature of poor white labor in the Old South?

Like Isham, most white laborers in the antebellum South performed a variety of tasks—ditching and mining as well as an assortment of other jobs—and like Isham, most white laborers moved around quite a bit. On the other hand, much of Isham's life was clearly atypical. After all, few white laborers—and few other antebellum Southerners, for that matter—were executed as murderers, and fewer still killed their employers. While all white laborers were extremely mobile, few wandered the southern countryside to the extent that Isham did. In addition, Isham's immensely fragmented family life was somewhat unique, as most white laborers maintained relatively stable family lives—resembling in this respect their wealthier neighbors—and relied on the labor of family members to ensure their economic survival.

Over the course of his short life, Edward Isham worked at a variety of tasks. During the 1840s and the early 1850s, Isham worked periodically as a gold miner in various counties throughout north Georgia. In between stints as a gold miner, he performed a number of other jobs. In the late 1840s, Isham labored as a rail splitter and tenant farmer in Walker County, in northwest Georgia. He then worked for a time on a railroad being built near Chattanooga, where his mother sometimes lived. He returned to the city periodically and often found temporary work on one of four railroad construction projects in the area during the 1850s. Isham also served briefly as a fireman on the Tennessee River during the late 1840s. Returning to Carroll County around 1850, Isham took a job driving a herd of his brother-in-law's cattle from Carroll County to Montgomery,

Alabama. He then went to nearby Macon County, Alabama, where two of his brothers lived; the trio "built a little shantie on the river and rafted lightwood to Montgomery."[5]

Sometime in the 1850s, Isham struck out for the West, perhaps in part attracted, like most landless people, by the promise of cheap land and economic opportunity that the frontier seemed to offer. Isham settled briefly in Johnson County, Arkansas, an upland county in the northwest part of the state with terrain similar to that of his north Georgia homeland. The Isham autobiography offers few clues about Isham's motives for moving to Arkansas and no evidence that Isham became a landowner once he arrived. Instead, Isham worked as a common laborer splitting rails for area landowners and as an independent contractor gathering firewood and selling it to local riverboats on the Arkansas River. He also supplemented his food supply, and probably his income, by "hunting deer and bees." Isham soon left Arkansas and returned to Alabama. After briefly resuming the logging operation with his brothers in Macon County, he headed to north Alabama and east Tennessee, where he worked as a laborer for brief periods for a series of individuals, including one stint as a laborer for a free black farmer who lived near the Tennessee River.[6]

After Isham completed his series of jobs as a common laborer in Alabama and Tennessee, he headed to the North Carolina Piedmont to look for work on the Western North Carolina Railroad, a line under construction in Iredell County during the late 1850s. Isham never reached the railroad construction site; instead, he began to work as a ditcher for various people in Iredell, Lincoln, and Catawba Counties. His last employer, James Cornelius of Catawba County, employed Isham to work on a ditching job, but after working two days, Isham quit and asked Cornelius to pay him eight dollars. Cornelius reportedly replied that "that was too much, but he was willing to pay what was right." Isham sued Cornelius over the disputed wage and received a judgment of five dollars; however, Cornelius had the judgment stayed. When Isham later confronted Cornelius about payment of the judgment, the two men fought, and Isham killed his former employer.[7]

The occupational mobility described in Edward Isham's autobiography was fairly typical for white laborers, most of whom worked at numerous and different jobs at a variety of locations over the course of their lives. For example, a landless laborer from Chatham County, North Carolina, worked at eighteen different locations in Chatham and Alamance Counties from 1844 to 1856, including farms, cotton factories, a furnace, a flour mill, and a sawmill. The Tennessee Civil War veterans' questionnaires collected in the 1920s provide many additional examples of poor whites who developed diverse skills in order to make a living in the slave South. Miner Cole of Tennessee recalled that his landless father found work before the Civil War as a farmer, a well-digger, a rail splitter, a land clearer, and a house carpenter. Similarly, James Powers remembered that his father made a living in antebellum North Carolina making rails, gathering herbs and roots, and clearing land.[8]

If most white laborers could match Edward Isham in the range of tasks they performed to make a living, few could equal his incredible record of geographic mobility. For Isham, relocation was often initially undertaken to avoid prosecution for various criminal offenses, not to look for work. Economic necessity, however, did require most white laborers to move frequently so that they could take advantage of often sporadic work opportunities, but these moves were generally neither as often nor as far as Isham's travels. Upcountry Georgia, for example, contained numerous landless whites who never left the area yet moved around a great deal. The sketchy details of John Poss's life during the 1850s illustrate this reality. Poss worked as a landless farmer in De Kalb County in 1850. In 1856 he was working as a laborer on the farm of G. B. Hudson in neighboring Gwinnett County, and by 1860 he had relocated with his family thirty miles west, to Cobb County, where he toiled as a landless farm laborer.[9] Few of the white laborers working alongside Edward Isham in Lincoln County, North Carolina, in the days before he encountered James Cornelius could claim to hail from a locale as distant as Isham's north Georgia. In fact, practically all of the laborers who headed households in Lincoln County in 1860 were natives of the state, and most had been born in Lincoln County or one of the six counties that adjoined Lincoln; only 4 percent of the county's laborers had been born outside the state of North Carolina. Even so, many of Lincoln County's white laborers regularly moved around the immediate area in the search for work. For example, Jonathan Anthony, born in Lincoln County and working there as a landless farm laborer in 1860, had worked as a landless farmer in nearby Gaston County in 1850.[10]

The existence of black slavery in the South dictated the kind of occupational and geographic mobility experienced by Edward Isham and other poor white laborers. Slavery both stunted the growth of industrial wage positions and limited the need for white workers, as well as the wages paid to them, in the region. Because many Southerners who needed additional labor for their various enterprises relied on slaves, the market for white labor in the antebellum South was one of infrequent work and low pay. Of course, rural laborers in other areas of the country during the same era, such as farm hands in the Midwest, also found their work to be seasonal. Farm laborers in the Midwest, however, could at least command high wages during the peak agricultural periods.[11] White farm workers in the South, and indeed all types of white laborers in the region, had to compete with slaves, and white laborers ultimately worked as a supplemental labor force, filling sporadic and temporary needs in various niches of the southern slave economy. William Banister, who grew up before the Civil War in Campbell County, Georgia, expressed this fact of poor white life succinctly when he recalled that his "father worked by the day when ever he could get work."[12] Thus in order to take advantage of what were essentially short-term work opportunities, poor white laborers had to possess a wide range of marketable skills, and they had to be willing to relocate regularly. In short, they had to be extremely flexible.

Within this world of shifting job opportunities for poor whites, some types of work were clearly more desirable than others. For instance, the mining that Edward Isham often performed did not always offer a steady income but could at times provide a life of relative independence. Isham grew up in the Pinetown neighborhood of the upcountry county of Carroll, where his father labored as a miner. Isham claimed that during his father's day "every one dug where he liked and could get a location." Especially during the early days of the country's first gold rush, which occurred in the southeastern Piedmont from North Carolina to north Georgia, mining offered landless individuals an independent means of making money. Some landless miners searched for gold on unoccupied land, keeping anything they found for themselves, while others leased property from landowners and payed as rent a percentage of any gold that they found.[13]

Other landless men, however, mined for wages on the land of wealthy individuals or emerging mining companies, a form of work that generally provided, by comparison with independent mining, only infrequent and relatively unprofitable employment for landless whites. For example, from 1852 to 1854 John Fowler worked as a miner on the property of Mary G. Franklin, who in 1850 owned land in Cherokee County, Georgia, that was worth over $25,000. Fowler and several other white laborers worked sporadically at Franklin's mine and at her sawmill, receiving fifty cents a day, compensation that Franklin generally paid in either food or clothing. These laborers, however, did not depend totally for their survival on the wages that Franklin paid. During the period he worked for Franklin, John Fowler apparently owned some livestock that he grazed on the open range; in one instance Franklin docked him for a day he had supposedly worked because he had actually been "looking for hogs."[14]

Edward Isham, however, seems to have worked as an independent miner in Georgia. When he searched for gold in Carroll County, Isham was apparently still able to mine unoccupied land into the early 1850s. His disputes with other people who tried to jump his claim to a particular piece of mining territory and his fights over area water to wash the gold suggest that no one owned the land Isham excavated in Carroll County. In fact, when Isham quarreled with Elijah New over a mining location, neither man apparently owned any land in the county.[15] Isham periodically worked as a gold miner as late as the early 1850s, but the north Georgia gold rush had peaked and begun to decline more than ten years earlier.[16] Thus by the time Edward Isham first went to work as a miner in the early to mid-1840s, the opportunities for independent gold diggers were declining. By the early 1840s, miners had already removed most of the gold from the area, and the increasing resettlement of the north Georgia region by whites following the federal government's successful removal of the Cherokee Indians made unclaimed or unoccupied land less available in the region.

Isham considered a return to mining in North Carolina in the days before he murdered Cornelius, but he apparently had little interest in joining the local miners of iron ore who worked in Lincoln County; rather, Isham envisioned a return to the gold mining he had learned from his father. Although the iron ore miners in Lincoln County appeared to be independent diggers, not wage miners, Isham might have considered such mining more arduous and less profitable than the more familiar life of gold prospecting. What Isham perhaps did not know was that the gold-mining area to which he thought of going, the Gold Hill district in Rowan County, was a mining area dominated by corporately owned mines and worked by white wage and slave miners. Had he ever gotten there, Isham would have found at Gold Hill little of the independent gold digging he had practiced in north Georgia. The independent digger's way of life had essentially disappeared in the North Carolina Piedmont by the late 1850s.[17]

Isham also occasionally toiled as a logger, another form of work that offered a fair amount of independence. When Isham cut and sold timber with his brothers in Macon County, Alabama, during the 1850s, opportunities apparently still existed in the county for small and independent logging operations, despite the growing presence of corporately owned sawmills and wage loggers. In 1850 fifty-four employees worked in eight Macon County sawmills. One sawmill, the Steam Mill Company, was sizable enough to employ fifteen men. Likewise, when Isham moved to Arkansas and worked at "the business of getting lightwood for the boats," he undoubtedly worked as an independent contractor collecting timber from land he did not own. In fact, Isham's efforts in this area apparently conflicted with those of other people who were similarly engaged. At least some of these disputes may have involved the right to appropriate a particular stand of timber, a battle similar to the one Isham waged with Georgia miners, fighting over the right to dig in a particular piece of ground owned by none of the contestants.[18]

Many poor whites worked as independent miners, loggers, hunters, or herders, and Edward Isham seemed to favor such a lifestyle, whenever possible, over wage labor. At one point, Isham left a job on the railroad to become a gambler, trading the regimented life of building railroads, with its regular wage, for an uncertain but more unconstrained life spent trying to part his fellow rail hands from their earnings. Isham obviously had a quick temper and a violent personality, so it is hard to imagine him taking orders easily from anyone for very long. Isham, however, likely had no choice but to work occasionally for wages — on the railroad, as a farm laborer, as a ditcher. The independent laboring opportunities readily available when his father was a young man had gradually constricted as most of the South was transformed from a frontier to a settled, agricultural society and as the market economy penetrated farther into the southern backcountry with the passing of every year.

Although most poor white laborers were increasingly forced to work at some point in their lives as dependent wage earners, white wage laborers, especially those who did agricultural work, were generally employed only to fill short-term labor needs, often by individuals who had little or no access to slave labor. When Isham went to Walker County, Georgia, in the late 1840s, he worked temporarily as a rail splitter for James Fulcher, a landless farmer with no family. Fulcher, who likely had a specific task to complete but no one in his household to help him, employed a transient white laborer such as Isham as perhaps the least costly answer to a temporary labor problem. Likewise, George Hudson of Gwinnett County, Georgia, who in 1850 farmed sixty improved acres but owned only one slave — a seven-year-old girl — hired white labor to work on his homestead almost every year from 1847 to 1856. During this period ten different white laborers worked for Hudson, but most worked for only limited terms. For instance, D. C. Rutledge, who farmed as a tenant himself, worked brief stints for Hudson in January 1850 and 1851.[19]

Individuals who had capital to spare and had more substantial labor needs generally bought or hired slave laborers, workers whom employers could subject to a greater degree of control and discipline than white laborers.[20] A frequent complaint among employers of white labor was that white laborers were irresponsible and would never stay with any one task for a sustained period. In fact, employers often suggested that the short terms of employment for white laborers sprang simply from the fickleness of poor white workers. John Wilkes, who ran a sawmill near Charlotte, North Carolina, in 1856, complained to his father that the white labor he employed was undependable. Wilkes claimed that he had "had enough of white labor in this country—for it appears to me that they are the gentleman & I the workman—they absent themselves when they please, throwing more work on my hands." His laborers' "independence" meant, he complained, that "tommorrow morning I may have 7 or 8 at work or I may have only one." Wilkes had only employed white laborers because, beginning his enterprise in midyear, he had been unable to get black slaves, most of whom could be hired only at the beginning of each year for an annual term. Wilkes obviously wanted a labor force he could more easily control, and he had already made plans to secure slave labor for his operation once the new year began. Despite Wilkes's open displeasure with white labor, the white laborers' work must have been at least minimally satisfactory, for Wilkes's sawmill was developing so well that he had made plans to build a gristmill nearby.[21]

Poor white laborers could obviously exercise more independence of movement than slave laborers, and many white laborers did leave their wage jobs when they felt like it. Isham quit his job splitting rails for James Fulcher once he "got money enough to bring my mother and Mary" to Walker County. And why should he not have left? After all, Fulcher would have turned Isham out once the task at hand was complete. Isham planned to make a crop in Walker County; the rail-splitting job was merely a temporary expedient to acquire some ready cash.[22]

What the Charlotte sawmill owner John Wilkes and other employers of white labor often perceived simply as irresponsible behavior on the part of white laborers may thus actually have reflected shrewd calculation regarding available opportunities. For John Wilkes's white laborers, the construction of railroads through the North Carolina Piedmont during the mid-1850s temporarily swelled the number of available jobs for white laborers and in the process increased the value of other types of labor that poor whites normally performed. In 1855, a Piedmont observer noted that "labor is high here . . . It is the railroad that makes labor high here."[23] Thus the white laborers on whom Wilkes had to rely in 1856 to cut his lumber probably had several other, more attractive and more profitable employment options available to them.

Similar recognition of the range of obtainable employment may have led Edward Isham to turn to ditching soon after he arrived in the North Carolina Piedmont. With area railroad construction increasing the number of job opportunities for poor white laborers, Isham and other white wage workers in the area had the rare luxury of choice among a variety of employment opportunities. If he had to work for wages, Isham undoubtedly favored the often unsupervised lifestyle of a ditcher over the more structured regimen of a railroad worker. After all, when Isham did his ditching task for James Cornelius, the latter reportedly "was gone to market." Since railroad construction had also raised the price paid for other types of poor white labor in the area, ditching, although difficult work, held out the promise of very attractive wages for white laborers. While Cornelius had balked at paying Isham more than seven dollars for less than two days' ditching work, a court had decreed that five dollars was a fair wage; however, this sum far exceeded the typical wages (generally no more than a dollar a day) paid to poor white ditchers.[24]

Besides increasing the number of employment opportunities for poor whites and raising the value of poor white labor, the construction of railroads throughout much of the South during the late antebellum period also eased the movement between jobs that was often desired by or required of poor white workers. A northern traveler who briefly encountered a white laborer on a train in upcountry Georgia in 1856 discovered that the man was en route to a job making shingles but had recently worked at several other occupations, including labor on a riverboat, at a sawmill, and as a farmer. The

Yankee visitor noted that the laborer had come aboard the train with a bag containing about a week's worth of provisions; the poor white man indicated that he would return to his wife and children once he finished making shingles. Likewise, a landless man named James W. Overcash planted a crop of wheat in Rowan County, North Carolina, in the spring of 1860, and then in May, he took the train south to Charlotte, North Carolina, and secured a job working for wages. Although his exact task is unknown, Overcash clearly did not like the work. He told his brother that "I have to do a good many things hier that I do not like and for that reason I will not stay hier longer than I can get money to go some wair els." Overcash especially disliked the close supervision his employer exercised over his employees. In less than a month, Overcash apparently raised enough money to travel to Panola County, Mississippi, and by June 1, he was working as a plow hand for a Mississippi cotton farmer. His quick relocation to Mississippi suggests that he traveled to his new job at least partly by train.[25]

Although white laborers often made frequent moves looking for work and seeking economic opportunity, they did not wander the countryside aimlessly. Many journeyed to locales where family and friends provided them with job opportunities.[26] Isham often relied on family to help him make a living. When he mined for gold in Forsyth and De Kalb Counties, Isham worked the property of landowning relatives, an arrangement that probably offered as much freedom and profit as his squatter mining efforts in Carroll County. Isham's brief stint as a livestock driver involved transporting his brother-in-law's herd of cattle, and when lumbering in Macon County, Alabama, he worked with his brothers who lived in the county. He also relied on his mother on more than one occasion to provide him with both a physical haven and an economic one.[27]

Although Isham, like many other white laborers, could often count on kin, especially more prosperous relatives, as sources for work, Isham's family arrangements did not resemble those of the vast majority of his poor white peers. In fact, Isham's failure to maintain a stable household for any length of time clearly distinguished him from most poor white laborers. While few of Isham's 1850

Pinetown neighbors remained in the district ten years later, even most of those who had migrated in search of work largely managed to keep their families intact. For example, William Peoples, who had been a miner in Pinetown in 1850 but was working as a tenant farmer in De Kalb County in 1860, lived throughout the decade with his wife, Nancy, and their five children.[28]

White laborers often counted on the labor of spouses and/or children as an important contribution toward ensuring household survival. Some wage positions for white laborers, especially farm laboring jobs, offered opportunities for white laborers to use all of the available labor of their households, providing in the process greater financial compensation than would have been earned by an individual working alone. Just as unclaimed mining or timber lands helped numerous white laborers avoid total destitution, opportunities for the employment of the entire family enabled white workers to offset the fleeting and sporadic nature of the demand for wage labor in the antebellum South.

Some wealthy Southerners who sought white laborers actually preferred those with a family. When Calvin J. Cowles of Wilkes County, North Carolina, sought a white laborer for one of his farms in late April 1861, he instructed his agent that "it would be best to get some fellow who has a family & wants to hire" to move to a house on the property "& take charge of the farm[,] work for wages on it[,] etc." Cowles undoubtedly desired a laboring man with a family not only because he wanted to avoid locating a drifter on his farm — someone like Edward Isham — but also because a man with a family would have a wife and children who could provide additional labor around the farm, generally at reduced wages.[29] George Hudson regularly received the advantage of such arrangements when he hired poor white families to work on his farm in Gwinnett County, Georgia, in the 1850s. When William Duck's family worked there in 1856, Duck and his three boys did all kinds of general farmwork — from ditching to plowing to harvesting. Hudson paid William Duck fifty cents a day and the boys twenty-seven cents. In addition, the Ducks mended shoes for the Hudson family, a task that Mrs. Duck probably helped to perform. When Elizabeth Bradbury's family worked for Hudson off and on between 1849 and 1852, the Bradbury labor pool encompassed Elizabeth, two of her sons, and one of her daughters. The sons generally did farmwork, including picking cotton; the daughter worked at domestic chores for the Hudsons, and Elizabeth performed both kinds of labor.[30]

Edward Isham, temperamentally unsuited to preserving a settled family life, obviously failed to reap the kind of economic benefits that many poor white laborers often wrung from their families. In this and other ways—such as his frequent and far-flung travels around the South—Isham's life differed importantly from that of most white laborers. Yet the autobiography also suggests that many of Edward Isham's experiences as a poor white laborer were quite typical. Isham made a living both by taking advantage of unused or unclaimed resources and by working for wages. In addition, like most other poor white laborers, he essentially formed part of a casual, mobile labor force for the slave South, meeting an intermittent and temporary demand. Poor white laborers did not have to be criminals to experience the kind of job instability reflected in Isham's autobiography. In a mature, settled slave society like most of the antebellum South during the 1850s, the market for poor white labor would always be varied, fleeting, and unstable. The life of the laborer ultimately offered survival, though not generally advancement. Even so, few poor white laborers ever lashed out at their employers as Isham did. Most white laborers, facing Isham's situation with Cornelius, undoubtedly just moved on to the next temporary employment opportunity.

3

A Stereoscopic View of the Frontier: George Swain, Edward Isham, and the Resettlement of the Cherokee Country

DAVID H. KLEIT

While the American frontier has long been portrayed as the arena for triumphant individualism, John Mack Faragher, in his study of life on the Illinois prairie, has perceptively shown the importance of family and community for successful frontier settlers.[1] Other recent scholarship has drawn attention to the many people who did not prosper on the frontier.[2] Like thousands of other American settlers, aspiring planter George Swain and backcountry brawler Edward Isham each arrived on Georgia's frontier with the Cherokee Indians during the decade before the United States forcibly removed the Cherokees in 1838. They both lived many years on and near what had been the land of the Cherokee Nation, an area that was called the Cherokee country even after the Cherokee people had left. Considered together, the lives of these two very different men provide a more three-dimensional perspective on the frontier than could be achieved by examining more similar individuals. Their experiences suggest that the support of family and friends often made the difference between success and failure for the wide variety of people who resettled the Cherokee country.

Edward Isham and his poor white peers have remained largely

out of the view of historians. In preparation for Isham's 1859 trial for murder, however, Isham's attorney recorded a detailed account of Isham's life. This document provides a rare and valuable counterpoint to the more accessible lives of his wealthier neighbors like George Swain. Swain arrived in the Cherokee country as an already prosperous adult planning to achieve great wealth by trading land and building a plantation. Isham grew up not far from where Swain settled, but Isham's family was poor. George Swain received substantial financial support from his North Carolina family, especially his brother David, but his associates in the Cherokee country did him more harm than good. Isham's family had little money to give him, but his many relatives and friends in and near the Cherokee country regularly provided him with important assistance in other ways. Swain pursued a series of high-risk endeavors that wasted his brother's money. Isham made quite resourceful use of the help available from his family and friends throughout almost all of his life. Dissimilar in many ways, Swain and Isham both relied heavily on assistance from other people in their efforts to seek success and to elude misfortune. Ultimately, neither man succeeded.

By the time George Swain arrived in the Cherokee country, he had substantial resources available to use in trying to make the fortune he craved.[3] Born in 1792, he grew up in Buncombe County, North Carolina, in a religious and prosperous family.[4] His father, also named George Swain, was a slaveholding postmaster, merchant, hat maker, and doctor who also operated a small farm. Historian John Inscoe has called him "one of Asheville's earliest and most prominent citizens."[5] The younger George Swain moved to Georgia when he was twenty-five. His wife died a decade later in 1827.[6] According to the 1830 federal census, George Swain then lived in the Georgia upcountry with his young daughter and eleven slaves.[7] In 1832, Georgia gave out by lottery the over 6,000 square miles of Cherokee land it claimed. Swain enthusiastically entered the booming land market that followed.

Swain settled in Paulding County in January 1837, and he hoped his nascent farm there would grow into a plantation.[8] Swain later recalled that he had started up his farm "in the woods and amongst the indians."[9] Although the Cherokees still lived in the area, the Treaty of New Echota had been announced a year before George Swain's arrival. This fraudulent removal agreement settled any lingering doubts that the Cherokees would indeed be forced to leave. Swain's plans rested on more than his own skills and capital. His father had died in 1829, but he knew he could depend on monetary assistance from his younger and wealthier brother. David Swain was president of the University of North Carolina and had previously served as governor of that state.[10] George Swain was thrilled with the potential of the land he bought for his home farm, and he confidently purchased additional "scattered" lots elsewhere. In his opinion it was "the best time to procure land in this country we shall ever see." He usually planned to pay for his purchases with the profit he expected to make by selling later. At the height of the boom, George Swain raved about his certain success, informing his brother David: "I have laid out all the money I can command for land & if I had $10,000 I could without any risk Double the Amt. in 3 years."[11]

Edward Isham's background, resources, and age contrast sharply with those of George Swain, and as a result Isham pursued quite different endeavors.[12] Isham's family did not have the means to pursue George Swain's dreams of land trading and plantation building, but the Cherokee country also had attractions for poor people like the Isham family. Many whites came, hoping to achieve independence by farming lands that did not attract the wealthy. The biggest initial draw of new people of all kinds into the Cherokee country, however, had nothing to do with agriculture. In 1829 a major gold rush erupted within the part of the Cherokee Nation that had long been claimed and would soon be taken by the state of Georgia. Edward Isham's father was among the thousands who came in search of gold.

Early in the 1830s, the Isham family settled just outside the Cherokee country in Carroll County, Georgia, and here Edward Isham had a very different upbringing from that of George Swain.[13] Born in Jackson County, Georgia, in about 1827, Isham grew up poor in Carroll County at a time when Carroll County was a particularly rough part of the rough-and-tumble backcountry.[14] With a father he himself described as "dissipated," Edward Isham had essentially no formal education, and organized religion made no impact on his life.[15] Instead, Isham learned from an early age to settle disputes and establish his status through direct physical combat. At the age of ten he fought another boy, hurting him with a rock. Edward "went home scared" of the consequences, but his father told him he was "a fool for being scared." Shortly thereafter an opponent soundly beat Edward while holding him by his long hair. Edward's father promptly cut his son's hair short, and Edward "went back and whipped" the other boy.[16]

Isham's impoverished backcountry childhood trained him to do more than fight. Like many other poor whites, he of necessity learned how to do a wide variety of work. His father had moved to Carroll County to mine gold, and Edward himself made money by mining as a teenager. He was usually most comfortable in the unruly, hard-drinking, hard-fighting mining culture in the hills and mountains of the Cherokee country.[17] Isham returned repeatedly to mining both in Carroll County and in a variety of other locations in and near the Cherokee country.[18] He usually made money either as a miner or as a gambler separating miners from their earnings. Yet he lost his money almost as quickly as he gained it. When not mining or gambling, Isham found work farming, ditching, splitting rails, working for the railroad, and doing most anything else that would pay.

Edward Isham worked because he needed the money, which made him rather different from George Swain, who schemed to rise above the comfortable prosperity he already had. The newly available lands of the Cherokee country provided many opportunities for well-backed newcomers like George Swain, but they also held risks for the unwary. Swain's lack of trustworthy associates in the area where he lived deprived him of the advice and support that might have offset his personal limitations. Instead, Swain's poor judgment and impractical nature neutralized the advantages he should have reaped from his brother's backing. When the financial crisis of the late 1830s finally spread to the South, Swain's grand dream of making a fortune turned into a nightmare. Swain struggled during the 1840s just to avoid complete impoverishment. Like many others, he was unprepared for the collapse of the speculative boom. To make matters worse, the Cherokee country was a particularly unfortunate area in which to be so dramatically overextended. Money was tight everywhere during the 1840s, but in the newly resettled Cherokee country people were clearing new farms and had no surplus capital. In addition, while many of the new residents had counted on the Western and Atlantic Railroad to provide market access, construction of the railroad halted temporarily due to the lack of funds. Largely as a result of land trading, George Swain had thousands of dollars in debts, and a variety of individuals owed him a total of over $10,000.[19] Swain could not collect what was due him, and he in turn could not pay his own debts. Moreover, Swain had recklessly secured substantial notes for others. He regularly found himself sued for these debts as well. Within a few years he began losing property—including land, slaves, and crops—in forced sales to pay his debts.[20] George Swain needed repeated infusions of David Swain's money to remain afloat financially. While David frequently provided the money that George needed, George's demands and the general financial crisis together strained even David Swain's considerable resources.[21]

Despite overwhelming evidence, George Swain only slowly recognized the depth of his financial problems.[22] When he finally did begin to confront his true difficulties, his approach to solving his problems made a very bad situation much worse. He refused a fortuitous offer of $10,000 for his farm, holding instead to the persistent belief that the "real" value of his property would soon reassert itself and allow him a substantial profit.[23] Needing money to pay his debts and restore his hopes of making a fortune, he turned to what he still thought he knew best. George Swain's now married daughter, who lived in Jefferson, Georgia, wrote David Swain: "You know his love of trading & experimenting, this feeling clings to him in all his troubles, with greater force if possible than formerly."[24] Both his increasing desperation and his questionable judgment are evident in repeated unsuccessful efforts to persuade David Swain to fund his proposal to buy hundreds of ungranted lots. The individuals who had won these lots in the land lottery had concluded that they were not worth even the nominal fee required to take out title, but George Swain thought he could make a "certain" profit by buying and re-selling these otherwise unwanted lands.[25]

Swain consistently made visionary plans requiring considerable initial commitments of both time and money, and he then followed through haphazardly. For example, persuaded by an alleged expert to build three different mills, Swain made substantial efforts over several years and invested about $500 in an ill-conceived project that never earned him a dime.[26] In a similar episode, he built a massive distillery including a stillhouse measuring thirty feet by sixty feet, despite the sharp opposition on moral grounds from the brother on whom he relied so heavily.[27] George Swain abandoned the project as a failure after several years. Each unsuccessful plan gave way to a new attempt to generate profits. At various times Swain invested time and money in tobacco, a tannery, orchards, livestock, rice, and Irish potatoes.[28]

Meanwhile, George Swain often neglected his farm, and as a result it failed to produce the significant income it might have yielded even in hard times. Indeed, the more troubled his situation became, the more hope, time, and energy he placed in new experiments and trading. With relatively little attention from its owner, the farm deteriorated instead of developing over time. Swain had bought enough land to build a plantation, but he did not have the money or slaves to do so. Therefore he usually rented out substantial portions of his land. Unfortunately, he consistently had trouble both collecting his rents and getting tenants to live up to their agreements. Yet he nonetheless allowed many of the same tenants to return year after year.[29] After George Swain had lived on his Paulding County farm for twelve years, his nephew, George Coleman, reported to David Swain that the land had "been taken just such care of as Uncle takes care of every thing. [Everything] waisted [and] nothing applied to the improvement of the place. Fencing all to rack, grass & briers over run the whole place, [and] not one of the tenants cultivated the place agreable to contract."[30]

George Swain's tenants were not the only people to take advantage of him; many of his difficulties came from not knowing whom he could and could not trust. Since everyone had arrived in the area only recently, he had few associates that he had known for long before the panic. Furthermore, Swain appears to have been a poor judge of character. He guaranteed other people's debts and then complained bitterly when he had to pay what they could not or would not. He repeatedly trusted self-styled experts to design his projects, and they inevitably proved unworthy of his confidence. His closest associates were traders and schemers like himself, and their opinions frequently proved no more perceptive than his own. When Swain's friends had better judgment than Swain himself, they often had no scruples about liberating him from his money. His few relatives in the area either relied on him for support or competed for David Swain's charity. Moreover, George Swain never remarried. Thus he did not regain the assistance that a wife might have provided him.[31]

Edward Isham had many more friends and relatives in the Cherokee country than did George Swain. But then since Isham had both little money and an extremely combative nature, he had to move frequently, and everywhere he went he needed all the help he could get. The document recording Isham's life story was prepared for his murder trial, and it may well overemphasize violence. Nonetheless, the fighting was clearly frequent and brutal. Isham fought for any and every reason: to protect himself or his interests, for status, for women, and sometimes, it seems, for the sheer thrill of fighting. He made use of knives, guns, rocks, and most every conceivable blunt object. He participated in planned set fights, spur-of-the-moment brawls, and every sort of conflict in between. Edward Isham and his opponents often felt no need to fight "fair"; if an opponent was drunk, or sleeping, or surprised in an ambush, then so much the better. Isham killed at least twice and caused numerous serious injuries. He sometimes suffered injuries himself. The damage came not only from weapons like guns, knives, and rocks but also from the ferocious nature of even unarmed backcountry brawling, where sharpened, lengthy fingernails were common and eye gouging was widespread.[32]

Many poor whites migrated frequently in order to find employment,[33] but because Isham could not stay out of trouble, he moved
more often than most. Even if Isham made it through a particular
battle without serious injury, mobs, committed enemies, and/or officers of the law frequently chased him afterward. As a result, he often
moved suddenly. For example, he once settled in Walker County,
Georgia, and earned enough money to bring his wife and his mother
there to join him. In his words, "Here I raised one crop but getting
into several fights, at a log rolling and at Gordons Grocery, I sold out
and went up to Chattanooga to work on the Rail Road."[34]

Edward Isham could not have survived his violent lifestyle for
long by himself, and he did not wander aimlessly from place to
place. Isham's relatives assisted him in fights, helped him escape
from lynch mobs or the law, and provided him with places of refuge.
Edward's three brothers and his brothers-in-law provided him with
occasional work opportunities, sometimes in the form of partnerships. More important, Edward's brothers also sometimes fought
at his side, lent him weapons, gave him warnings, and helped him
to make his escapes.[35] When fleeing danger, Isham sought specific
places of comparative safety and anticipated assistance. The crossing of a county line provided significant security from the law, and a
state line helped even more. His brother's home in Macon County,
Alabama, was a good place to avoid troubles in Georgia. A brother-
in-law provided him with refuge on more than one occasion, as
did aunts and uncles in Forsyth County, Cobb County, and De
Kalb County, Georgia. This form of family cooperation was so self-
evident as to lead to his discovery by his pursuers on at least two occasions. Similarly, his mother's home in Chattanooga provided a
base of operations at the intersection of three states. Once when
warrants there made it impossible for Edward to remain, he moved
himself and then his mother just across the state line to Ringgold,
Georgia. Although he most frequently moved within or near the
Cherokee country, Isham got as far west as Arkansas and spent time
in at least five different states.[36]

In addition to his family, Isham also relied heavily on a wide variety of other people. His male friends included free blacks, a mixed-

blood Indian in Arkansas, and a "wild" slaveowner, as well as gamblers, miners, and laborers like himself.[37] Despite his considerable geographical range, almost everywhere he traveled he found old friends or brought them with him. To be a friend of Edward Isham, a man pretty much needed a willingness to lend him weapons or to fight on his side against all comers. He was more than willing to do the same for his friends.[38] One example makes clear how a friend could be a welcome stand-in for one's own family: "I got into a difficulty with one Bratch Ward and we fought desperately, his sons and nephews joined him, and Jeff Chambers a friend of mine joined me—We fought at a grocery, and we finally whipped them and they shut themselves up in the grocery, in the fight I accidentally struck Chambers with a heavy stick and nearly killed him. I helped him home." The conclusion of this incident displays the manner in which Isham's violent lifestyle required his impressive mobility: "The other party gathered a crowd to kill us and we fled to the woods—I then came back to Carroll county and commenced mining."[39] While friends like Jeff Chambers could be invaluable, Isham understood that the boundary between friend and enemy could be quite thin—a fight could readily break out among friends, and an opponent might or might not become a friend when the battle ended.

Like Isham's blood relatives and male friends, many women played an important part in his life. By Isham's account, wherever he went he found women who became lovers and sometimes wives, although the distinction for him was not necessarily a great one. Isham frequently abandoned his lovers or they him, but these women also sometimes defended him, brought him weapons, or brought him money in times of need.[40] Isham felt no need for faithfulness on his own part, and he occasionally encouraged a woman to abandon her lover or husband to run away with him.[41] The mobility of both men and women meant that an effective divorce required simply moving on. Running away with Isham apparently could provide a woman with escape from the domination of a husband, lover, or father. A woman who entered a relationship with Isham might evade other men in her life even without moving. Disputing Isham's claim meant a violent confrontation with him. None-theless, more than one man was willing to fight Isham to reassert his own prerogative. Indeed, Isham frequently fought with other men over women, either in driving these men away from their women or in defending his own claims.[42] The only recorded major conflict be-tween Edward and his family resulted when he had an affair with the sister-in-law of his brother John. This liaison provoked a fight be-tween Edward and John, who drove Edward away by breaking a chair over his head.[43] Many of Edward Isham's relationships were entirely transitory, while others lasted intermittently for years.

Edward Isham's family and friends thus made it possible for him to stay alive and out of jail. In contrast, George Swain could not avoid financial ruin, even with the assistance of thousands of dollars from his brother David. Despite David's frequent loans, George had to sell his five remaining slaves in 1844 to meet some of his debts. David Swain then bought George's farm to provide the additional money needed to pay George's creditors. This maneuver stemmed the tide of debt for only a few years, and in 1849 David sold the property for $9,000.[44] David used the proceeds to fund George fur-ther rather than reimbursing himself for the extensive loans that he had made to his brother. David then generously offered George the opportunity to reestablish himself farther north in the Cherokee country, on land that George had himself selected and bought for David in Murray County, Georgia. David gave George complete freedom to run the property as he wished, but George did not stay there long.[45]

George Swain had only a limited interest in building his brother's farm, and he asserted his independence in a way that ensured he would remain unsuccessful even after the recession of the 1840s had given way to another boom in the 1850s. Before he left for Murray County, George asked David for $2,000 to buy land for an experi-ment with Irish potatoes and to "give me in a new place some little standing in society." His ambitious goal was to profit enough to pay back his brother and "secure a *home* of *my own again*."[46] He bought a variety of small, relatively inexpensive lots in the mountains and set about to restore his fortunes by raising Irish potatoes.[47] George conceded that David's lands were more valuable, but he argued that his own less impressive, less accessible mountain tracts would produce more profit.[48] He was wrong once again. His efforts at raising and marketing potatoes failed miserably.[49] Meanwhile, he lent at least $2,000, half of which was David's, to several men headed to California in the gold rush!

During the 1850s, George Swain roamed northern Georgia from project to project, unwilling to be tied down to one place under his brother's support and unable to succeed even with monetary assistance. Scrambling to stay ahead of his creditors, George Swain performed increasingly substantial amounts of manual labor during the late 1840s and the 1850s.[50] In 1852, for example, he hired out himself and his horse, plow and gear, to plow for others. He even plowed for his niece's husband, who was farming the Murray County land George himself had rejected. Swain complained bitterly when his relative refused to pay him for his time and trouble.[51] Swain continued to dream big dreams, and the copper-mining boom just over the Tennessee line at Ducktown attracted him to try mining on the Georgia side of the border.[52] Alone and in partnerships he bought land and tested it for precious metals, without success. Swain provided much of the labor himself, working for many hours at a time despite his advanced age. Although there is no record to suggest that he met Edward Isham, Isham and at least one of his brothers mined and gambled in the Ducktown area at about the same time.

Through all his misadventures George Swain continued to think of himself as a land trader and entrepreneur. He even tried to persuade his brother to sell his Murray County land to finance George's hopes to buy land near Rome, the major transportation center in Floyd County. David wisely rejected this proposal.[53] He usually also declined to fund George's other planned enterprises, such as growing extensive orchards, starting a turpentine business, and raising honey bees. George Swain's management capabilities, limited in the best of times, declined further in the later years of his life. David Swain apparently gave George control (but not ownership) of David's lands in Murray County as a way to provide support, but this arrangement did little to solve George's more fundamental problem.[54] In 1860, one of George's friends asked David Swain to relieve George of the management of David's farm in Georgia, for George could not fulfill the role and was still pursuing "his vision-ary course of making money." As the friend commented, "he is not calculated to contend with the dishonesty of mankind" or with any sharp traders. Consumed with his plans for wealth, "he has no stated home and is just rambling about from place to place. It makes me sorrow for him."[55]

David Swain's judicious assistance kept George Swain's increas-ingly fanciful dreams alive, but for Edward Isham the absence of a support network at a critical time helped lead to his very real death. After years of violence, it is not coincidental that when Isham was ultimately hanged for murder, the execution took place in North Carolina, well away from the people on whom he had relied for so many years.[56] In about 1858, Isham came to North Carolina seeking work, and he settled for a time near Statesville. He married, bought ten acres of land, and raised a crop. When his wife died after having a child, Isham turned to heavy drinking. James Cornelius, a slave-holding farmer, hired Isham to clear some ditches, but when Isham completed the job he demanded more in payment than Cornelius was willing to pay. Surprisingly, Isham sued and won a compromise judgment in court for five dollars. Although Cornelius stayed the judgment, Isham soon confronted him and demanded the money anyway. When Cornelius refused to pay, Isham struck him with a stick and then fatally stabbed him with a knife.

Isham fled immediately, but he was far from his family and his usual friends. The people he saw on his way out of the area gave him little aid and then testified against him in court—saying that he had threatened them to keep them quiet, that his clothes were bloody, and that he left the bloody clothes behind and stole replacements.[57] Isham managed to reach Tennessee, but he never made it to his friends and family. The Cornelius family offered a $500 reward for his capture, and this inducement quickly produced the desired re-sult. Isham received as good a defense as his conscientious and tal-ented young attorney could give, but the evidence was overwhelm-ing. Isham was convicted and then hanged for the murder.[58]

The experiences of George Swain and Edward Isham serve as a

reminder that the frontier was no place to be an isolated individual. The people who sought to exploit the opportunities inherent in newly acquired Indian land confronted many dangers and uncertainties; the numerous migrants who came in groups of neighbors and relatives did so for good reason. While the contrasting resources and backgrounds of Swain and Isham usually steered them toward very different endeavors, both men frequently relied on assistance from other people. Indeed, they often needed help just to avoid disaster. When Swain moved to Georgia, he left behind dense networks of family and friends in western North Carolina. His new associates in the Cherokee country caused him at least as much harm as good and significantly undercut the benefits he gained from his brother's extensive support. Because Isham grew up on this frontier and came from its most mobile segment, he had friends and relatives to assist him throughout the Cherokee country and at some points farther west. He needed their help frequently, and he made good use of it.

An individual's success or failure is not solely determined by family and friends, no matter how large a role they may play. Both of these men contributed mightily to their own problems. Swain wanted to achieve wealth and planter status, but he pursued one unlikely scheme after another. Ultimately, he preferred these enterprises, the independence they offered, and the fortune he hoped for to accepting life as a farmer dependent on his brother's generosity. George Swain never ceased to regard himself as a master trader despite repeated evidence to the contrary. Edward Isham, in his own less respectable domain, proved to be more adept and more pragmatic. Yet no matter how hard he worked, how much help he received, or how quickly he moved from place to place, Isham's lifelong inclination toward violence placed him at continual risk and denied him the opportunity to establish a long-term home. Isham remained defiant to the end. Facing the likelihood of his own execution, Isham called the murdered Cornelius "a damned dog. It is hard to be killed for one damn dog."[59]

"I Have Killed a Damned Dog":
Murder by a Poor White
in the Antebellum South

SCOTT P. CULCLASURE

In May 1859 the farming community around Sherrill's Ford in Catawba County, North Carolina, heard the stunning news of neighbor James Cornelius's death. Cornelius, a prospering yeoman farmer, was brutally murdered by a white laborer from Georgia named Edward Isham for a debt of a few dollars. Although he was able to flee Cornelius's farmyard, where the fatal assault occurred, Isham was soon captured, indicted, and, after being granted a change of venue, tried in neighboring Gaston County. Those involved in the trial appeared to know Isham only by his alias, Hardaway Bone, which he had adopted in an earlier flight from trouble in Georgia. Considering the testimony about Isham's defiant speech both before and after the stabbing of Cornelius, the young lawyer appointed by the court to serve as counsel for the penurious defendant faced a difficult task. Nevertheless, Lincolnton attorney David Schenck appealed the guilty verdict to the state supreme court. The appeal, based on Schenck's contention that two prejudiced jurors had been unfairly seated, proved fruitless. On May 25, 1860, a year after the murder, the thirty-two-year-old Edward Isham was hanged. Newspapers that had printed blaring headlines deploring the crime scarcely mentioned the execution. The notorious Hardaway Bone seemed quickly forgotten.[1]

Edward Isham, however, made it possible for his true self to be remembered. His appeal to the state's highest court required a complete transcript of his trial, thereby preserving the voices of those who testified. More remarkable is the account, prepared with the help of his counsel, that Isham left of his own life. The man known as an illiterate transient laborer named Hardaway Bone was fortunate in one respect: Isham's counsel, though privately acknowledging in his diary that his client was guilty, conscientiously prepared the case for the defense. Sometime before the trial, likely when Isham was jailed in Catawba County, David Schenck met with the defendant. When he visited the jail at Newton, he took with him an eight-by-thirteen-inch leather-backed and marble-papered notebook that he had used as a commonplace book. Perhaps Schenck asked Isham to relate his life's story in the hope of bringing to light some circumstance that might prove helpful during the trial. Assuming that Schenck did ask, the striving young lawyer thus revealed his passion for scribbling. Already he had copied into his book admonitions for dealing with adversity, descriptions of the qualities of beauty, and evidences of what constituted wisdom—all those ideas and more supported with quotations from the likes of Horace, Shakespeare, Pope, and Longfellow—along with a list of cases that set precedents for assault and battery. Now, across twenty-seven pages, Schenck carefully transcribed the life history related to him by a man whose only defense consisted of the claim that James Cornelius's death was not premeditated.[2]

One individual like Edward Isham cannot represent the complex experiences of an entire group of white southerners dispossessed of wealth and power. So difficult is the task even of defining who the antebellum poor whites were that only a few historians have attempted it. Contemporary observers, more concerned with either condemning or justifying slavery, contributed to the difficulty of making those people seem real by constantly stereotyping the "po' white trash." The poor themselves helped to tell of their lives only indirectly. Often they can be glimpsed in census reports, and frequently they can be heard in petitions to state legislatures or executives. Court proceedings also seem to have ensnared large numbers of the poor who encountered trouble; Isham's case captures the desperation of an individual at odds with the community. Other evidences of the lives of poor whites appear more sporadically, and rarely in letters or diaries.[3] Edward Isham's autobiography, therefore, offers with startling immediacy a life lived in what Bertram Wyatt-Brown has termed "shamelessness."[4] Isham tells a harrowing story in which violence provides the framework for his life and transience offers the only possibility for survival.

Because Isham possessed a ferocious temper, it is tempting to view the fatal stabbing of Cornelius as the result of sudden anger rather than premeditation. Isham left little doubt that, whatever his personal culpability, he had been steeped in a culture of incredible violence. He grew up along what Frank Owsley called the "inner frontier," for Isham, near the recently vacated Creek and Cherokee country of northwestern Georgia.[5] Carroll County, in which Isham spent most of his life, suffered the banditry of gangs like the Pony Club, described at length in William Gilmore Simms's 1834 frontier novel *Guy Rivers: A Tale of Georgia.*[6] The steadiest of the many occupations Isham held was gold mining, work reputed throughout the South for its lawlessness. The criminal behavior Isham demonstrated reflected much of the culture he knew. His actions could not have had worse consequences. Living a life on the run, Isham eventually came to North Carolina, where the clash between the violent culture of his youth and the more stable existence among the farming communities along the Catawba River easily targeted him as a dangerous outsider.[7]

Still, cultural environment alone did not make Edward Isham a violent man. Isham's personal experiences, marked with a seeming inability to form lasting relationships, further shaped his mercurial nature. His drunken father, before abandoning a common-law wife and family, taught his namesake never to avoid fighting and always to win, no matter how. Economic considerations may have forced the young Isham more than once to leave a poor county where gold mining was in decline and small farmers had to scrape for a living. Nevertheless, of at least equal importance to understanding his transience is the fact that Isham could not stay out of trouble long enough to settle in one place, so that it became harder for him to create secure bonds with others. Isham apparently formed an attachment that approached constancy with only one woman, a wife named Rachel Webb, among the many women he knew and occasionally fought over. Her presence seemed to bring the few stretches of peaceful existence Isham knew, and he praised her as he did few others by noting that "she was an easy good tempered woman and never quarrelled with me." Similarly, the death during childbirth of a later wife seemed to affect him so much that it could be considered, coming as it did during a time of personal failure, as a factor in the steep decline that led to the murder of James Cornelius.

His defiance so threatened the people of Sherrill's Ford that Edward Isham soon found himself in jail, talking to a defense attorney who was younger than he. Had the two men reflected on that setting, they might have been struck by each other's circumstances. One individual was a promising lawyer, well regarded by his peers, who looked forward to a marriage that would fulfill the longings expressed in his diary. The other, perhaps still clad in the working clothes described in newspapers advertising for his arrest, may well have been combating the effects of exposure and exhaustion after two weeks that he had spent as an outlaw. From his origins in Georgia, Isham's pursuit of work and purpose and his escape from the law had taken him to five southern states. This time there would be no more escaping. For a short time after coming to North Carolina, Edward Isham had tried to live an acceptable life. He had married, only to have his pregnant wife die; he had farmed, only to lose his crop; he had sued to collect a debt, only to have his efforts thwarted by a member of the community with greater standing. In his rage, Isham had shouted bloody threats and taken bloodier action against those who represented a society that appeared determined to marginalize him. Nothing written in his account, nothing said during his trial, and nothing uttered even as he stood on the gallows suggested any remorse on his part.[8]

Just as he challenged the people who lived along the Catawba River, so too does Edward Isham challenge those who wish to understand how someone so in conflict with society could survive for as long as he did. His story can help to frame the questions necessary for a better understanding of antebellum poor whites. To what extent did poverty foster transience, thereby adding to that group's invisibility? Did tendencies toward violence characterize poor whites to the degree asserted by antebellum observers? If violence defined poor white existence, then what does it signify — part of broader cultural behaviors fostered by frontier conditions and southern conceptions of honor, or an outward manifestation of the psychological and social pressures that resulted from poverty's dislocating effects?[9] Is it possible to determine the extent of bitterness and hostility felt by poor whites who resented a society that seemed so closed to them? The tale of Isham's life and trial can help historians consider issues raised by antebellum poverty that have been left too long to neglect and the realm of stereotype.

Edward Isham was probably born in 1827 in Jackson County, Georgia. If he knew the year of his birth, he did not tell it to David Schenck. Instead, Isham remembered being five years old "at the time of the cold Friday and Saturday." The autobiography contains many such obscurities; Isham's quickness of intellect combined with his lack of schooling assured that he would express himself in ways different from ones his more learned counsel might have employed.[10] The spelling of the family name also remains unclear. Schenck consistently spelled it "Icem," perhaps reflecting what he heard an illiterate man say. The federal census spelled the name "Isham," although the 1840 manuscript from De Kalb County, Georgia, where Isham said two of his uncles lived, provides a third alternative by recording the Christian names given by Edward for his uncles — Charles and James — with the surname "Isom."[11] More striking than the variety of spellings, however, is the alias by which people in North Carolina knew Isham. Shortly before coming to the state, he adopted a name that was a corruption of "Harland Bone," an otherwise unidentified individual living along the Coosa River with whom Isham had hidden while fleeing an earlier shooting in Alabama. Though he knew his informant's given name, Schenck used only the alias when writing of Isham in his diary. "Hardaway Bone" became the label that marked Isham as someone different, threatening, and not a part of the farming communities along the Catawba River valley.

Sometime in the early 1830s the impoverished family of Edward Isham, father and son, moved, likely because the elder Isham had, in the words of his son, "spent what property he had." The family left one part of the Georgia Upcountry, Jackson County in the east, for another, Carroll County in the west. At just that time, William Gilmore Simms published a novel that the unlettered Edward Isham could not have read. *Guy Rivers,* one in a series of popular romances that Simms wrote, portrayed the dangerous passions unleashed in humanity by living along the southern frontier. The novel was set in the northwestern region of Georgia where the Isham family settled. Simms captured the desolation felt by southerners uncomfortable with the wildness of places like the new gold fields of Carroll County: "There still stretch the dreary wastes, the dull woods, the long sandy tracts, the rude hills that send out no lights for the encouragement of the civilized man." [12]

Simms's protagonist, the aristocratic Ralph Colleton, flew to the frontier to escape personal disappointment and heartbreak. In the gold-mining village of Chestatee, Colleton encountered a culture in which order was as absent in the conduct of society as it was in the layout of the log buildings. For Colleton, as for Simms, the frontier threatened established ways. Eventually Colleton fled eastward to escape lawlessness and a manner of justice that thoughtlessly and harmfully challenged legitimate authority. Edward Isham also left the region to come east. Unlike Colleton, however, Isham did not return to aristocratic values and an acknowledgment of personal failings. Rather, he entered communities that saw him as the embodiment of "unregulated passion" and "ill judged direction," in the words of Guy Rivers, the condemned outlaw of the novel. [13] Antebellum society likely viewed Isham as a threat because of his personal failure to subdue the violent passions that other southerners had overcome. [14]

Isham described his father as "dissipated." Before the son was fully grown, the father "had taken up with another woman and left my mother alone." Even though he figured only briefly in the narrative, the elder Isham profoundly influenced his son's life. Young Isham attended school for only five days before he got into trouble.

Isham was ten years old when, at school, he hit another boy with a rock; he offered no explanation of what caused the fight. Returning home shaken, Isham confided to his father, who "told me I was a fool for being scared." Other fights soon followed, including one with William Garthard. Holding Edward tight by his long hair, Garthard beat him mercilessly. Young Isham again ran to his father. This time, the father cut off the boy's hair "so I could have a fair chance," and Isham returned and whipped his opponent.

A pattern of life familiar to many white southerners developed in the Isham household. With an upbringing dominated by a father who taught his son to live by his fists and by a mother who is only a shadow in the narrative, even though she continued to live with her son long after the father abandoned them, Edward Isham grew up an aggressive boy.[15] Added to the inculcation of violence was the uprooting of migration. If the family expected to find greater prosperity in the gold mines of Carroll County, it doubtless met with disappointment. Living "in the suburbs" of Pinetown, near the gold-mining center of Villa Rica, the Isham family settled in a neighborhood of miners and small farmers, few of whom, according to the 1850 census, owned either real or sizable personal property. Like most of their mining neighbors, the Isham household possessed neither cow nor horse and raised no pigs or corn. Most of the heads of households were illiterate, and while many of the children had attended school, the question remains whether their experience was much better than Isham's. Most of the residents were natives of Georgia, although a sprinkling of people from North Carolina lived in the community. Family arrangements reflected the area's poverty. By 1850 the elder Isham was living with a woman slightly more than half his age and with four children ranging in age from ten years to six months. The twenty-three-year-old Edward lived in a neighboring dwelling with his seventeen-year-old wife, Rachel, and his younger brother William.[16]

Increasing numbers of fights marked the years of Isham's childhood and adolescence in Carroll County. Few social institutions existed that might have moderated the effects of Isham's upbringing.[17] For example, although he joined a Methodist congregation, Isham was soon "turned out" for fighting. In any event, evangelical Protestantism could have little effect: "No preacher could live or preach in Pinetown; one lived there once and they tore down his fences and ran him off." Left with little to restrain him, Isham developed a fearsome reputation as his belligerence grew. A fight ensued with two young men named McQuister from Hickstown; Isham claimed to have "whipped them both." During a more serious argument with Tom Godfrey, his mining partner, over water for sluicing, Isham was hit with a shovel. Isham fought back by throwing rocks and ran to his father's house for a gun. One of Godfrey's friends went to town for a warrant, only to find himself pursued and apparently beaten by Isham with a hickory stick. Isham was arrested and jailed at Carrollton, the county seat, where he escaped that night by crawling through a hole in the floor. In a behavior that he would often repeat, Isham returned home long enough to eat supper and then fled to De Kalb County to live with his uncle Charles. Increasingly during the decade of the 1850s, Edward Isham found himself fettered by two mutually reinforcing shackles: economic hardship, made worse by continual rashness, and criminal wrongdoing encouraged by his poverty and social standing.

The degree of Isham's transience, coupled with the variety of jobs he held, stuns the imagination. He spent much time moving from one county to another in the Georgia Upcountry and the foothills farther north, often staying with relatives and continuing to work as a miner. According to his account, before reaching maturity Isham had lived with uncles in De Kalb and Forsyth Counties to escape trouble in Pinetown. More than once he journeyed to Macon County, Alabama, where his brother John resided. There he made shingles, cut lumber, and rafted goods to Montgomery, also the destination of a cattle drive that Edward had undertaken. In Chattanooga, Tennessee, Isham worked on the railroad and as a fireman on the Tennessee River's *Sam Markin,* where he observed returning Mexican War veterans. With Jim Waters, Waters's wife, and his own wife, Rachel Webb, he next traveled to Johnson County, Arkansas. For nearly six months, Isham "enjoyed myself better than ever before in my life" as he split rails and hunted deer and bees.[18] After stopping in Memphis and Paducah, Kentucky, he returned to his brother's home in Alabama to launch a combined fishing and gambling enterprise. Eventually Isham came to North Carolina, expecting to work on the railroad but turning instead to digging a well, farming, and ditching.

Isham operated within a wide circle of contemporaries equally given to a roaming existence dictated by opportunity and necessity, suggesting that his transience resulted from his status in society as well as a personal sense of purposelessness. Some of his "intimates," as Isham termed them, had an entrepreneurial nature, like Jim Ingles, whom Isham met in Chattanooga and encountered again in Smithland, Kentucky. For a time Isham and Ingles jointly plied their trade as gamblers along the Ohio River, until they both lost what money they had.[19] Other individuals, like longtime Carroll County associate Jeff Chambers, were expected to help in fighting. Chambers seconded Isham in a fight with Dick Fenley, who, Isham admitted, "got the best of the fight," leaving Isham with a gouged eye and a bitten finger that soon became infected.[20] The multiplicity and tenuousness of Isham's relationships underscore the extent to which he divided his life into segments of only a few months; any relationships had to endure his propensity for traveling. What Isham called friendships were something much more ephemeral, as he likely discovered to his mortification when he heard the damning testimony of those who knew him at his trial for the murder of James Cornelius.

The most troubling of Isham's relationships, in the view of the white supremacist society in which he lived, were the ones he formed with black southerners, both slave and free. Isham claimed that a Methodist congregation churched him because he attempted to knife "a negro," presumably a slave, in a dispute over a fishing pole. Whether the disciplinary action resulted from the fight or from the relationship remains unclear. Not long afterward, Isham was choked by a free black at a swimming and drinking party. Stopping at a grocery on the way home, Isham waited to regain his sobriety, whereupon he attacked the freeman "and beat him severely." Significantly, however, the two "afterwards made friends."

Such relationships, Eugene Genovese has noted, required relentless squelching by planters, who feared what might happen if "degraded" whites realized that a "genuine sympathy might exist across racial lines."[21] Those relationships may have constituted a less serious offense in places like the Georgia Upcountry than they did in areas more densely populated by slaves. On the frontier, black southerners lived in fewer numbers and often, in the words of Steven Hahn, "shared a close living environment, worked side by side at similar tasks, might attend the same church, and could engage in casual fraternization" with whites. Even so, Hahn reports at least one example, in a study that concentrates on the Upcountry counties of Isham's birth and primary residence, of a white resident's being taken to court in Jackson County for fraternization similar to Isham's.[22] White-black alliances fostered by shared economic deprivation and societal contempt were anathema, particularly to slaveholders worried about too much contact between white laborers and black slaves. Even if Isham did not mind the opprobrium of fellow whites, he felt its sting. Becoming "too intimate with a free girl" caused trouble when he took the woman to Warner Lyons's grocery near Pinetown. An argument ensued with Lyons's girlfriend, Betsy Wedding. Made furious by Isham's insulting manner, Wedding produced a shotgun while Lyons barricaded the grocery door. Isham knew what it was like to be reviled for crossing the racial barrier. Considering the frequency of his later associations with black southerners, however, the stigma must have had little effect on him, except perhaps as a further inducement to fighting. Isham's shameless behavior may represent his expression of the contempt he felt for a society that had rejected him.[23]

Nowhere does Edward Isham illustrate more clearly his casual regard for others than in his relations with women. True, he implied that he cared enough for his mother to move her to Chattanooga so that she might live near him. (There "she sold cakes and whiskey and boarded work hands for a living.") And Rachel Webb, the woman who became his first wife, thought enough of her husband to take him his rifle on one occasion after hearing him yell at a nearby fight. In Isham's eyes Rachel Webb deserved praise because "she never complained" when he began to spend more time in the company of a girlfriend named Beck Caldwell. In one sense Isham provided for his wife, as when, during flush times gambling in Tennessee, he "dressed well, had plenty of money, and supplied my wife with all necessities." Even so, Isham mentioned in the same sentence his affair with Caldwell. Isham's attitude toward women, one by no means confined to poor white men, was utilitarian; women were regarded much like slaves. Therefore, Ann Baldwin merited taking to Pinetown and away from an angry father in Ringgold because she had money that Isham "concluded I would get." Mary Dagget was a pretty girl whom Isham hired as a cook while he was digging for gold in Cobb County, Georgia. They soon "took up together," but having little luck in the mines, Isham abandoned her at Isley's grocery. The children produced in these relationships, at least the ones who survived childbirth, held no greater claim on Isham. James, a son by Rachel, was the only child mentioned by name, and James apparently never knew his father. Isham's propensities are interesting less as they reveal poor whites' sexual mores, which southern evangelicals found objectionable, than as they hint at a larger, overarching pattern of male-dominated and, in its extremes, oppressive southern behavior. While such behavior may have been exaggerated among poor whites, all classes shared its underlying attitudes toward women.[24]

Like the men of his acquaintance, the many women Edward Isham knew lived within interconnecting social circles, affording his life more cohesiveness than might otherwise appear. For example, a twenty-year-old woman named Mary became engaged to marry Isham when he met her during a stay at his brother's Alabama residence. Returning to that state after creating trouble in Georgia that caused a crowd to chase him, he found that during his absence Mary had married Peter Windley. Undaunted, Isham persuaded Mary to return with him to Carroll County. Domestic bliss proved elusive, however, as Isham soon complained that "she did not treat me kindly and I became jealous," an emotion that only increased when Isham spied on their cabin from atop Bald Hill and saw her walking into another man's house. Mary left for Ringgold and there married

Hiram Brown. Meanwhile, Isham again journeyed to Alabama and began living with Mandy Hatch, who was both Mary's sister and the sister-in-law to his brother John. Now Edward found himself quarreling with his brother over the new relationship; whether Edward's reputation was at issue in the argument is unclear. After a fight in which John hit his brother in the head with a chair, Edward returned to Pinetown with his sister but apparently without Mandy. When he next visited Ringgold, Isham cohabited with Caroline Brown, the sister of Mary's husband. Finally, when Caroline "became pregnant," Isham "quit her and married Rachel Webb." Not only did Edward Isham freely consort with a large number of women; the women he knew—along with their other lovers—often knew each other as well. Although he moved across an expansive geographical terrain, at the same time Isham frequently wended his way within a familiar circle of acquaintances.[25]

Did the apparent purposelessness in Edward Isham's life reflect a belief that, regardless of the undertaking, he would never overcome his poverty? Isham's account lacks a sense of reflection about what happened to him, making the demarcation between the individual's qualities and the opportunities provided within society difficult to discern. On only one occasion did he mention thinking about where his life was taking him. An acquaintance in Chattanooga slipped up behind Isham after he had gotten drunk and had begun quarreling, possibly at a brothel, and knocked him senseless.[26] Isham awoke the next morning at his mother's residence, badly hurt and scared. "I reflected on my course," he said, "and for awhile was disposed to do better, but warrants [were] issued for me and I fled." In too much trouble to settle down, Isham took flight, only to meet with other bad men and bad times. Whatever originally motivated him recklessly to pursue ruinous ends—from seeking vengeance to undertaking risky gambling enterprises—Isham was being sheared by the cutting blades of violence and poverty. For him, as for many southerners, reputation counted for much. The reputation for fierceness and cunning that he created, and in which he appeared to revel, probably served him well in the rough-and-tumble worlds of gold mining and river steamboats. When those qualities failed to help,

Isham often outran justice's pursuit. In more settled areas, however, Edward Isham would find neither tolerance nor escape.

Sometime in 1857 or 1858, Isham moved to North Carolina. Once again, he was on the run. In Macon County, Alabama, an "old feud" with Jim Runnels had turned violent. Hearing from the mother of his girlfriend, Susan Proctor, that Runnels was carrying a loaded pistol and had voiced his intention to kill him, Isham, after a drink of liquor, declared that "this fuss has been going on long enough and I would end it." Isham found Runnels at Proctor's door and, as Runnels stumbled into the yard, fired at him with a shotgun borrowed from his brother. Runnels reeled behind the house shouting "Oh Lord," and Isham fled to the Coosa River. Not until later—perhaps when his brother overtook him and ferried him across the river to Harland Bone's residence—did Isham learn that Runnels had died. For the first time but not the last, Edward Isham had killed a man.

Isham speedily crisscrossed northern Georgia and southern Tennessee, "avoiding all public notice." At Ducktown, Tennessee, he sold his gun and gambled at cards for money. Isham fell ill and was too sick to work by the time he returned to Rabun Gap, Georgia. Crossing to the Tennessee River, he "worked for a free negro." His journey then took him to North Carolina, where he traveled from Brindletown in southwestern Burke County to the county seat at Morganton. Even though this area was known for its gold mining, Isham apparently sought railroad work, so he followed the tracks from Morganton to Statesville and took up residence in Iredell County near that town, according to a newspaper account.[27] Instead of railroad work, Isham found the farm of James Lesley, who hired him to dig a well and, eventually, allowed him to marry his daughter Mandy.

Isham appeared ready to settle down, as he "bought 10 acres of ground from Charlie Carlton" and began to raise a crop. The appearance of stability was misleading. At election time in the summer of 1858, Isham fought with a man who afterward secured against him a county court grand jury indictment for two counts of assault and battery.[28] Isham's threat to kill another individual who had insulted him and his mother-in-law resulted in a warrant for his arrest. "To avoid the officers," Isham remembered, "I went up near Taylorsville [the seat of neighboring Alexander County] and remain[ed] a week or more, gambling with some white men and free negroes and won some money." When Isham moved southward to Lincoln County, he lost the crop he was growing in Iredell County, presumably because of his legal difficulties. As far as the residents who knew him in Iredell County were concerned, Isham was an outlaw known only as Hardaway Bone. When Mandy died during childbirth, he lost his last mooring. Isham had begun working as a day laborer for local farmers, and he crossed into Catawba County, where James Cornelius "hired me to clear out some old ditching."

The Cornelius brothers, James and Austin, were successful members of a family that represented well the Piedmont's image of sturdy farmers. James Cornelius was a prospering forty-nine-year-old bachelor in May 1859. His farm of 236 acres lay along the southern edge of Catawba County next to the river bearing the same Indian name. The county's list of taxables for 1859 valued his land at $3,540, which, together with his four slaves, was assessed for $18.76. Even more impressive were the neighboring holdings of Austin Cornelius. Austin was two years younger than James and had fathered by his wife, Ann, a family of nine children. The two eldest were sons, Henry F. and James H., who had nearly come of age and would soon possess their uncle's estate. The federal census of 1860 listed the value of Austin Cornelius's real estate at $14,000 and his personal property at $18,000, wealth that had likely been augmented by his status as James's executor and trustee for Henry and the young James. With his sixteen slaves, Austin produced on his 300 acres of improved land 2,000 bushels of corn and 430 bushels of wheat in 1859. Sizable numbers of pigs, sheep, and cattle added to the value of an Upcountry farm that grew neither cotton nor tobacco. Few of the nearly 800 residents who lived in the twelve dozen households surrounding the Sherrill's Ford post office could match the wealth of the Cornelius brothers.[29]

The *Iredell Express* reported that James Cornelius contracted Edward Isham on a monthly basis to work on his farm. After only two days of labor, Isham "went on a Sunday morning to Mr. Cornelius, who is a bachelor and resides alone with only his negroes on the farm, and demanded a settlement."[30] Isham said simply that Cornelius "hired me to clean out some ditching while he was gone to market." When he returned, Cornelius "expressed himself satisfied" but objected to Isham's price of seven dollars. For once Isham assumed the role of plaintiff and brought suit before a magistrate. He was awarded just five dollars but hoped to collect the money soon in order "to redeem my gun which I had pawned to Dr. Motte." On Saturday, May 7, 1859, Isham learned that James Cornelius had succeeded in staying the magistrate's judgment. That night Mrs. Susan Reed, at whose house a then drunken and morose Isham had left his infant child, heard him mutter that if Cornelius "don't pay me my money I will cut his bowels out." Thomas Lemly advised Isham that Cornelius had acted within his rights, which provoked Isham to respond, "God damn him; if he stays it I will kill him." Isham left Reed's house early Sunday morning after stating his intention to go "to the fishery." He stopped along the way through the river bottom to trade knives with Washington Sherrill, exchanging his "small worthless knife," according to Sherrill's testimony, for one with a blade nearly four inches long. Then after cutting a small sweet gum stick about an inch in diameter, Edward Isham went to the house of James Cornelius, whom he saw "sitting just inside the door washing his feet in a bowl."[31]

When James Cornelius watched Edward Isham walk to the porch of his house, he saw a thirty-two-year-old man described as standing erect at five feet nine or ten inches tall and as having light hair, a fair complexion with a smooth, bony face, and gray or blue eyes. Isham, said to be "well-formed and rather good looking," had "mild eyes" that nevertheless conveyed "a bold look." Isham had lost his right thumb; he said it was blown off by a bursting gun when he was a child. He spoke "slowly but determined." Several quirks of behavior added a disquieting element: Isham often held "a knife in his hand when talking with any one or sitting alone, having his head slightly inclined one way or the other" as he talked. His wardrobe included "a black cloth frock coat with velvet collar, much worn, a pair of black cashmere pants and a pair of summer pants with red stripes, and black wool hat with a broad band and a tolerably high crown." Even if Cornelius shared in the estimation of "Hardaway Bone" as "a very bad man" possessed by propensities for liquor and gambling, his brother Austin said that he showed no concern for his safety when Isham appeared at his door.[32]

As Edward Isham related, the encounter between him and James Cornelius began peaceably. The men exchanged greetings, and Cornelius invited Isham to come inside. "I walked [in] and stood leaning against a table in the middle of the floor," Isham remembered, and "I then told him I had come by to get that little money he owed me." Isham claimed to have expressed his willingness to accept only four dollars, with the remainder paying the court costs incurred by his suit. Unconvinced by Cornelius's excuse that he had only twenty-five cents in the house, Isham sneered when Cornelius declared that their dispute could be settled if necessary with the gun hanging over the door. Austin Cornelius later testified that his brother had made no such threatening remark and, furthermore, had quoted Isham as saying, "I will have my money, or one of us must die."

Isham and Austin Cornelius agreed that when James stepped onto the porch to empty his washbasin, Isham struck him with the stick he had been carrying.[33] Isham continued to beat Cornelius as they lurched into the yard. According to Austin, his brother defended himself as best he could bare-handed; Isham said that Cornelius returned his blows with "a piece of plank or shingle" he picked up once the fighting had begun. Cornelius broke away from Isham and ran toward the kitchen, crying for help from his slave Jim. "Another negro man and two negro women came," the court record showed, "the man having picked up a . . . piece of a fence rail." When Isham again attacked Cornelius, the slave with the rail attempted to separate them. Acting desperate and frenzied, Isham drew his knife and repeatedly stabbed Cornelius. Once released, Cornelius staggered toward the slave women, who helped him mount a horse that had already been saddled for the morning's ride to church. Isham threatened the male slave, who he thought was

being restrained by the women, with a rock, then flung it at the fleeing Cornelius. Isham left Cornelius's farm and returned to Susan
Reed's house, still wearing his linen coat with its blood-soaked left
sleeve.

Word of the assault probably reached nephew Henry Cornelius
before James himself did, because Henry found his uncle "sitting
in a corner of his own fence, his pantaloons covered with blood."
Henry carried James, who was too weak to walk, to his father's
house. There Austin Cornelius, with help from neighboring farmer
Henry Barkley, physician J. J. Mott, and brother Jesse, washed and
dressed James's wounds. Most distressing was the fearsome gash
James had suffered between the ribs on his left side. Three inches
long and six inches deep, the wound showed marks from the knife's
handle guard. Air could be heard rushing through the wound, and
food would exit from it. Even without Dr. Mott's opinion, James
understood the seriousness of his condition. Jesse Cornelius remembered his saying, "I am cut all to pieces and cannot live long."
The stricken brother described what had happened and, on May 21,
1859, dictated his last will and testament. Later that day, James
Cornelius died.[34]

As Edward Isham escaped from Catawba County, he left behind
a number of witnesses who would testify about his words and actions. William Sherrill, for example, met Isham coming from the
Cornelius farm shortly after the assault and was warned by him that
"if you tell any one you have seen me here I will kill you." Observ-
ing his bloody clothes when he returned to her house to collect a
gun, powder, and lead, Susan Reed accused Isham of having killed
someone. "No," he replied after she repeated her charge, "I have
killed a damned dog." Isham's bloodied linen coat was found later
in Thomas Lemly's yard, and Lemly declared that in its place Isham
had stolen his own coat. Likely the last one to see Isham before he
left the county was Albert Nance, who ferried him across the Catawba River and was informed by him that he would leave William
Reed's gun "where he can get it."[35]

As he fled, Isham quickly grew despondent. He had been drinking heavily since the death of his wife and complained that he "was

sick and was very tired." He ate supper on Sunday evening at Daniel Fink's Iredell County farmhouse; too uneasy to rest, however, he left as soon as the moon had set. That night he slept by the road on which he was traveling. Near Taylorsville in Alexander County he heard horses galloping across a bridge. "So tired and sore I could hardly walk," Isham managed to elude capture, although the posse passed close enough for him to recognize Charlie Carson.[36] By Monday night, Isham was treading mountain roads and huddling beneath a tree for shelter from a driving rain. A few days later, as the rain continued, he approached Taylorsville, Tennessee, just as the stagecoach mail arrived, delivering handbills that called for his arrest. Storekeeper William Waugh chatted with Isham about his travels and quickly realized that the stranger carrying a gun was wanted for murderous assault. After a short pursuit and even briefer struggle, Waugh and A. B. Slimp overpowered Isham in Carter County, Tennessee, near the North Carolina border, and bound him with ropes. "I cut Jimmy Cornelius bad," Waugh reported Isham as saying, "but I did not know that he was dead . . . He was a damned dog. It is hard to be killed for one damned dog." In an obscure comment directed perhaps at Austin Cornelius, Isham declared that "if I could kill one more I would die willingly." Isham was transported 105 miles to the Catawba County jail in Newton. During the journey he made a final attempt at escape. Waugh and Slimp shared the $500 reward that Austin Cornelius had offered for Isham's capture. The death of James Cornelius, occurring soon after Isham's jailing at Newton, justified the charge of murder that newspapers had bandied about for two weeks. So clear was Hardaway Bone's guilt that the Sherrill's Ford community likely accepted willingly the grim assessment of his fate offered by the *Asheville News:* "He will probably swing."[37]

The Charlotte *Western Democrat* printed two articles in its issue of May 10, 1859, that related to each other in a way not immediately evident. The first was an advertisement written by Austin Cornelius that contained information about Hardaway Bone's stabbing of James Cornelius. The second, a notice about David Schenck, reported that "our friends in Gaston speak of Mr. Schenck as a young gentleman of ability and high character, and as possessing an amiable and pleasant disposition which makes him a favorite with his acquaintances." David Schenck had established his practice as the only lawyer living in Dallas, the seat of Gaston County, formed during the previous decade from the southern part of his native Lincoln County and presumably offering opportunity for a twenty-five-year-old attorney. Schenck took his "sweet and sympathizing" new wife, Sallie Wilfong Ramsour, to reside in the home of a Dallas merchant named Jacob Pegram. Fellow boarders in the household managed by Pegram's wife, Mary, included a schoolteacher, a clerk, two physicians, and two medical students. "*Our* little room," Schenck confided in his diary, "holds two very comfortably and we are living in happy seclusion in this little town until our means justify a removal to a more congenial and pleasant residence."

Like many young lawyers, Schenck periodically left his wife to ride the court circuit, which in the autumn of 1859 brought him to the Catawba County courthouse in Newton. There he met superior court judge Robert R. Heath. Schenck soon held a high opinion of Heath; the judge was "firm but courteous" and possessed a "master intellect and legal learning" that commanded "the most profound respect." Thanks to Heath, Schenck also made another acquaintance, one whom he would not regard so highly. Edward Isham had been sitting in the Newton jail through the summer, penurious and charged with the murder of James Cornelius. Because Judge Heath appointed Schenck to defend him, Isham would at least be represented by counsel.[38]

Schenck believed Isham's assault constituted "certainly the most cool and deliberate murder I ever investigated." Nevertheless, court records suggest that he labored dutifully on behalf of his new client. After being presented with the grand jury's indictment that he "feloniously wilfully and of his malice aforethought did kill and murder" James Cornelius, Isham submitted an affidavit that claimed he could not receive a fair trial in Catawba County because of prejudice against him. Judge Heath ordered the venue changed to Gaston County and bound witnesses for their appearance. On Wednesday morning, October 26, 1859—five months after Cornelius's death and barely two weeks since meeting his counsel—Edward Isham went to trial for his life.[39]

The jury that sat in judgment of Hardaway Bone consisted of citizens who were more nearly the peers of James Cornelius than of Edward Isham. Of the ten jurors listed in the 1860 federal census, most were farmers with real estate values that ranged from $500 for Lawson Mauney to $5,101 for Andrew Jackson Dickey. Those who did not farm found stable employment elsewhere: James U. Craig was an overseer, Samuel P. Pasour, Jr., was a blacksmith whose household included a female weaver, Ephraim Linebarger was a carpenter, and Eli J. Robinson smithed in addition to farming. To those jurors—hardworking men possessing some degree of property and status—Isham's resort to violence represented more than a criminal action. The poor, transient laborer called Hardaway Bone had threatened the stability of a society centered on what Edward Ayers describes as "a pattern of local and personal power." Edward Isham would have his day in court, but it would be brief.[40]

Two contentions emerged from the defense that David Schenck provided Isham: that the method of jury selection was prejudicial to the defendant and that the assault on Cornelius constituted voluntary manslaughter rather than premeditated murder, a distinction that would have kept Isham from going to the gallows. In a thicket of common law, the defense's arguments about the impaneling of jurors and the admissibility of evidence maintained that Isham was guilty only of manslaughter and would have required jurors to disbelieve much of the testimony they heard. Nonetheless, Schenck tried diligently to defend a cause he considered hopeless.[41]

The sheriff of Gaston County summoned seventy-five men to constitute the case's jury panel. As the process of selection began, Schenck announced his intention to challenge each juror for cause, and both he and Solicitor William Lander consented to Judge Heath's acting as trier. Schenck penciled two names, Wincester Pegram and Alexander Rutledge, on a piece of paper as jurors whom the defense challenged. Both men told the judge they believed the defendant to be guilty, with Pegram explaining that his opinion had been formed by hearing rumors to that effect when he passed through the neighborhood of the Cornelius farm four days after the assault. Pegram and Rutledge assured the court, however, that the rumors had not produced so strong an impression that they could not listen to the testimony and accord the defendant a fair trial. Judge Heath found both jurors competent and tendered them to the defendant. The defense excepted Pegram immediately. Schenck then requested that the defendant be allowed to postpone showing cause for challenging Rutledge until the entire panel had been reviewed (in the hope that less biased jurors could be found). Judge Heath denied the request, holding that only the state could claim that right. The defendant's counsel then excepted Rutledge, and the impaneling of the petit jury was quickly completed. The overruling of counsel's request later provided a basis, however weak, for appeal to the state supreme court.[42]

The trial produced a string of witnesses whose unfavorable testimony added to the hopelessness of Isham's defense. Members of the Cornelius family, Austin in particular, rallied to provide accounts of James's stricken condition and what he told them of Isham's unexpected assault. Thomas Beaty graphically described James's knife wounds. Thomas Lemly and William and Susan Reed quoted the language employed by Isham when he learned that the magistrate's judgment had been stayed. Isham's warning to William Sherrill not to tell anyone that he had been seen fleeing Cornelius's farm was recounted. Washington Sherrill identified the murder weapon as the knife he had traded to Isham at Isham's request the day of the assault. Isham's bloodied linen coat, having been thrown down in Lemly's yard, was produced, and Lemly pointed to his own coat stolen and worn by the defendant. Sheriff Jonas Cline and William Waugh, the storekeeper responsible for Isham's capture in Tennessee, related the prisoner's confession to the stabbing and his fierce disregard of what he had done. Apparently having no friendly witnesses on whom to call, Schenck attempted to have much of the adverse testimony expunged and, in its place, to argue for a case of manslaughter.[43]

The most damning testimony came from witnesses who quoted direct conversations with either the victim or the defendant, and

Schenck accordingly attempted to have such words stricken from the record on the ground that they constituted only hearsay evidence. Each time Schenck objected to the testimony being received, however, Judge Heath overruled him, which in turn resulted in the defendant's entering an exception. The defendant's counsel objected to Solicitor Lander's request that Austin Cornelius relate what his brother had told him of the assault. A similar objection occurred when Jesse Cornelius recounted details of the fight as James had communicated them to him. All the declarations made by William Waugh of Isham's lack of remorse over having killed "a damned dog" again brought counsel's protest without success. In fact, the only motion Judge Heath sustained was one made not by Schenck but by the solicitor, who objected to receiving evidence from the defendant that he had made a second confession the day after his arrest in which he stated that he killed Cornelius only in self-defense.

Discounting the testimony of those who reported Isham's angry words would allow Schenck to try persuading the court that the unlawful killing of James Cornelius was the result of manslaughter. While that strategy may appear farfetched, it was not totally ludicrous. The contention that premeditation was not proved, for example, was supported by the observation that Isham had not been seen leaving the Reed house that Sunday morning with the stick he used to strike Cornelius. Furthermore, Schenck attempted to exploit a tiny discrepancy between the testimonies of surviving brothers Austin and Jesse Cornelius. Jesse differed from his brother in stating that, as he understood from James, Isham had begun stabbing him only after James shouted for help from his slave Jim. For the defense, the distinction of when Isham brandished his knife was an important one; Schenck used Jesse Cornelius's declaration to argue that the assault turned lethal in the excitement generated by the approach of the slaves, one of whom carried a piece of fence railing. That sequence of events, Schenck asserted, demonstrated that malice aforethought, a necessary element for proving premeditated murder, could not be shown.

Unfortunately for the defendant, Schenck was not allowed to incorporate his manslaughter argument into the instructions given the jury. Judge Heath further undermined counsel's position by declaring that the approach of the slaves had little to do with whether Isham was guilty of murder because the stick with which he struck Cornelius had been recovered and was itself a deadly weapon. The question for the jury to decide was whether the defendant exhibited malice aforethought when he first struck his victim, and Heath informed the jurors that evidence to that effect had been introduced, if they chose to believe it.

"Duty must be consulted before taste," Schenck commented in his diary about another unpleasant case he undertook in the fall of 1859. The jury that heard *State v. Hardaway Bone* appeared to show little hesitation in executing its distasteful duty. Upon the return of a guilty verdict, the Gaston County Superior Court sentenced Edward Isham to be hanged for the murder of James Cornelius. An appeal to the North Carolina Supreme Court was immediately prayed, and Isham's insolvency necessitated the state's waiving security for costs. Schenck wrote, "We appealed but only with the view of delay. My friends complimented my effort but I thought the speech was almost as bad as the case." [44]

The North Carolina Supreme Court did not hold a much higher opinion of the case. Associate justice Matthias E. Manly wrote an opinion that speedily dealt with the issues Schenck had raised. Beginning with how the jurors had been selected, the court held that there was no error in declaring competent a juror who admitted to having formed an opinion based solely on rumor about the defendant's guilt but who was willing to afford the defendant an impartial hearing. In addition, the defendant had no right to postpone showing cause for challenging a juror; only the state, which in common-law tradition had lost the right of peremptory challenge, could exercise that privilege. Other defense arguments received even less attention: principles too familiar for the court to review regarding the admissibility of testimony would have addressed each of counsel's objections, and the instructions Schenck requested for the jury were predicated on the unfounded assumption that there was mutual combat between the defendant and his victim. "Clothe it in the details of the evidence," Justice Manly solemnly concluded, "and it is a very bad case." The supreme court found no error, and, in the spring term of 1860, Isham stood before Judge James W. Osborne and was sentenced "to be taken to the place of public execution and on that day [May 25] between the hours of Eleven O'Clock A.M. and Three O'Clock in the afternoon to be hanged by the neck until dead." [45]

In the autobiography he narrated to David Schenck, Isham recounted nearly threescore fights, beginning with a childhood scuffle and ending twenty years later with the murder of a farmer. Sometime after the ink of the account had dried, Schenck abruptly ended his notebook entry of Isham's life with the penciled notation "Hanged 25 May 1860." By that time, James Cornelius had been dead for a year. Whether or not the execution of Edward Isham generated public excitement in Dallas is unknown. "We learn he made no remarks on the gallows," the *Iredell Express* reported, "but remained unconcerned to the last." Presumably Isham received only a pauper's burial. His infant child—a daughter called Margaret Bone—survived, growing to adulthood and almost certainly knowing what her father had done. That any of Isham's relatives in Georgia or Alabama learned of his fate is doubtful. The survival of Schenck's notebook probably accounts for the fact that at least one local history remembered his story as much as seventy-five years after his crime. [46]

James Cornelius was buried, according to his deathbed wishes, on the land he farmed in Catawba County. The will he devised that bequeathed the bulk of his estate to Austin and Austin's sons was contested by other members of the Cornelius family, and probation was delayed until a final trial could be conducted in Catawba County Superior Court during the fall term of 1860. Like Isham, James Cornelius was remembered long afterward when the county's Department of Public Welfare authorized the relocation of Cornelius family headstones, including his and Austin's, so that Duke Power Company could fashion Lake Norman by inundating the Catawba River valley. [47]

David Schenck profited from the fall circuit of 1859. Referring to the court session in Gaston County, he wrote, "I made here about $200 in Cash and added something to my reputation and practice." Of the $254 in earnings he recorded, he did not indicate any remuneration received for serving as Isham's counsel.[48] A courtroom adversary also helped his practice. So impressed was Schenck with the "most powerful advocate I ever listened to" that he entered into a law partnership with solicitor William Lander in 1860. Their Lincolnton firm enjoyed a respect in neighboring counties that lasted until Lander's death in 1868. By that time, Schenck's renown as a trial lawyer encouraged him to pursue a larger career in the state's judicial and political arenas.[49]

Tightly intertwined strands of poverty, violence, and transience bound Edward Isham's life. He learned both violence and transience from his drunken father, a drifter himself, and a barren existence in the Georgia Upcountry reinforced the lessons. For Isham, the fearsome individualism said to have been fostered by the frontier was perhaps a less significant influence than the relentless struggle for financial survival. The decision to fight for water at the gold mine or the attention of a girlfriend or to avenge a potentially crippling insult required as little rational consideration by Isham as the decision to leave home to escape the law and search elsewhere for another chance. Violence and transience nurtured each other while serving as the only means by which Isham could protect his meager social and economic standing. Such behavior may have been common at other levels of southern society, but in the lives of poor whites it assumes a more somber, brutal overtone. Poor whites might be mocked for their perceived buffoonery, but those who so quickly scorned them and readily stereotyped them had reason to fear them.

Isham's bitterness, the fruit of a lifetime of purposelessness and frustration, eventually found an outlet certain to lead to his condemnation.[50] James Cornelius represented the wrongs Isham believed he had suffered. Whereas Cornelius enjoyed the labor of slaves, Isham had been reduced to working for a free black. While Cornelius surveyed his productive farm, Isham's meager ten acres were taken from him. Finally, after Isham undertook the most unskilled of labor, digging ditches along the edge of a field, Cornelius succeeded in manipulating the legal justice system to forestall payment of the wage due.

The murder of Cornelius was remarkable because of the comparative rarity of such incidents in the antebellum South. The posse, handbills, and newspaper advertisements promising a reward for Isham's arrest, however, indicate that the crime was significant in a way not immediately evident. A society concerned to prevent grievances from transcending racial barriers could not allow the murder of a slaveholder by a poor white to go unpunished. Edward Isham committed a crime not so much by taking the life of another as by undermining the legitimacy of social authority. Today the voices of the dispossessed are hard to hear unless, like Edward Isham, they shouted. It remains for historians of the South to find ways to hear these voices and to listen as the shadowy figures behind them speak.

5

Edward Isham and Criminal Justice for the Poor White in Antebellum North Carolina

SCOTT P. CULCLASURE

Edward Isham was not a nice man. His life on the lam, however, came to an end when he met his match in the form of a family outraged by the murder of one of their own and with enough standing to ensure that Isham did not this time escape the rule of law. Justice in the antebellum South was swift: in the year after James Cornelius's death, Isham was arrested, tried and convicted, refused a retrial by the state supreme court, and hanged. He was hanged and forgotten (except, surely, by the families he left grieving). There is no gravestone inscribed with Hardaway Bone, the name by which he was known in North Carolina.

Perhaps David Schenck recoiled, finding that his client lacked remorse either for the life he had taken or for the purposeless life he had apparently lived.[1] Regardless, the notebook containing Isham's account of himself signified little until a later generation discovered it anew. The most remarkable aspect of Isham's account—the degree to which violence structured his life—is also a sobering reminder to the historian attempting to understand antebellum society. The sword of violence cuts two ways: it defines deep-rooted social values and attitudes and, at the same time, degrees of deviation from expected behavior. Edward Isham's uniqueness should make us cautious about generalizing from his life. Most southerners, after all, did not find themselves prosecuted for affray, mayhem, or assault and battery, much less murder. At the same time, Isham's experience opens multiple lines of inquiry about how poor whites interacted with their world during the antebellum years.[2]

If Edward Isham's treatment represents the response of an established community to fits of unmoderated passion, then the question follows: does the historical record offer further support for the contention that in a region reputed for lawlessness and violence, justice was meted out swiftly to poor white southerners whose actions were perceived as threatening the social order? I searched for such evidence in a source richly mined by Bill Cecil-Fronsman for his recent book, *Common Whites: Class and Culture in Antebellum North Carolina:* [The North Carolina Governor's Papers and Governor's Letter Books].[3]

My study's central conclusion is that the answer cannot be posed as concisely as the question, largely because of the nature of the evidence. This study rests upon the memorials and petitions resulting from homicide convictions that supporters and detractors submitted to the governors of North Carolina during the 1850s. The documents suggest that the combination of violence, transience, and poverty assured these poor white southerners of sterner treatment when they came before the courtroom bar. Yet because this collection of cases is limited by geography to one state and by time to one decade, I have not attempted to apply my findings to southern legal and social history generally. Instead, I have used the memorials and petitions in two ways: to recover the voices of humbler classes of southern whites too often neglected in historical studies and to delineate issues of criminal justice suggested by Edward Isham's experience. Further study of available records from across the South is clearly needed.

A search through the papers and letter books of the North Carolina governors who served from 1850 to 1860 uncovered memorials and petitions for executive clemency on behalf of thirty people convicted of either manslaughter or premeditated murder, two degrees of homicide. These cases each involved the taking of a white southerner's life by another white southerner. To avoid the complicating factor of how slaves were treated in the criminal justice system, a few crimes involving black southerners were purposely omitted from the study. The line between manslaughter and murder was not always clearly drawn; solicitors and attorneys general often advised governors of cases where the prosecution had to content itself with a conviction of manslaughter rather than murder.[4] The memorials and petitions often described the crime, the prisoner, and the deceased and offered evaluations of community feelings, albeit from a one-sided perspective (and a perspective not necessarily favorable to the prisoner). Murder trials were usually appealed to the state's highest court, with the *Supreme Court Reports* often providing concise information about the crimes, how they were prosecuted, and any legal issues that were raised during the trial. Sensational crimes tried in larger towns attracted the attention of newspapers that occasionally printed summaries of testimony.[5]

Finding the homicide cases and locating the petitions is a haphazard process. The Governors' Papers and Governors' Letter Books, housed in the North Carolina State Archives, remain inadequately indexed.[6] Trial court records remain as they were in 1855 when a correspondent of Dorchester, Massachusetts, asked Governor Bragg to send homicide statistics for North Carolina. Bragg lamented in his reply that such information was not at his disposal; one would have to comb through each county's superior court minute dockets to compile the requested information.[7] Various governors' repeated pleas to the General Assembly that such data be collected went unheeded.[8]

Because murder convictions like Edward Isham's rarely resulted in petitions to the governor, the most compelling evidence of how poor whites fared in the antebellum criminal justice system likely lies undisturbed in stacks of docket books. A perusal of minute dockets for two counties' superior courts supports this contention. One docket covering the decade of the 1850s showed a case of manslaughter that was never petitioned to the governor and a murder conviction that was; another, more populous county's docket listed six manslaughter convictions that did not result in pardon petitions.[9] This short list suggests that manslaughter convictions in cases where the state had charged murder usually did not give rise to petitioning. In their correspondence with governors, solicitors often commented on the greater willingness of a community to acknowledge that a murder had been committed than to return a murder conviction. Punishment for manslaughter was usually no more than branding and a few months' imprisonment, and such convictions were usually entreated to the governor only when community members considered the prisoner's actions justified or the punishment unduly severe. Many manslaughter convictions therefore failed to wend their way to the governor's office.

The simplest breakdown of the decade's thirty petition collections shows that thirteen stemmed from manslaughter convictions and seventeen resulted from murder convictions. Of the prisoners found guilty of manslaughter, seven were pardoned and six were not. Democratic governors David Reid and Thomas Bragg—the chief executives whose terms covered most of the 1850s—each granted three pardons and refused another three. The seventeen applications for clemency of murder convictions received a similar overall response, with eight pardons granted and nine refused. Each governor, however, acted differently. Whereas Governor Reid issued four pardons, one outright refusal to pardon, and one reprieve of sentence, his successor, Governor Bragg, refused to grant a pardon in any of the six cases studied.[10] Perhaps Governor Reid, whose political reputation rested upon his campaign for universal manhood suffrage, sympathized more readily with the prisoners whose cases he reviewed.[11] A comment Reid added to a letter accompanying an 1854 pardon of a nonhomicidal crime offers insight into some of the frustrations that attended the petition process: "I send you a Pardon for Hux. The petition was quite long, but omitted to set forth the material fact of the offense of which he was convicted. I have guessed that it was for Assault and Battery, & have written the pardon accordingly. If I have not pardoned him for the right offense therefore it is not my fault."[12]

In the final busy months of 1859, Democratic governor John Ellis pardoned four murder convictions but declined to pardon a fifth one.[13] Governor Ellis might have agreed with the observation

Superior Court Judge Robert Saunders made a year earlier to Governor Bragg: capital felonies appeared to be dramatically increasing in number, perhaps as much as 25 percent in the last twenty years.[14] Even so, execution remained an uncommon occurrence. The prisoner Governor Ellis refused to pardon was a man named John Starling, guilty of murdering Sally Cotton. Together with Edward Isham, whose conviction no one cared to bring before the governor, Starling went to the gallows as one of only two men executed by the state during the year preceding the taking of the 1860 federal census.[15]

The fact that cases involving friendless poor white southerners like Edward Isham remained unrecovered became evident immediately during research for this study. After all, memorials and petitions in homicide cases resulted from the actions of friendly parties—or, in instances of counterpetitioning, from those who opposed a pardon—and only rarely from the direct efforts of a prisoner. No one in the Catawba County community of Sherrill's Ford where James Cornelius was murdered dreamed of petitioning for the pardon of Isham.

Individuals and communities torn by the most serious of capital offenses struggled, however, to make the judicial system correspond with personal views of justice. White southerners of humbler means appeared to be treated with consideration if the community putting them on trial could recognize shared bonds of personal character or appreciate circumstances they judged to mitigate the crime. Prisoners deserved pardon, petitioners repeatedly argued, because a killing resulted inadvertently from a drunken fight or because the victim was of disreputable character. Even more dramatic are the glimpses that many cases provide of the societal tensions that also existed just beneath a surface of consensus and just beyond the view of historians. These cases, sometimes directly but often obliquely, illuminate the intersection of legal principle, social class behavior, and community expectations.

Nearly one-fourth of the petitions demonstrated the volatility of relations between men and women, especially among humbler social groups. The arguments presented in court, the justifications offered in memorials and petitions, and the responses of governors hint at the struggles of antebellum communities to define justice in the relations between men and women.[16] The women in these cases did not fare well: drunkenness could excuse a husband's behavior, and a woman's hesitation in fleeing an assault might be understood as meaning that she was in no immediate danger of losing her life. Even in a case like Alvin Preslar's, where a husband's compelling cruelty led to the murder of his wife, two trials were required before a conviction could be reached that withstood appeal to the North Carolina Supreme Court.[17]

Alvin Preslar of Union County owned land valued at about five hundred dollars and an equal amount in securities. He was married to a woman named Esther (who remained unnamed in court records) and, according to the 1850 census, had fathered two girls and four boys. The only surviving description of Esther Preslar from the time of her husband's trial was that she was "a fat woman." During the afternoon on November 21, 1855, Esther Preslar met the wrath of her drunken husband.[18]

The quarrel instigated by Alvin Preslar concerned "a tract of land," but the exact circumstances are unclear. For nearly two hours Alvin had repeatedly threatened Esther with a knife and an ax and had kicked, choked, and beaten her across her bonnet-clad head with "a sound piece of sap pine wood." This account was uncontested. When Alvin had finally finished with her and lay down, fully dressed, to rest, Esther sought escape. She collected her nine-month-old baby, a quilt, several yards of spun cotton, and extra clothes and beseeched her eighteen-year-old son, Noah, who had witnessed her abuse through the chinks of the family's log cabin, to walk with her to her father's house, a distance of about two and one-half miles.[19]

Still recovering from earlier bouts with chills and the mumps, and walking in the evening through rain-dampened woods, Esther Preslar was unable to complete her trip. Despite repeated stops for rest, she told her son that instead of continuing, she would spread her quilt by the road and sleep the remainder of the night. Her stepmother found her the next morning only about a hundred yards from the house and feebly struggling to catch her runaway infant. Esther was unable either to stand or to lift her arms. Her body was swollen and covered with bruises especially across her abdomen, and all she could swallow was a little coffee. That evening, she told her sister Lecy that she was dying, for her husband "had kicked her about to death." Esther Preslar died early the next morning.[20]

The opinion of the examining doctor was that neither Esther's beating nor her exposure after she left her house was in itself sufficient to cause death. The question for the court, as the judge charged the jury, was one of assigning responsibility: had Alvin Preslar murdered his wife by driving her from home in a weakened condition after severely beating her, or had Esther Preslar caused her own death by leaving of a free will and needlessly exposing her weakened self to the elements? Of the three counts of murder brought against the defendant, the jury returned a guilty verdict on the one that alleged that Esther Preslar died from the combined causes of the beating and subsequent exposure. Alvin Preslar was convicted of deliberately causing his wife's death.[21]

The supreme court, however, found no evidence that Esther Preslar had been forced to stay out in the open air for the entire night. Her preparations after her husband went to sleep suggested to the court considerable deliberation rather than hasty flight. Certainly, her decision to stop by the road so near to the shelter she sought and spend the night outdoors could not be blamed on Alvin Preslar. The court found error and ordered a new trial.[22]

Preslar was convicted a second time, this time on the charge that the blows he inflicted were in themselves sufficient to cause death. By December 1856, Governor Bragg had received petitions presented by Alvin's brother, Elias, that were signed by over 200 people. Alvin Preslar, the petitioners claimed, had killed his wife in what general opinion held was the "result of a drunken frolic." He "appeared unconscious of having done any serious injury to his wife," and he remained at home unaware of her death until his arrest. But the worst of his circumstances was the fact that, after a year of being "locked up and chained down in a dark and solitary dungeon," Preslar was being defrauded of his possessions by a doctor who had testified in the first trial on behalf of the prisoner and the doctor's brother. Preslar had signed his property and securities over to the two men to prevent the state from recovering them for an earlier, unspecified court judgment. Now the two men had refused to help the prisoner post bond for a second supreme court appeal! One petition stated that this fraud, added to the forlornness of the prisoner's "helpless little children," who were brought to the county seat with frostbitten toes, had aroused considerable public sympathy. Surely the eighteen-year-old Noah could not be considered helpless, but petitioners often spoke of forlorn children about to lose their surviving parent.[23]

In the closing days of 1856, solicitor William Lander—the same individual who later prosecuted Edward Isham—responded to a plea from Governor Bragg to clarify what had become a complicated situation. Lander acknowledged the fraudulent conveyance of property and how the case might appear worthy of pardon if one had looked only at the supreme court decision. For Lander, however, the crime was clearly proved at the second trial, where medical evidence supplied by doctors other than the one who was allegedly cheating Preslar of his property convinced the jury that blood found within the abdominal cavity meant that the blows in themselves had been fatal. The refusal of the first jury to convict on this count and its decision to settle instead on a more equivocal one could be explained by the fact that one of Preslar's relatives had somehow been seated on the jury, where he had threatened to deadlock the proceedings. "I think it was considered to be an aggravated case of murder by all concerned as well as by the whole community," Lander concluded in an estimation of public opinion strikingly different from the tone of the petitions. "I can only add that the case disclosed against the prisoner more cruelty and barbarity towards his wife . . . than any other case I ever witnessed."[24] Governor Bragg was unwilling to do anything more than grant a reprieve for one month, which meant that Alvin Preslar would go to the gallows in February of 1857.[25]

Not surprisingly, few prisoners were thought incorrigible by their supporters. Joseph Benson Starns, for example, was convicted in Union County in 1852 for the manslaughter of Samuel A. Garey.

Petitioners described him as having "heretofore sustained a most unexceptionable character for honesty, truth, propriety of demeanor and steady habits." Some defendants were also vilified by their detractors in counterpetitions that were probably subject to the same degree of exaggeration. To his detractors, Starns "exhibited a ferocity of nature & a depravity of heart in the murder that is seldom equalled in the annals of crime"! He stabbed Garey "in the darkness of night with a suddenness & ferocity from which there was no retreat." Victims likewise were described in extreme terms; they were either dissolute reprobates or innocents dying in the presence of loved ones. Garey, the victim of Starns's attack, was represented by partisans for Starns as "a fierce, irascible, overbearing, tyrannical and dangerous man." Those who mourned Garey for stab wounds inflicted by Starns said that he died "in the very arms of the heart broken mother."[26]

Reputation and social standing—whether of the prisoner or of the deceased—often determined how a case would appear to both the local community and the governor's office.[27] If a victim consorted with the hated class of free blacks, the community thought he probably deserved the ill treatment he received, but even someone as much a stranger as an Irish immigrant like Florence McCarthy could receive public support if he shared in values like hard work and minding his own business.[28]

Reputation of the victim apparently played a role in Governor Reid's decision to pardon Abram Thomason for the 1854 murder of Ivey Jones. Thomason remains a shadowy figure; his name does not appear in the census reports for Brunswick County, and little is said of him in the single petition found in the Governors' Papers.[29] Ivey Jones, however, was more clearly perceived. A thirty-one-year-old man whose property was worth only eighty dollars, he and wife Elizabeth were the illiterate parents of two children.[30] The petitioners described Jones as "a man of low bad character" disliked by his neighbors. They believed they had good reason for their estimation. This "very powerful, strong, and athletic man" was widely known as a liar and a thief. This list culminated with the victim's worst trait: Ivey Jones was an associate of "free negroes."[31]

Apparently Thomason stabbed Jones after great, though not legal, provocation. The record does not describe the cause of the assault. Of the three wounds, Dr. Lucas testified that the one that cut out Jones's bowels killed him. Help came when neighbors heard Jones shout, "I am stabbed!" He was found lying in the arms of a free black, and he instantly blamed Thomason. When Jones died a few days later, he left behind no friends who would send a petition to the governor's office to counter the claims for mercy afforded by the many people who wanted the prisoner freed. Abram Thomason received Governor Reid's pardon for the murder of Ivey Jones on October 23, 1854.[32]

Florence McCarthy also benefited from the efforts of others, although in many important ways he remained a stranger in Chatham County. In 1856 McCarthy was one of four Irish immigrants working as a laborer near Lockville on the canal project of the Cape Fear and Deep River Navigation Company. The four, McCarthy especially, were bullied unmercifully by a native laborer named Silas Pollard. For two weeks McCarthy withstood Pollard's abuse of his country, occupation, and politics. The fight that Pollard finally provoked led to his death and charges of manslaughter against the Irishmen.[33]

Three of the workers were acquitted, but McCarthy was found guilty within what Judge Person admitted was a strict application of the law. The petitioners quoted the judge as expressing surprise that any individual "endowed with common feelings and passions of humanity could have experienced so much forbearance as the prisoner did." According to the *Greensboro Patriot,* Judge Person even refused to have McCarthy branded, a punishment usually administered in the court's presence as soon as the sentence was pronounced.[34]

Too poor to post bail, McCarthy was sent to jail for three months. What most concerned McCarthy's petitioners was how imprisonment had disturbed his equanimity. Petitioners feared that a man noted for being "remarkably industrious and attentive to business" was now losing his mind. "He fancies that his life is in continual danger from cutthroats & demons—A mouse is sufficient to fill him with indescribable terror."[35] A laborer vulnerable because of his isolation from the common culture in which he worked, and yet appealing because of his habits of industriousness, Florence McCarthy had aroused the sympathy of the community. How he fared after receiving Governor Bragg's pardon of December 4, 1856, was not reported.

If a poor but hardworking stranger could meet with public approval, someone of greater social status might be condemned for liberties taken with humbler folk. Cases like these point toward limits on behavior insisted upon by the local community and rarely undermined by governors.[36] The richly documented case involving Wilson W. Boyd illustrates clearly how quickly a killing across social lines could bring feelings of resentment to the surface. A merchant and partner in dry goods with John Stacy, Boyd had originally come to Anson County's Wadesboro as a peddler. He was said to have been born "of poor obscure" but "nevertheless respectable" parents, very unlike his victim. Boyd's troubles began in October 1851, when the store in which he worked was visited by Colonel Martin J. Pickett. Coming from a large and locally well known family, Pickett's father had been a prominent attorney who had served in the state legislature. His son now bore a military title that reflected more the respect with which the family was held than any real military experience.[37]

Supporters of Boyd said that the "turbulence" of Pickett's character went back to his boyhood. This characteristic surfaced when Pickett visited the store of Stacy and Boyd and asked Stacy if he owed the store any money. Stacy replied that his only transaction was five dollars Boyd had charged, an amount that included a loan of cash and the purchase of a few small items. Later, as Boyd and Pickett examined the account book, Pickett disputed the debt, lost his temper, and accused Boyd of dishonesty. Boyd returned the insult by characterizing Pickett as "a damned rascal," which nearly provoked a fight. Pickett leaped over the counter and came at Boyd with a bowie knife before being restrained by Stacy. From this time forward, hard feelings between the two men festered. Before long, Boyd was known by his friends to be carrying a pair of pistols: "He would not be caught with his breeches down again," one witness remembered him saying. Tensions ran high the day before the fatal confrontation, and Pickett, conducting business as a magistrate in a room of Sigman's Hotel, was accused of threatening the merchant with a chair when Boyd came into his presence.[38]

The killing took place on August 22, 1852. On that Sunday morning, Pickett was walking down the street from his house toward Sigman's Hotel, where Boyd boarded. As he approached the hotel, he saw Boyd lounging on the piazza with other townsmen, including the sheriff, who sat in a chair leaning against the wall next to the parlor door. Pickett crossed the street, put his foot upon the piazza step, and, leaning forward with his uplifted cane, told Boyd he knew Boyd was his enemy and repeated a warning about "peeping" at him with a glaring eye. Boyd rose from his seat and began to retreat toward the parlor. Most witnesses testified that Pickett struck Boyd with his cane, at which point Boyd fired a pistol. As they fell into the street, Boyd fired a second round point blank at Pickett, leaving powder burns on Pickett's clothing. Pickett lay mortally wounded. In a dying statement, he protested his innocence and accused Boyd of harassment.[39]

Wilson Boyd's trial was moved to neighboring Richmond County at the instigation, his petitioners claimed, of Pickett's friends, who knew that the Wadesboro community would refuse to convict the prisoner. In a letter to the governor, P. M. Powell claimed that the trial judge was prejudiced against Boyd and too drunk to see justice done. After Boyd was found guilty of manslaughter and sentenced to be branded, but before the sentence could be executed, fifty people in the crowded courtroom clamored to free the prisoner by force. Although counsel for the defense dissuaded the crowd from such action, Powell thought that a mob of as many as a thousand people was prepared to storm the jail in which Boyd was to be imprisoned for twelve months.[40]

Community support for Boyd was palpable. In the middle of October, a meeting of citizens was held in nearby Lilesville to approve resolutions affirming their law-abiding nature but insisting on Boyd's liberation. Another meeting was scheduled to attract supporters from all the counties neighboring Anson, so widely was

Boyd's case known. The petitions eventually sent to Governor Reid included the signatures of over 3,000 citizens! Boyd was described in one memorial as a "poor young man" of twenty-six years who would benefit from the $600 that had been raised to cover the costs of his prosecution, which his sentence required him to pay. Boyd's defense lawyers provided the governor with their recollection of all the trial testimony, and the clerk of superior court sent a suggestive affidavit saying that his transcript of the evidence had been removed from his files.[41]

Only one letter came to the governor from someone sympathetic to Pickett, and that statement most clearly puts into relief the prevalent social tensions. J. Medley, who said he had been friends with both parties but was personally interested only in principles of justice, explained the excitement of the community as growing "out of an unfortunate prejudice owing to the deference [difference] of there [*sic*] positions in society[,] Col Pickett moving in the higher circles of life[,] Mr Boyd being in the more humble walks of life. . . . the lower classes seem to be deranged upon the subject." In short, the common people believed that because Pickett "was a rich man and struck a poor man with a stick they seem to think it was right to take his life."[42] Medley's voice was a lone one, but it might have resonated with others who felt it too impolitic to speak out against Boyd. The memorials and petitions sent on behalf of Wilson Boyd were overwhelming, and Governor Reid pardoned him on November 23, 1852.[43]

Historians have noted how formal justice can be understood only within a context of societal values.[44] The degree to which poor whites in antebellum North Carolina were singled out for punishment by the criminal justice system remains an open question, largely because they were the ones least likely to have their pleas carried to the governor's office. The memorials and petitions that do exist reflect the paradoxes that often afflicted antebellum attitudes. Communities condemned those who associated with free blacks, yet sympathized with honest, bullied underdogs. Circumstances like the abuse of alcohol or denied opportunities for education were, it was argued, mitigating factors in fatal assaults. At the same time, juries tended to believe that each individual, even a victimized woman, acted as a free agent of his or her will. An appearance of consensus among white social groups could quickly be punctured by feelings that a less privileged individual had been abused by one of greater prestige. If the drama of the courtroom represents extremes in antebellum behavior among southern whites, it also provides a unique opportunity to examine tensions that often escape detection elsewhere. The voices of many southerners can be heard today only in the memorials and petitions that rest in archival boxes.

6

Mothers, Lovers, and Wives: Images of Poor White Women in Edward Isham's Autobiography

VICTORIA E. BYNUM

In many ways, Mary Brown lived a life as ordinary as her name. A white woman born in Alabama, she married at about the age of twenty, gave birth to several children, and probably died before the age of forty.[1] Yet her life did bear a certain distinction. She was once the mate of Edward Isham, a notorious murderer known as "Hardaway Bone" in western North Carolina, where he was hanged in May 1860. And if one believes Edward's confession to his lawyer, she was one of the few women who, rather than endure his abusive behavior, rejected him—twice in fact.

Edward's autobiography suggests that a poor white southern woman might negotiate her future at least somewhat within the sorely limited parameters of the antebellum backcountry. According to Edward, Mary was twenty years old, "very pretty," and already married when she ran off with him to Georgia around 1848. They first met when he visited his brother—Mary's brother-in-law—in Macon County, Alabama.[2] Edward and Mary became engaged, but then he wandered back to his native state of Georgia, presumably expecting her to await his return. Instead, in perhaps a calculated move, she quickly married Peter Windley. Upon Edward's return to Alabama, nothing would do for him but to win Mary back; he persuaded her to ditch Peter and run off with him.[3]

Mary seemed not to blink at abandoning one husband for another. The swiftness with which she replaced Peter with Edward suggests that these "marriages" lacked formal legal sanction. Indeed, Edward's allusions to his own and others' marriages frequently referred to cohabitations that over time could have qualified as common law unions but in the short run lacked the sanction of either state or church. Informal and fleeting marriages bespoke the precarious nature of domestic life in a region known for its economically distressed and highly transient laboring population.[4]

Like his new wife, Edward was born and raised in the southern backcountry during an era in which raw physical struggle was a fundamental fact of life. Poor men labored, mined, or farmed small tracts of land merely to survive; to compensate for their lack of wealth and social prestige, many earned their badges of masculine honor through gambling, brawling, drinking, and debauching women.[5] The same traits that likely attracted Mary to Edward—his powerful build, "mild blue eyes," and "rather good looking" countenance—perhaps allowed Edward to indulge his penchant for violence and lawlessness longer than most men of his class would have dared.[6]

Like many lower-class men, Edward seemed to take pride in shocking genteel society. Unable to achieve economic or political prowess, he instead intimidated others with his toughness and fists. Edward proudly described his early twenties to his lawyer as his "prime," a period in which he had been "a great wrestler" and "could not be thrown down." He recounted—and probably embellished—tales of bitings, fingernail slashings, and eye gougings. At age ten, he explained, a gun blast had blown off one of his thumbs. Despite the ignoble death that lay before him, Edward laid claim to a life of "manly" behavior.[7]

The fact that Edward left behind an autobiography, not a diary, that compiled tales of male prowess is important. His memories were surely selective, some of them chosen to exhibit the strength and power he craved.[8] By dictating his life's story to his lawyer, he contributed to antebellum America's voluminous store of oral and written tales about life in the "wild" southern backcountry. Popular literature of the day was filled with both serious accounts and "tall tales" that celebrated the most primitive rituals of manhood in a frontier theater. As Elliott Gorn and Carroll Smith-Rosenberg have argued, such tales inverted the genteel principles of eastern society, evoking fantasies of individual freedom in an increasingly market-driven society while warning of the dangers of disorder. "Nature," writes Smith-Rosenberg, "was a chaotic power that simultaneously enticed and demanded taming."[9]

Women appeared frequently in rough-and-tumble tales of the backcountry and were as likely to flout conventions of ladyhood as men were the conventions of gentlemen. Particularly in the Davy Crockett Almanacs, popular between 1835 and 1860, stories about "wild" women titillated eastern audiences with images of a world in which women were as untamed and as sexually aggressive as men.[10]

The letters of Peter D. Swaim, Esq., to his friend Benjamin Elliot vividly expressed the influence of such images on one "gentleman" forced to live in the North Carolina backcountry. After Swaim went to work in 1841 for a doctor in Montgomery County, he complained that his new home was a "heathenish, outlandish part of creation." The region was filled, he wrote, with "hills and valleys, Mountains and rivers . . . even Wild Cats." Although he found the county to be "dissipated" and its churches without preachers, who in any case would have had no "hearers," the "gals" were "modals of pure [physical] perfection."[11] Living in this state of nature physically invigorated Swaim. On August 29, 1843, he wrote that his experiences in "these mountains have made me a heap '*Tougher.*'" For emphasis, he added "'*Tough, Tougher, Toughest.*'"[12]

In the same letter, Swaim offered his own tall tale about life in Montgomery County. He described meeting "a female giant" along the road, "a perfect 6 foot specimen—a real two hundred pounder."[13] The two began to tussle, with the woman clearly gaining the upper hand. As was common in frontier tales, Swaim intertwined sex and violence by fusing images of sexual intercourse with images of the battlefield. He wrote that he finally "threatened to bring my battering ram into my service—but so far from its intimidating her, it only done her good to think I would resort to such a means of defence.—She insinuated that her *castle* had been stormed with Battering Rams and all other impalements of war without the least injury.—But I carried my plan into execution . . . . When peace was declared I resolved never to go into another engagement with such unmerciful big '*Generals.*'"[14]

In keeping with the genre of frontier literature, Edward Isham described women who freely engaged in sexual relationships, drank alcohol, and took up arms with and against men. His narrative did not, however, provide explicit descriptions of sexual activity even though stories of flirtations, adultery, and thwarted love abounded. Perhaps because Attorney Schenck wrote his client's autobiography in his capacity as a lawyer, he may have edited its contents. He twice deleted a word used by Edward to describe what in legal terms were probably "disorderly" or "bawdy" houses. Schenck's deletions seem to indicate a distaste for overtly sexual language.[15] He displayed no squeamishness, however, about reporting details of Edward's innumerable tales of mayhem. Raw violence seemed to shock his genteel sensibilities far less than did raw sex.

Edward's relentlessly violent behavior revealed the dark side of masculinity taken to excess. It also revealed the class limits of his male prerogatives. When he killed James Cornelius, he did not merely commit murder—an act he claimed to have attempted several times in the past and to have succeeded at once before. He killed a respected slaveowner from a community in which he himself was an outsider. By hanging "Hardaway Bone," North Carolina's law-abiding citizens purged their society of a man they viewed as menacing and uncivilized. They also reinforced the cultural and class boundaries between propertied and landless men.[16]

What can we learn about women from this autobiographical saga of brutal manhood? Although many women appear on its pages, insights into their world are particularly limited by the manuscript's "confession" mode, which dictated that Edward explain himself to the world, not his world to others. He "confessed" his interactions with women in order to explain his own actions. Whether writing about his mother, wives, or lovers, Edward used women as markers for the high and low points of his tumultuous life. They alternately provided him with refuge, nurturing, and sex. His mother, for example, regularly sheltered him from the desperate situations created by his penchant for raucous living. His three wives enabled his fitful attempts at sobriety and stability, and his many lovers gratified his insatiable craving for adventure, excitement, and escape from personal responsibilities.

Poor women waged difficult struggles in this male-dominated world in which norms of masculine behavior undercut their own ability to gain personal fulfillment and a measure of prosperity. For men like Edward, women were "prizes" to be protected or stolen from one another in contests for mastery. Jane Mobley, for example, became the object of Edward's affections when he "fell out about her" with Jim Fletcher, another suitor. She must have felt a mixture of fear and excitement when Edward "got a double barrelled gun and went up to see" her. Edward reached above his class, however, when he took up with Anne Baldwin, who, he said, "had some money . . . [and] I concluded I would get it." After successfully driving off Anne's "old beau" with a rock, Edward tangled with her father, who "cursed me for being with his 'gal' and fired a horse pistol at me but missed." [17]

Perhaps it excited Jane Mobley and Anne Baldwin to have lovers and fathers fight over them with such fierceness. These battles, after all, established their value in a world ordered by men. But as in the case of Mary Brown, male competition also offered women opportunities to escape unhappy situations they were otherwise powerless to change. Women's ability to manipulate or instigate male struggles over "ownership" of them constituted their major sphere of power.

Edward described one woman who even dared enforce rules of competition over women. He recalled a time when he "got too intimate with a free [black] girl" and raised the ire of Betsy Wedding, a white woman being "kept" by Warner Lyon, the owner of a "grocery store" or tavern. White men frequently crossed the color line in search of sexual partners, but Edward violated an important taboo when he escorted the African American woman to Warner Lyon's tavern. Betsy, he reported, almost shot him with a double-barreled shotgun a few nights later.[18] Maintaining taboos against inter-racial courtship protected poor white women's "superior" value over black women, thus providing some compensation for their inferior class standing. In practical terms, enforcement of racial boundaries limited the number of women who competed for men.

There were stark limits, however, to female power. Jane Mobley changed her mind about running off a second time with Edward when she discovered that he already had a wife. Anne Baldwin may never have realized that Edward wanted only her money. And although Betsy Wedding struck a blow for men's obligation to display public deference toward white women, she was powerless to prevent their clandestine transgressions of the racial line, which were far more frequent. As poor white women struggled to find male protectors (preferably husbands), they risked debauchment and abandonment by men seeking pleasure and profit, not wives. As the words of a popular folksong warned, "He will hug you and kiss you and tell you more lies than leaves on the green tree or stars in the skies."[19]

Curiously, in a manuscript replete with violence, Edward recounted no violence committed by men against women. When one considers the purpose of his confession to Schenck, however, this is perhaps not surprising. By striking a woman, a man exhibited masculine prerogative, not masculine prowess. Even though husbands could legally beat, or "chastise" errant wives, striking a woman was not considered an honorable act.[20] In 1857, a North Carolina newspaper applauded the "sternly righteous" Superior Court judge who fined wife-beater Stephen Cole $500 and sentenced him to ten days' imprisonment for exceeding the boundaries of this right. Similarly, in 1859 another North Carolina newspaper editor congratulated a man who beat up his sister's husband for indulging in what the editor sarcastically called the "*manly* pastime" of beating women.[21] In his final representation of himself to the world, Edward Isham strove to display male bravado and prowess. Stories about men fighting *over* women, not *with* them, furthered this end.

Neither Edward's silence in regard to male violence against women, nor newspaper editors' denunciations of it, meant that men refrained from beating women or received punishment for doing so. North Carolina's governor, for example, reduced Stephen Cole's fine to $250 after Walter L. Steele, a prominent planter, petitioned on Cole's behalf. Steele described Cole's wife as "lewd," a "brutal vixen," and a "she-devil." Society tolerated, even approved, men's battering of unruly or déclassé women. The court records of the Old South are replete with cases that reveal widespread tolerance for violence by men against women.[22]

The manuscript's limits as a tool for gauging men's physical abuse of women are strikingly evident when we compare it to the antebellum diary of William Johnson. Johnson, a free black barber and slaveholder who chronicled events in Natchez, Mississippi, for almost sixteen years, frequently recorded the violent actions of both men and women.[23] As an African American, Johnson's consciousness of racial inequities made him particularly sensitive to abuse of black women by white men. He told, for example, of one white man who forced a free black woman to walk through the market "with her cloathes hanging all off at each shoulder. Her back was very much whipped." In another entry, he expressed disgust for a white man who beat a free woman of color so badly that she eventually died from her wounds. Despite a court trial, the white man "got clear of the charge . . . Rascally. Rascally."[24]

Notwithstanding Johnson's disgust with these wanton beatings of the most powerless of women, he accepted violence as a tool for controlling one's underlings. In one entry, he noted that he was ready to beat "old Mary," his mother's slave, "untill I make her faint," for stealing biscuits from a city hotel. On another occasion, he gave a "few cuts" of a whip to his own mother, who regularly embarrassed him with her public quarrels. He also wrote with amusement about a white man who chained his daughter in irons to prevent her from marrying a woodchopper.[25] As long as men's physical coercion of women remained intraracial, Johnson accepted it as a natural expression of male authority.

While Edward Isham did not admit to acts of violence against women, he often demonstrated his lack of any particular respect for them. He casually recounted seducing, impregnating, and abandoning women. In one case, he mentioned hiring a "pretty girl named Mary Dagget" to cook for him while he was digging gold in Cobb County. When work ran out, he took her to De Kalb County and simply "left her" there when he decided to return to Pinetown in Carroll County. In another instance, he mentioned seeing a woman whom he had impregnated years earlier. "She met me up the road," he said, "and had the child with her but I did not know her." [26]

In regard to all but his third "marriage," Edward admitted to committing adultery. He also admitted to stealing from women. In addition to seducing Anne Baldwin in order to get her money, he cheated the wife of an acquaintance out of a pair of shoes and stole a pocketbook from a drunken "old negro woman." [27] Thus, although Edward did not specifically cite physical abuses of women, by him or anyone else, time and again he described treatments of women that revealed his shameless disregard for the traditional female prerogatives of deference and protection from men. In such an environment, violence seemed certain to have occasionally erupted between him and women.

Edward's antisocial behavior only increased as he entered his thirties. Yet a decade before his arrest for murder, when he brought his new wife, Mary, to his boyhood home of Pinetown, it appeared that he might embrace mature manhood. He left Mary in Pinetown only long enough to find work in Ringgold, near the Tennessee border. He then returned for her and his mother (also named Mary), who now came to live with them. According to Edward, "I went up to Walker County to hunt a house, and split rails . . . til I got money enough to bring my mother and Mary up there." [28] But despite this promising foray into respectable life, he raised only one crop on his new farm. He soon began hanging out at the local taverns, where he frequently engaged in fights with other neighborhood men.

Edward's dissolute behavior soon got the best of him and his marriage. He abandoned farming for railroad work in Chattanooga but soon encountered "a difficulty with some Irishmen boat hands about some lewd women." Meanwhile, Mary remained in Georgia, where Edward presumably expected her and his mother to keep company quietly until he returned. After spending an undisclosed period of time carousing in the Chattanooga area, he returned home and seemed genuinely surprised to find "something wrong with Mary, she did not treat me kindly." Mary, it seemed, had decided not to remain the wife of a man given to drinking, gambling, and adultery.[29]

At first, Edward was unable to grasp that his wife had abandoned him. Jealous, he secretly followed her as she performed her daily tasks. Around dusk, as she walked to a well for water, Mary visited the cabin of one Noah Vineyard. Edward "slipped up" to find Noah "sitting on a bed with her and [with] his arms around her." Pandemonium ensued. Startled to find her husband at the cabin door, Mary ran off. Edward, of course, immediately challenged Noah to a fight, firing on him three times but failing to hit him.[30] In the end, Edward claimed to accept Mary's rejection of him, saying he "had but little to do with her" anymore, although she continued to live in Chattanooga, probably near his mother.[31]

In conducting a romance with Noah, Mary adhered to a familiar female pattern of escaping one man by taking up with another. Both her affair and her impulse to run when "caught" by her husband made perfect sense in this ardently patriarchal world.[32] To have stood her ground before Edward might have been dangerous. Personal boldness in a woman equaled "sauciness"; aggressive behavior transformed her into a shrew or, worse, a whore who warranted physical discipline. In the traditional literature so revered by white southerners, meekness, chastity, and self-sacrifice emerged as cardinal characteristics of both upper- and lower-class "good" women.[33] Yet these very characteristics promised Mary a life of misery with Edward Isham. She chose, instead, to freeze him out and, most important, to find refuge in the arms of a new male protector.

Geoffrey Chaucer would have sympathized with Mary's dilemma and would have appreciated her solution. The English chronicler of "good women" understood the self-defeating paradox faced by women shackled to classical notions of true womanhood. A good woman's only true virtue—chastity—was superior to man's, yet she lacked his reason and physical prowess and thus needed his protection. In return, she ministered to man's most intimate needs for nurture and sex.

While the ideal of true womanhood permeated both upper and

lower classes, its practical applications might differ. As Chaucer's Dido, the ruler of Carthage, remarked of Aeneas, the Trojan object of her desires: "He has such manly virtues, I can tell, / And he can do so many things so well / That all my love, my being, he has won." Destined to attain her highest nobility in self-sacrificing love, Dido was also doomed to become Aeneas's sexual victim. When he proved untrue, she could only wail: "You will not from your wife thus foully flee? / Alas, that I was born! what shall I do?" She did, of course, what all good women thwarted in love must do: she ran a sword through her heart in the name of martyred womanhood.[34]

Mary, however, did not martyr herself. Showing more the spirit of Chaucer's frankly sexual and self-interested Good Wife of Bath, she also exhibited the practical concerns of a poor woman—she quickly married husband number three, Hiram J. Brown. By 1850, she and Hiram lived in Ringgold, surrounded by Brown kinfolk. Hiram worked as a mechanic while Mary tended their six-month-old son.[35] Good looks and flirtatious ways had finally gained for Mary what every ordinary southern girl knew she must obtain: a steady, hardworking husband who would "make her a living." This was no small accomplishment in a region where, as Elliott Gorn notes, a poor man's role "was defined less by his ability as a bread-winner than by his ferocity."[36]

Perhaps Mary better understood the implications of remaining with a man like Edward because of the fate of her mother-in-law, Mary Isham. After all, the senior Edward Isham provided the model for the behavior of Edward, Jr. In his earliest recollection of boy-hood fights, Edward recalled that his father belittled him for be-ing scared and later cut his hair after an opponent held him by it and whipped him. He further described the elder Edward as a "dissipated" man who wasted his property and moved his family frequently.[37]

Sometime after 1840, Edward, Sr., left Edward's mother and took up with twenty-five-year-old Cynda Elkins.[38] Mary Isham, im-poverished, middle-aged, and the mother of perhaps seven chil-dren, did not likely anticipate or seek remarriage. Like many south-ern women, she had married at the earliest bloom of womanhood.

She was born between 1806 and 1810, and by 1828 had given birth to at least two sons and one daughter.[39] When abandoned by her husband in midlife, she entered the world of menial labor. Edward reported that she sold cakes and liquor and took in boarders.[40]

The younger Mary managed to avoid her mother-in-law's fate. She shed two mates before she reached twenty-one, apparently avoided being impregnated by either, and employed her youthful charms to gain a third husband quickly. Multiple liaisons did not prevent her from eventually forming a stable relationship that modestly improved her economic status. She died sometime between 1860 and 1870, while still in her thirties. Had she lived longer, of course, she might have suffered the same fate as her former mother-in-law. Certainly, Hiram Brown wasted little time in marrying a younger woman and beginning a new family after her death.[41]

At times, it seemed that the elder Mary Isham merely traded life with a dissipated husband for one with a dissipated son. When railroad work beckoned, Edward moved them over the state line to Chattanooga. Mother and son had not settled long before Edward hit a man with a brickbat, stole a horse, and fled back to Georgia to evade arrest. When he returned to Chattanooga after engaging in a series of scraps, his mother sheltered him until he hit the road once again.[42]

Mary may have preferred her son to remain on the lam, since his returns home inevitably created chaos. A months-long binge of "drinking & gambling" on the road ended when Edward was "knocked . . . senseless" by a stranger and returned to his mother's home "hurt badly" and "scared." For the one and only time in his confession, Edward reported that "I reflected on my course [in life] and for awhile was disposed to do better."[43] He had, after all, lost his wife and, now, almost his life. If Mary Brown earlier saw her mother-in-law's life before her, surely Edward now saw his father's before him.

Despite his reflections, however, Edward changed his address rather than his course in life. In a renewed quest for safety and work, he again disrupted his mother's life, much like his father before him. Fined by a Chattanooga court for participating in a "fuss," he now moved himself and his mother down to Ringgold, Georgia, where she resumed selling cakes and he resumed gambling. For Mary Isham, hard work, frequent moves, and disorderly men were facts of life. Loyalty and interdependence characterized the relationship between this mother and son, reflecting the value of kinfolk in an economically uncertain and frequently dangerous world. Only once, when she later moved back to Chattanooga without Edward (probably to make a better living), did Mary appear to act independently from his needs.[44]

When mother and son moved to Ringgold, they gained Mary Brown as a close neighbor. Despite Edward's claim that he ignored Mary after she rejected him, he impinged on her life during the year following their breakup. Just before moving to Ringgold, he indulged in an affair in Alabama with Mandy Hatch, who was Mary's sister and a sister-in-law to Edward's brother John. Edward hinted at the mischievous nature of this affair when he described John's response: "He struck me with a chair and cut my head badly."[45] Edward retreated to Georgia, and after briefly laying low in Pinetown, turned up in Ringgold to pester his former wife.

Perhaps Edward hoped that Mary would leave her new husband, as she had earlier left Peter Windley, and run off with him. If so, his hopes were dashed. He soon began an affair with her husband's sister Caroline, who apparently lived in the Brown household. Like his affair with Mandy Hatch, this one seemed calculated to create a fuss, perhaps even a fight with Hiram Brown, particularly after he abandoned Hiram's now-pregnant sister. To Schenck, Edward reported only that he "quit" Caroline and instead married seventeen-year-old Rachel Webb, the daughter of a neighborhood widow.[46] Edward did not offer any details about Mary's response to all this, but she likely harbored no regrets about ending their marriage.

In making Rachel his new bride, Edward assured that he would not again be bested by a woman. Not only was she a teenager, but she also possessed a temperament quite different from Mary's. Rachel appeared to be the quintessential "good" woman who suffered her husband's dissolute ways and lived only to serve his needs. After a rocky beginning that included Edward's usual indulgences in drinking and fighting, the couple moved to Pinetown, where, amazingly, Edward "went to work, kept sober, and made some money and was peacable for six months"—surely a record for him.[47]

Despite this promising interlude in his marriage, Edward soon returned to a cycle of degradation. Drawn by a "noise" at the neighborhood grocery one night, he broke his fast and began brawling again. Forced as before to escape town, he and Rachel took refuge in his mother's home in Chattanooga. Never able to resist his addictions for long, Edward indulged them with such abandon in Chattanooga that he decided to send Rachel home to her mother.[48]

For a time, Edward's marriage competed with his dissolute ways for control over his life. He reconciled with Rachel, moved five miles above Chattanooga, and found work on the Nashville Railroad. Again, he "was civil and worked hard for about six months."[49] One senses genuine, if pitying, tenderness in Edward for his young wife. Their reconciliation seemed precipitated by his discovery that she was sick. Recalling in his confession that Rachel gave birth to a stillborn child, he also remembered her as "an easy, good-tempered woman . . . [who] never quarrelled with me." After a particularly successful binge of gambling, during which he "dressed well" and "had plenty of money," he seemed proud to have spent part of his winnings to provide Rachel "with all necessaries."[50]

Despite his brief moment of economic success and domestic felicity, Edward's private excesses with women increasingly mirrored his reckless public behavior. He proved incapable of channeling his need for immediate self-gratification in directions that would enable him to maintain either prosperity or intimacy. In the same breath that he told of "supplying" his wife with goods, he admitted to spending more time with a girlfriend, Beck Caldwell, than with Rachel. "But she never complained," he noted.[51]

Rachel continued to endure her husband's ways, even after his cheating at cards forced them to move West. Edward and his cheating partner gathered their wives and moved to Johnson County, Arkansas, where Edward achieved another six months of sobriety and hard work. This time, separation from old friends and familiar neighborhoods in Georgia, Alabama, and Tennessee seemed to ease the grip of old habits. Sadly, however, though he reminisced that he "enjoyed myself better than ever before," he once again destroyed his marriage's peace, this time by tussling with the "greatest bully in the county" and again nearly losing his life. By Edward's account, Rachel displayed boundless loyalty. His description of her heroic defense of him, reminiscent of the legendary Dido's efforts to keep Aeneas's ships "well-supplied in every way," offered a familiar frontier inversion of womanhood. Edward claimed that his meek, mild-tempered wife wielded an ax against his attackers and later, amid flying tomahawks, rocks and sticks, brought him a gun.[52]

Despite Rachel's prominent role in the fracas, the action centered, as usual, around Edward. Ultimately, she was a rather minor player in his life. Not long after describing her heroic defense of him, he noted without explanation or apology his abandonment of her and their infant son.[53] Indicative of her inferior position in his life, and unlike Mary, Rachel disappeared from Edward's life story as soon as he shifted the narrative to his return to old haunts in Georgia, Tennessee, and Alabama. When he reported taking a third "wife" in North Carolina, it was as though his marriage to her had never happened.

Edward's life spiraled downward after he abandoned Rachel in Arkansas. He committed his first murder in Alabama, assumed the alias of "Hardaway Bone," and eventually fled to North Carolina. There, in a last fitful effort at stability, he sought self-control through work, marriage, and, presumably for a time, sobriety. Sometime after James Lesley (Lasley) of Iredell County hired him to dig a well on his land, Edward married Lesley's daughter, Mandy. This marriage proved even more short-lived than the previous two when Mandy died shortly after the birth of their only child.[54]

Mandy's death hit Edward hard. Time and again over the years, he had depended on his mother or a wife to pull him back from the edge of self-destruction. Always, except for Mary and now Mandy, women had sheltered him until his dormant addictions demanded gratification. Mandy's death left him stranded on the desert between desperation and debauchery. Depressed, he returned to the all-too-familiar cycle of drinking and carousing, becoming sick in the process. Finally, precarious economic circumstances sparked his ferocious temper. He attacked James Cornelius for refusing to pay the wages that even a court of law agreed Cornelius owed him. When Cornelius died of his wounds, there was no one to shelter Edward and certainly no one to take up arms for him. He was quickly captured, charged with murder, convicted, and sentenced to hang.[55]

As her son's life moved toward its fateful end in North Carolina, Mary Isham struggled on in Chattanooga, where she worked as a domestic, took in boarders, and managed to acquire a modest home.[56] Her next-door neighbor, Susan Isham, age twenty-six, was probably her daughter-in-law. Susan was also likely a sister to Mary Brown, which might explain why Mary and Hiram Brown also lived in Chattanooga in 1860, only ten households away from Mary and Susan Isham.[57]

In 1860, the Brown household contained four children ranging in age from two to ten years. Thirty-two-year-old Hiram Brown had changed his occupation from mechanic to house carpenter, and the couple apparently owned their own home. Like Mary Isham, Mary Brown had made modest progress toward achieving economic security. Her attainment of greater respectability and stability contrasted with Edward's own descent into degradation and poverty.[58]

The exigencies of making a living and rearing children no doubt absorbed the attention of both women as Edward faced the consequences of murdering James Cornelius. Sitting in a North Carolina prison cell, awaiting his execution, he must have wondered whether his mother, brothers, or former wives knew of his fate. At age thirty-two, Edward's luck had run out; he had killed a "damned dog," as he put it, and would himself now be executed. The man who lived in a rage for manhood died without the final comforts of the "good women" so vital to the definition and service of that manhood.

Because they were kin to a murderer who left an extensive account of his life, we know far more about the lives of women connected to Edward Isham than we would otherwise. None came to weep at his hanging; none appeared to claim the tiny daughter he and Mandy left behind. It was the infant Margaret who ultimately bore the full weight of Edward's dismal legacy to "his" women. Margaret "Bone" inherited her father's murderous pseudonym and nothing more. She apparently grew up kinless in the household of William and Susan Reed, a married couple who had testified against her father at his trial.[59]

7

The Worlds of
Nineteenth-Century
Condemned Men

JOSEPH P. REIDY

By many standards, Edward Isham was not a likable man. During his comparatively brief life, he drank, fought, gambled, whored, stole, and spread mayhem across a wide swath of the Southeast. His unrestrained proclivity for violence proved his undoing. At his demise, many of his contemporaries must have sighed with relief to see a bad man getting his just deserts.[1]

Yet Isham's story fascinates. On the supposition that no man is an island, the present essay seeks to understand him in his native habitat. Doing so requires placing Edward Isham in the economic and political landscape of his region and time, in the social atmosphere of his family, neighbors, and associates, and—perhaps most important—in the comparative context of other nineteenth-century murderers.

To the extent that the child fathers the man, understanding Isham requires beginning with his youth. Although the autobiography lacks full details, his childhood was tumultuous. His "dissipated" father "spent what property he had," then abandoned the family to seek his fortune digging gold in Carroll County, Georgia.[2] While not forsaking contact with his mother, Isham lived with his father at the mines. Like many another son of the southern yeomanry, his apprenticeship in the arts of fighting began when he was ten under his father's tutelage.[3] Even before he was grown, he recalled, "I . . . began to work for myself in the mines," a rough-and-tumble world in which his father's lessons would stand him in good stead.[4]

In some respects, Edward Isham's world displayed aspects of a backcountry frontier.[5] His father, like other upcountry settlers, occupied land that the Cherokees had reluctantly ceded during the 1830s. Although Isham may have laid eyes on comparatively few frontiersmen of the Daniel Boone stripe, he surely knew others whose attraction for the wilderness prompted frequent excursions from home and family. In such a setting, where hostile Indians, dangerous animals, and assorted other hazards of the forest might take fierce vengeance upon the uninitiated, men developed a violent culture of masculinity. During the first generation of white settlement in the upcountry, increasing density of population and cultivated fields did not erode the foundation of this masculine culture.

As Steven Hahn has demonstrated for Georgia and Charles C. Bolton for North Carolina, the eastern foothills of the Appalachian Mountains endured economic, political, and social pressures during the late antebellum period that threatened to undermine the independence of the yeoman majority.[6] Although Isham attributed his family's landlessness to his father's dissipation, alcohol alone cannot explain the difficulties yeomen faced in maintaining their independence. Like many of his contemporaries whose ties to the land had been severed, Isham pursued a livelihood mining gold, cutting shingles, driving cattle, rafting lumber, farming, and working for wages. Given the irregularity of such employment, young men such as Isham moved about frequently in search of employment.

Fighting figured prominently in the routine social interactions among these men.[7] Often a matter of recreation or sport, fighting also represented the means whereby a man safeguarded what meant most to him: his person, his family, his possessions, and his honor. Any man who shied away from physical contests, regardless how frivolous the pretext, was a coward. Yet not every fight pitted man against man in defense of honor or in demonstration of individual prowess, as Isham's relationship with Jim Waters, with whom he had agreed "to go 'halves in cards and in our fighting,'" suggests.[8]

Fighting among the lower classes followed conventions that in some respects mirrored the tightly orchestrated duels among the gentry.[9] There were prearranged "set fights," wherein the principals had their seconds and wherein the outcome might settle old scores, if only provisionally. Commonly accepted rules held that if a man "hollered," this admission of defeat ended the fight. More specific rules of engagement agreed to before the contest determined what, if any, weapons were admissible, but the combatants and their seconds generally carried and often employed weaponry that violated the rules. Such "foul play" produced a melee as relatives, friends, and bystanders joined in the fray.[10] Yet even the seemingly deadliest of encounters might end with the combatants "making friends."[11]

The land over which Isham and his kinfolk ranged—Georgia's upper piedmont and the proximate regions of Alabama, Tennessee, and North Carolina—felt increasingly strong commercial pressures during the 1840s and 1850s, much of it tied to railroad construction and the commercial development that ensued. Although commercialization threatened the stability of traditional yeoman practices and values, its effects were much more sweeping and insidious. On the one hand (and as Isham found), commercial enterprises such as railroads offered some prospect of employment to the dislocated. But on the other hand, commercial development initiated more sweeping—and ultimately more disruptive—changes. Individuals such as Isham might have mastered the rails, but they did not understand the system that was coming into being.

Though Isham the independent man strides confidently through the autobiography, Isham the caring son, good brother, hardworking nephew, loyal friend, and peaceable neighbor also appears, however fleetingly. Given that yeoman ideology prized family and community as much as manly independence, it should scarcely surprise that Isham reflected such values. Moreover, popular myths to the contrary notwithstanding, not even the most habitual lawbreakers or the most callous murderers of Isham's time mixed only with their own kind. Isham's account mentions scores of persons by name, including family members, friends, consorts, associates, antagonists, and strangers. Although the lot included a murderer or two, most shied away from hanging offenses, even if they drank, gambled, fornicated, and fought with some degree of regularity. In short, they were a representative cross section of the white lower class.

Nearly every person Isham identified hailed from the ranks of displaced farmers, landless laborers, and frontier entrepreneurs. His landowning uncles Charles Icems and John Everett were exceptions. So was his mother in that, having "sold cakes and whiskey and boarded work hands for a living" while she resided in Chattanooga during the 1840s, she managed to accumulate a nest egg by the eve of the Civil War.[12] Isham's father squandered his landholding in drink; his brothers in Alabama made their living in the forests and on the rivers; his brother-in-law William Bivings was a landless laborer. Isham's wives and consorts all came from similar backgrounds.

As Isham's account also suggests, the members of this lower class observed social mores that often differed markedly from those of the gentry, the solid yeomanry, and the middle classes. At times the mores overlapped, but rarely did they coincide. From a social perch above his own, Isham might have appeared as a ruffian with a death wish, but from the angle of the lower class, he may well have looked like an unlucky bastard whose defense of honor took a deadly turn.

The narratives of condemned murderers shed as much light on the phenomenon of public execution during the nineteenth century as on the lives of the men they portray. In fact, "biographies" such as Isham's were a central part of the rituals of capital punishment during the nineteenth century. According to the legal scholar Lawrence M. Friedman, the criminal justice system performs a "boundary-marking" function in the sense that it serves as "a kind of social drama, a living theater" of "morals and morality."[13] In capital cases, execution provides the climactic final scene. The life history of the condemned man, generally accompanied by a confession of his dastardly deeds, represented another stock component of the drama.[14]

Generally intended for publication, the confessions were frequently the product of attorneys, newspaper editors, or ministers, who stood as intermediaries between the criminal and society at large and assumed certain responsibilities to each party. Isham's autobiography departs in some respects from the confessions of the time, largely by virtue of Schenck's relationship to the proceedings as Isham's defense attorney. As Scott P. Culclasure suggests, Schenck's interest in crafting a plausible defense may explain both why he interrogated Isham and why he chose not to publish the account.[15] In such circumstances, Schenck's motives may have been largely personal: an adroit defense would have enhanced his reputation and advanced his career.

Notwithstanding these differences, other strong similarities between Isham's autobiography and the confessional literature of the time persist. The intermediaries typically sought to determine "the truth" about the crime, both to safeguard the interests of the accused murderer and the public at large and to advance the development of professional standards in law and journalism. Whereas the publicists of the early nineteenth century placed strong emphasis on the condemned man's repentance in preparation for the life hereafter, that concern receded as the century advanced, as Schenck's apparent indifference to the state of Isham's soul illustrates.[16] Though hardly above moral posturing — of which Schenck's reaction to Isham's apparent use of the term "whorehouse" is a typical example — these men sought to understand and not simply pass judgment.[17]

Even as they discharged responsibilities to the condemned, the intermediaries labored to serve the interests of society, positioning themselves as guardians of public morality, particularly of the Protestant Christian variety. In this regard, their commitment to the truth aimed to prevent the circulation of vicious rumors. Publicists in such disparate times and places as Thomas R. Gray of Southampton County, Virginia, in 1831, and H. A. Rockafield of Lancaster County, Pennsylvania, in 1858, made prefatory statements "To the Public" affirming this responsibility. Gray, who took the confession of Nat Turner, a slave condemned for leading the most famous slave insurrection of the antebellum period, insisted that he presented "a faithful record" of Turner's statements.[18] Rockafield, who promulgated the account of Alexander Anderson, a chimney sweep condemned for his part in the rape and murder of two women, pronounced his publication the only *"authentic"* account of the crimes.[19]

In complementary fashion, the intermediaries attempted to protect polite sensibilities from the most lurid or ghastly details of the crime, although in the process they frequently fanned public interest in precisely such details.[20] By disseminating the confession of the condemned, the intermediaries offered object lessons to the impressionable that crime does not pay. To the wayward and to the parents and guardians of youth, they aimed to identify the experiences and influences in the murderer's life that foreshadowed abominable deeds to come. Through repetition over time, the major players ritualized these roles to such an extent that only rarely did the condemned man, the intermediaries, or the public fail to play their respective parts.[21] As a result, posterity beholds the condemned through the eyes of others and hears his tale secondhand.

Isham's account of his youth echoes themes present in the confessions of other nineteenth-century condemned men. The image of troubled childhood in the confessional literature of the time reflected both the public's stereotypical expectations and the reality of lower-class life: poverty, unemployment, disease, premature death, dislocation, alcoholism, and physical abuse. Families struggled to make ends meet, and pursuit of this goal often entailed the employment or apprenticeship of children. Contending with such circumstances, many a lower-class youth succumbed to evil influences and to petty crimes even if only a few replicated Isham's progression to hanging offenses.[22]

Physical mobility, especially that associated with the search for work, routinely exposed boys and young men to vice and its roughneck practitioners. Condemned men routinely identified a rogue's gallery of bad masters and fellow apprentices, soldiers and sailors, and "river hands, brick-yard men and colliers" as the source of their introduction to ill-defined "rude tricks," to "cursing, swearing, lying and stealing," and to loose women.[23] Isham's almost casual reference to "a difficulty with some Irishmen boat hands about some lewd women" concisely reproduces one range of stereotypical images and behavior.[24]

From early in their youth, lower-class boys fought with their peers. As one condemned man explained, the initiation into this combative world often began with "quarreling and fighting."[25] Apart from honing self-defense skills, the fights established hierarchies both among individuals within a group and between one group and another. Many fights, if not most, grew out of a desire to defend the honor of an individual or the group against a real or perceived insult. One lad later recalled having threatened with death a group of boys who "had given me offense."[26] Another murdered a fourteen-year-old who "had given me some abusive language."[27] Lower-class youth cultivated a sense of honor that they defended with great determination and — on occasion — deadly violence.[28]

Just as condemned men recalled strikingly similar images of a difficult youth, they also outlined broad similarities in their adult experiences despite the presence of some distinctive regional patterns. Men living in the cities of the Northeast, for instance, cited the lure of the nightlife, wherein dance halls vied for patronage with drinking establishments, gambling dens, and brothels, and a new breed of independent woman was making her presence known.[29] For men from the small towns and rural areas of the North and the South, the palette of alluring vices contained less numerous and exotic colors.[30] But economic change—particularly in the form of the market revolution—was producing social dislocation in the South as well as the North, casting individuals and groups adrift from their traditional moorings. Their narratives of adulthood — whatever their chroniclers may have hoped for—represented not so much a steady slide to doom as a holding pattern in a world marked by physically demanding, unsteady, and generally unremunerative work; alternating cycles of relative comfort and stability on the one hand and abject poverty and dislocation on the other; and binges of drinking, gambling, whoring, and fighting that as often as not ended in bouts with the law.

In Schenck's account, nearly every act in Isham's past pointed toward an eventual rendezvous with the gallows. Set in the context of the rites of execution, Schenck played his role perfectly. It is not difficult to imagine the scene: Schenck, with pen and ledger in hand, sits facing the prisoner, not entirely repentant yet not entirely sullen. "Recount for me, Isham, the incidents of your life. Let your memory carry back as far as it will, and spare me no detail, however unpleasant, in your journey to the crime for which you now stand accused." As Schenck scribbles the heading, "Biography of Edward Icem alias 'Hardaway Bone,'" Isham begins "I was born," which, in his haste to catch up, Schenck transcribes without the pronoun "I." Whatever else of Isham's account he would miss, it would not be the unpleasant details.

In Schenck's scripting, belligerence overshadows every other feature of Isham's character. No doubt Isham would have had reservations about exploring the dynamics of personal relationships—especially if feelings of unmanly tenderness might be revealed. And Schenck would have considered such sensibilities a distraction from the central plot. Nonetheless, Isham came as close to expressing affection for his parents, siblings, other relatives, friends, and associates as the circumstances permitted. In describing his wife, Rachel Webb, as "an easy good tempered woman [who] never quarreled with me," he fairly gushed with emotion.[31] Though less demonstrative regarding Mandy Lesley, his later wife, his admission that he "had been drinking" after she died in childbirth hints at a deep sense of loss.[32]

A peaceable Isham also makes a number of cameo appearances. On several occasions, for instance, he stayed with his uncle Charles Icems in De Kalb County; during one such stay, his uncle fit him out with a set of tools so that he could return to gold mining.[33] Even in the gold "diggings," the scene of so many scrapes, there were times when Isham "went to work, and continued sober and civil for some months and made a good deal of money."[34] While working for the railroad outside Chattanooga, he "was civil and worked hard for about six months."[35] After moving to Johnson County, Arkansas, he recalled, "I worked . . . splitting rails, hunting deer and bees and enjoyed myself better than ever before in my life. I stayed there six months and got along very well."[36] On several later occasions, he settled into farming. At an unspecified time during the 1840s, he sank roots in Walker County "and raised one crop."[37] And following his move to North Carolina in 1857 or 1858, he "cleared some [land] and raised a crop" on the ten acres he bought from Charlie Carlton.[38] As often as not, Isham forsook his regular haunts for the land to elude pursuing lawmen or adversaries. But other displaced yeomen employed similar survival strategies of moving from one place and one pursuit to another.[39]

At the same time, life on the lam did not extinguish Isham's propensity for trouble. Seclusion provided both the occasion and the excuse for "drinking, hunting and gambling."[40] During an uncharacteristically peaceful stretch of mining that lasted "four or five months," he "gambled every night and fought chickens on Sundays [in] a regular cockpit made for the purpose."[41] As a result, even when old rivalries did not resurface, new associations might turn sour and conflicts ensue. Isham moved on down the line.

The dispute over wages that precipitated Isham's demise demonstrates the links between a man's labor, his possessions, and his honor, the defense of which might require physical force and perhaps the risk of death.[42] Isham's narrative hints in a number of places at this interrelationship. On several occasions, either alone or in concert with his associates, he destroyed property in retaliation for a perceived wrong. After a dispute with rival miners over a dam he had constructed, he took to his heels in advance of the sheriff, but not before breaking up their "rockers and shovels."[43] By the same token, he joined two friends in destroying the grocery of a man with whom they had been feuding: "We . . . broke up everything he had decanters, glasses and barrels and his fiddle."[44] Bettering the man could be achieved by destroying his property, if nothing else. "Spite-work always cured my distemper," observed another condemned man, recalling an incident in which he had cut off the manes and tails of his employers' horses following a dispute over wages.[45] Withholding a man's wages threatened his honor, which in turn required compensation in property or in blood.

The women of Isham's narrative played a number of roles that, however sketchily drawn, exhibit a range of images and behavior.[46] Isham responded in kind. Toward his mother, sister, and wives, he occasionally expressed feelings of tenderness and of responsibility for their welfare. His amorous encounters with women often turned on forbidden love and elopement. Notwithstanding this variability, the autobiography also consistently suggests that Isham and the men of his social circle perceived women as subordinates who at their best were junior partners in the challenges of life and at their worst were mere possessions. Most strikingly, in virtually every account of Isham's relationships with women unrelated to him by blood, a male rival figures as prominently as the woman does.

While consorting with Jane Mobley, for instance, he first fought "[a] young man named Thompson [who] was courting her," then later "fell out" with Jim Fletcher over her "at a frolic."[47] He and Mary Windley, to whom he had once been engaged, "agreed to run off" from Macon County, Alabama, leaving her husband, Peter Windley, behind.[48] Isham later became "jealous," when he "found there was something wrong with Mary," whom by then he considered his wife. Perceiving that "she did not treat me kindly," he suspected the presence of another man, whom Isham identified and then challenged to a fight.[49] Still later Mary married Hiram Brown, after which she and Isham "never had anything to do with one another."[50]

The end of that relationship did not curb Isham's rivalry with men over women. He took up with Thursday Murphy after having had "a severe fight with a man who had been keeping her."[51] Then came "Mandy Hatch, (a sister to Mary Windley, whom I took from her husband Peter Windley, and a sister in law of my brother John)." Isham eventually quarreled with his brother, who "was very angry because, I had taken up with his sister in law," and the ensuing altercation left Isham with a deep wound in his head.[52] After consorting with Caroline Brown, impregnating her, then quitting her for Rachel Webb, he "took up with one 'Ann Baldwin' and finding out she had some money, I concluded I would get it."[53] His relationship with her successively embroiled him with "a man who had been her old beau" and her father, who "cursed me for being with his 'gal' and fired a horse pistol at me."[54] Isham's interest in Beck Caldwell precipitated "a fight one night about her with a fellow named Moore."[55] Though not lacking in strategies for negotiating this patriarchal world, the women of Isham's narrative operated within boundaries marked and patrolled by men.

Other nineteenth-century condemned men frequently showed similar disdain for women, particularly those of the independent variety. Alexander Anderson, for example, who was executed for murder in 1858 in Pennsylvania, narrated a history of relationships with women that was remarkably like Isham's. He admitted to "keeping a woman, besides my wife, for about *five years.*" He too confessed a proclivity for "house" women—one of whom once raised a ruckus when she insisted that he marry her—and other "bad women." He once found himself the defendant in a case of "fornication and bastardy" that a former consort brought against him. "I have had," he concluded with understatement, "considerable to do with women."[56]

Still other men lost all bearings when they encountered independent women. The New Yorker William Gross, for instance, alternately experienced pleasure, jealousy, and a frustrated impulse to dominate his consort, Kizia Stow, who frequented "dance houses" of evenings. Gross eventually murdered Stow in a drunken rage precipitated by her insistence that she did not have to answer to him for her comings and goings.[57] Other convicted murderers cast sweeping indictments of women and their charms. Richard Smith, executed for murder in Philadelphia in 1816, warned youth "wont to be dazzled with the blandishment of female beauty" to beware, lest they be drawn to a married woman with a jealous husband, as he had been. Although by later standards his case may well have been adjudged one of self-defense, he traced his predicament to the "arts and intrigues" of an "evil woman . . . versed in all the wiles and machinations of that diabolical spirit which possessed the heart of the first of her race, and caused the fall of mankind."[58] Like the biblical Eve, independent women posed a threat of historic proportions to men who believed firmly in the expediency—if not also the divine ordination—of traditional relationships between the sexes.

Besides violating the law, Isham and his associates also routinely transgressed racial conventions. Whereas polite society condemned these associations as subversive of the tenets of racial inequality, the transgressors seem to have taken a more casual view.[59] In the variety of his interracial contacts, Isham suggests their ordinariness. His expulsion from the Methodist church followed "a difficulty with a negro about a fishing pole," which presumably occurred while they were fishing. Not long thereafter, when a swimming party degenerated into a drunken brawl, a free black man named Wash Smith "choked [him] very severely." In retaliation Isham ambushed Smith and "fell on him with a rock and beat him very severely," but as Isham recalled, "we afterwards made friends."[60] His capers with Ben Harmand, the "half breed indian" in Arkansas, suggest an ongoing association that appears to have rested upon friendship.[61] Isham also hints that one of his sexual relationships—that with a "free girl"—crossed the color line.[62] He gambled "with a negro" on one occasion and "with some white men and free negroes" on another; the implication is that this practice was not unusual.[63] Perhaps rarer, but worthy of no greater alarm in the narration, were such instances as that wherein Isham "worked for a free negro named 'Fax.'"[64]

Isham's narrative adds to the growing body of evidence suggesting that lower-class southerners frequently violated the racial conventions promulgated by the planter elite. To some extent, these violations represented the influence of evangelical religion, which, despite its compromise with the slaveholding elite early in the nineteenth century, still held the potential to challenge beliefs in racial inequality through the spirit of Christian brotherhood.[65] Nat Turner, for instance, recalled his relationship with Etheldred T. Brantley, "a white man." After being persuaded by Turner's revelations that "the great day of judgment was at hand," Brantley, in Turner's account, "ceased from his wickedness." Their relationship deepened. In another revelation, Turner remembered, "the Spirit appeared to me again, and said, 'as the Saviour had been baptized so should we be also,'—and when the white people would not let us be baptised by the church, we went down into the water together, in the sight of many who reviled us, and were baptised by the Spirit."[66]

Other violations of racial taboos grew out of day-to-day interactions among those who performed manual labor in the antebellum South. In plantation districts, planters viewed such fraternization as subversive even if it stopped short of perfect equality. By the 1850s, a common refrain heard throughout the cotton South castigated unscrupulous white men for "trafficking" with slaves, serving as fences for stolen cotton and supplying liquor in exchange. Grand jurors particularly lashed out at grocery operators for thus subverting public peace, but neither words nor actions proved effective against such interracial contacts.[67] In urban areas of the slave states, where white artisans and laborers rubbed shoulders with free blacks and with slaves who hired their own time, the potential for interaction seemed limitless.[68] Although he did not directly say so, Isham surely found this to be the case in Chattanooga and Montgomery, the cities he frequented most.

In nonplantation regions of the South, small-scale slavery gave rise to a different dynamic of racial relations from that which prevailed in the Black Belt. The circumstances of life and labor in yeoman households enabled upcountry slaves to enter into relationships with their masters and with other white folks that might have been considered seditious, if not revolutionary, in their plantation counterparts.[69] Daniel Hundley described the slaves raised in such settings as "saucy and impertinent" and pronounced it "no cause of wonder that they impudently call their masters by their proper names, and, when permitted, address all other white persons in the same ill-bred and familiar manner."[70] As the spread of commerce eroded traditional bonds, slaves and free blacks had even greater latitude in initiating such contact along railroad lines and rivers, in logging camps and mining camps, as John Inscoe's study of slavery in western North Carolina makes clear.[71] A kaleidoscopic mixture of harmony and strife ensued from these interactions, even if the white parties to the fraternization might hold notions of superiority and take refuge in racial privilege when it suited their interests to do so.[72] Yet in the circumstances of day-to-day life, Isham's peers appeared largely oblivious to the racial politics of their elite contemporaries.

Despite its apparent straightforwardness in many respects, Isham's autobiography offers precious little self-reflection, much less self-criticism. In the confessions typical of the early nineteenth century, the voice of the condemned man that emerged through the intermediaries denounced the evil of his ways. "Oh God!" exclaimed one murderer overcome with remorse over his crime, "hanging is too good for so vile a wretch." Another declared that the "hand of Providence" had prevented his escape "that murder might not go unpunished."[73] Some men such as John Banks, who had murdered his wife because she "was a bad woman," at first demonstrated to the recorder of his narrative an "obduracy and unconcerned state of mind" suggesting "moral depravity almost without a parallel, and scarcely to be believed." Following repeated visits from churchmen, however, Banks eventually "joined with fervor in their supplications at the throne of mercy. Overwhelmed in tears, he lamented his crime, expressed his sincere contrition, and a trembling hope in the mercy of his God."[74] Although Nat Turner resisted self-condemnation for leading the rebellion, in the end he pronounced himself resigned to his fate.[75]

In one notable case, the convicted jailbreaker and murderer William Morris steadfastly refused to play his assigned part. Professing innocence, he resisted all pressure "to suppress the exertion of a manly spirit. I believe," he insisted, "that resentment of wrongs is as useful a principle, as nature has given to man, and that every man ought to support his own rights, even in his last moments." In that spirit, he even refused to "expose my own faults" to the intermediaries anxious to publicize details of his life, claiming, "The gratification of public curiosity shall not cause me to enumerate them."[76] If nothing else, the hammering on gallows outside their jail windows prompted most men to talk. It also dispelled the kind of boasting with which the men might, in other, less confining circumstances, have narrated their adventures.[77] Morris was the exception who proved the rule.

In recounting his past deeds, Isham positioned himself closer to the unsentimental William Morris than to the repentant Alexander Anderson, though he stopped shy of Morris's refusal to narrate the particulars. Isham's reference to joining the Methodist church, for instance, suggests a fleeting sense of vulnerability that returns only once again to the narrative. Following a fight at a whorehouse in which he was "knocked . . . senseless" by a rock, he conceded, "I was hurt badly and it scared me very much. I reflected on my course and for awhile was disposed to do better" until pursuing lawmen put him to flight; alighting with a gambler, he quickly returned to his old ways.[78]

Despite his bravado, heralded, for instance, in his claim that "everybody was afraid of me and no officer would attempt to take me," Isham also indicated that other men were more fearsome than he.[79] Of a convicted murderer with whose son Isham had fought, Isham confessed, "I was afraid of old Fletcher and thought he would kill me."[80] Yet his numerous encounters with "great bull[ies]" and "wild fellow[s]" clearly suggest that he did not view himself in such a way and, moreover, that he considered it something of a social responsibility as well as a personal challenge to defeat them.[81] He was also a decent man who could abandon a grudge when circumstances warranted, as he did when a friend of "an old enemy named McAustin . . . came to me and begged me off from it as McAustin had a wife and three children."[82]

In the end Edward Isham remains enigmatic, partially revealed yet largely concealed in David Schenck's rendering of Isham's autobiography. Such must be the fate of the condemned men who with nothing to gain by silence and nothing to lose by speech chose to talk. Despite the idiosyncrasies of each, the narratives collectively identify a remarkably consistent set of experiences: poverty and social dislocation in childhood; economic marginality in adulthood; the violent character of interpersonal relationships within the lower classes; the connection between liquor and crime. Yet it is precisely at this point that the image of Isham and the other condemned men slips out of focus, thanks to the ritualized nature of nineteenth-century capital punishment. Following the murder came the apprehension and incarceration; then the interrogation behind closed doors and the trial, conviction, and hanging in plain view. Publication of the condemned man's confession served to reaffirm the community's ongoing commitment to traditional moral values, though the affirmation occurred even in the absence of a printed confession.

The almost unbroken sequence of violent encounters in Isham's narrative suggests the weight of these expectations: as though all a murderer's life experiences led inevitably to the fatal encounter, only such events as demonstrated that progression were worth the telling. In that sense Isham's relationship to Schenck was thoroughly typical: it replicated Alexander Anderson's relationship with H. A. Rockafield in Lancaster County, Pennsylvania, in 1858, just as surely as it echoed Nat Turner's relationship with Thomas Gray in Southampton County, Virginia, in 1831. Understanding the condemned man's life requires seeing though the rituals surrounding his death.

Appendix A

Maps

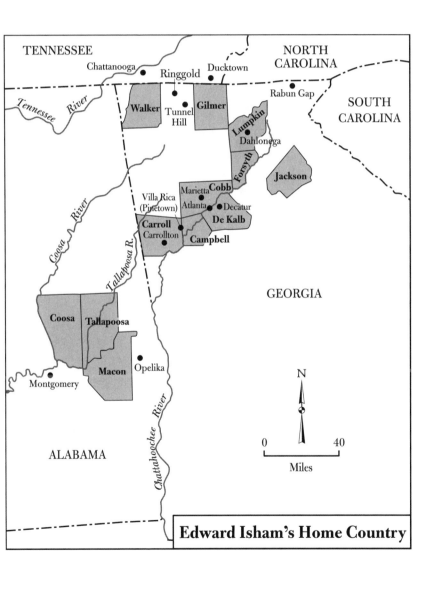

Edward Isham's Home Country

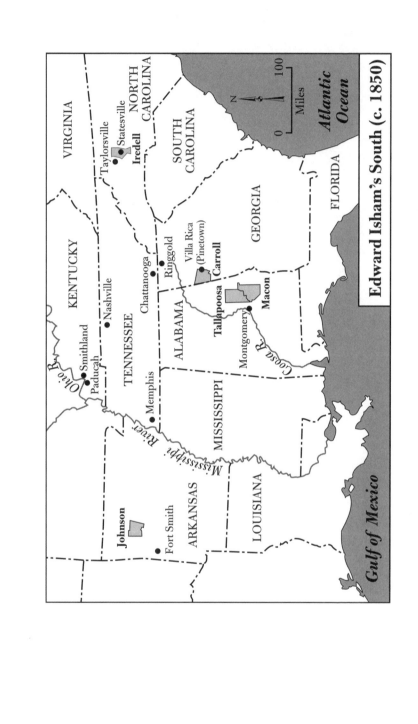

Edward Isham's South (c. 1850)

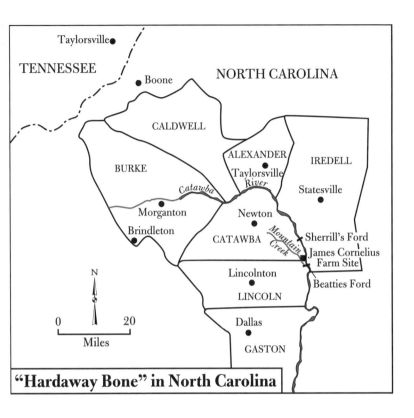

"Hardaway Bone" in North Carolina

TENNESSEE

NORTH CAROLINA

Taylorsville

Boone

CALDWELL

ALEXANDER

IREDELL

BURKE

Taylorsville

Statesville

Catawba River

Morganton

Newton

Brindleton

CATAWBA

Mountain Creek

Sherrill's Ford

James Cornelius Farm Site

Lincolnton

Beatties Ford

LINCOLN

N

Dallas

0   20

GASTON

Miles

Appendix B

Statement of the Case

State v. Hardaway Bone

by Superior Court Judge

Robert R. Heath

Judge Heath prepared this statement of the case against Edward Isham to accompany the defendant's appeal to the North Carolina Supreme Court. The first eight pages — not transcribed here — are copies of minutes of the superior court. The statement, together with copies of superior court minutes and supreme court justice Matthias E. Manly's manuscript opinion, may be found in Case 7858, Supreme Court Original Cases, 1800–1909, North Carolina Division of Archives and History, Raleigh, North Carolina. The court's opinion is recorded in *State v. Hardaway Bone, North Carolina Reports* 52 (1859): 121.

State v. Hardaway Bone

This was an indictment for murder, tried before Heath,[1] Judge, at Fall Term of the Gaston Superior Court of Law 1859.[2] Before the jurors were tendered to the prisoner, his counsel announced that each juror might be considered as challenged by the prisoner for cause, and by consent the Judge was permitted to act as trior. One Pegram[3] was drawn as a juror, & on being sworn, said he had formed & expressed the opinion the prisoner was guilty from rumors which he had heard in the neighborhood of the murder four days after it took place. The Court then asked the juror whether these rumors had produced such an impression on his mind that he could not listen to the testimony and give the Deft. a fair trial. He replied they had not produced such an impression, & he could listen to the testimony & give him a fair trial. The Judge ordered the juror tendered and defendant excepted. One Rutledge[4] drawn as a juror stated that he had formed & expressed the opinion defendant was guilty, from rumor, & the counsel for Deft. asked that the said Rutledge stand aside until the panel was gone through with. The presiding Judge declined to permit this saying this was the State's privilege & not that of defendant. Afterward, he was ordered to be tendered, and Deft. again excepted.

In order to show the defendant was the murderer of James Cornelius, deceased: the State introduced one Henry Cornelius,[5] his nephew, who swore that on Sunday morning May the 8th 1859 about 8 or 9 o'clock he found deceased in Catawba County, near deceased's house which he swore was also in Catawba County, sitting in a corner of his own fence, his pantaloons covered with blood. That said deceased was bleeding, seemed much exhausted and could not walk. That witness took him up and carried him to the house of witness's father, who was a brother of the said deceased & whose name was Austin Cornelius.[6] That said Austin Cornelius was a resident of the said county of Catawba in the State of North Carolina and in which county was laid Austin Cornelius's residence only a short distance from the residence of the said deceased in the same county.

The State then introduced said Austin Cornelius, who swore he was a brother of deceased. That he returned to his house aforesaid he supposed about nine o'clock in the morning, & found his brother now deceased on a bed at witness's house aforesaid. That said brother had on his person three stabs — one three inches long on the left side of his stomache, another on or near his left hip and a third higher up and further back on his body. That he had wounds on each of his hands — two bruises on his head, & his left arm was much bruised. That as he breathed the air could be heard distinctly passing in and out of the wound and that he died the 21st of May 1859 in said county. That from the time he first saw said deceased at witness's house on the morning aforesaid and up to his death, all his food passed out through the wound on the left side of his stomache. That when witness first came to the bedside of said deceased, said deceased told him he knew that he could not live but must soon die; others told him so. Though the physician who attended him expressed no opinion, he sewed up the wound and was compelled partially to open it again. That the deceased said this after & up to the time of his death. The Solicitor[7] then proposed to ask of the witness what the deceased said after these declarations were made as to who inflicted these wounds and under what circumstances they were inflicted. The defendant's counsel objected to the reception of this evidence. The objection was overruled, and the defendant again excepted. The witness then stated that his brother the deceased said subsequent to the declarations as to his belief he would soon die, that he was sitting in his own house in the county of Catawba aforesaid. That he was near the fireplace on said 8th of May 1859. That behind him and near to him was a table and deceased was engaged in washing his person preparing to go to church for which purpose his horse was saddled. That the defendant came with a stick in his hand and stopping at the side of the table said he wanted his pay and had come to get it. That deceased replied to him, "I have not got the money." The defendant said, "I will have my money, or one of us must die." The deceased finished washing and got up & threw out the water in which he had washed. That just as he got to the door, Bone the defendant commenced to beat him with a stick he had. That he struck deceased eight or ten times with this stick. That he protected himself as well as he could with his arms. That they both got into the yard about a rod from the porch of the house and defendant commenced to cut him with a knife. That the deceased hollored for his boy Jim. That Jim was not there & another Negro man & two Negro women came, the man having picked up a fence rail or a piece of a fence rail.[8] That the Negro man placed the fence rail between deceased & defendant and separated them & the two female Negroes helped deceased on his horse which had been saddled to be ridden by deceased to church & he rode off to near where he was found by his nephew. Deceased said all the wounds on him were inflicted by defendant. On cross examination this witness said that deceased remarked he had not suspected or had not thought Bone would hurt him. Deceased said nothing about any gun. The house of the deceased had two doors, one on the south side of his house. The gun of deceased was usually kept over the door and going from where deceased represented himself to have been when he started to turn the water out of the vessel in which he washed towards the door is in the direction where the gun is or was usually kept. Witness knows nothing of this or stick but what deceased told him since this. That on the Sunday aforesaid about 11 or 12 o'clock in the day witness went to his brother's house & yard where deceased said the stabbing & beating took place. That in the yard at the place spoken of near the porch he saw blood on the ground and found a stick on the ground nearly three feet long. He supposed it an inch to an inch & a quarter in diameter. It was of a size no good execution with the size of a good walking cane. Deceased said the cutting was all done before the Negro came with the rail & that he, deceased, did nothing but endeavor to fend off or act in defense.

The State then introduced one Beaty[9] who swore he reached Austin Cornelius's house about 12 o'clock P.M. on the Sunday aforesaid and found deceased there on the bed. Saw him again on Tuesday. There was a gash on his left side three or four inches long. The instrument or knife seemed to have struck a rib and to have run round it. There was a mark on each side of the wound, as if the blade had passed in the full length and the ears or ends of the handle had struck the edge of the wound. There was another wound on or near the left hip, another higher up, and a cut on each hand. All the food taken by deceased passed through the wound in his side & he could distinctly hear the air passing through the wound. He further swore he was present a few days before at the trial of a warrant[10] at the instance of defendant against deceased. That defendant claimed $7.87/100 for 1 & ¾ days work ditching for deceased & the Magistrate gave judgment for $5.00 and deceased prayed & obtained a stay of execution thereon on Saturday preceeding the Sunday aforesaid. On cross examination this [witness] swore he was no physician, that the wounds were washed & wiped and that the physician who attended deceased was not present. He saw him on Saturday & he complained he had rheumatism. This witness, the Physician, had been summoned.

The State then introduced Jesse Cornelius[11] another brother of deceased who swore that he saw the deceased on a bed at the house of Austin Cornelius at about 11 o'clock A.M. of the Sunday aforesaid. That he was wounded as stated by the other witnesses. That deceased said to him, "I am cut all to pieces, & cannot live long," and he seemed conscious of approaching death. The State then proposed to prove the subsequent declarations of deceased to this witness as to who cut & wounded deceased & defendant objected. The objection was overruled & defendant again excepted. This witness then swore to a statement made by deceased to him after he had expressed the opinion he must soon die or could not live long, in all respects similar to that sworn to by Austin Cornelius with this exception: that he understood deceased to say that defendant commenced to cut him after deceased called his man Jim.

The State then introduced Dr. Moore[12] who swore he was a regular bred physician of some fifteen years standing. That he had heard all the testimony. That such wounds as had been described ordinarily produced death. Though he had heard of recovering from such wounds he had no doubt the wounds produced the death of James Cornelius.

The State then introduced one Lemly[13] who swore he knew defendant. Saw him on Tuesday before the trial of the warrant aforesaid. Defendant said he had sued deceased & asked if deceased could stay it. Witness told him he could do so & defendant replied, "God damn him if he stays it I will kill him."

Mrs. Reed[14] was then introduced by the State. She swore that defendant came to her house on Saturday the day before the stabbing of deceased & remained there that day & night. Talked about a settlement with deceased & said, "If he don't pay me my money I will cut his bowels out." That deceased lived near her. That defendant left in morning (Sunday) & returned in about one hour with his cloths bloody and blood on the left arm of a linen coat which he had on. That he came in, said nothing & took down a small gun. That witness said to him, "Put up that gun. You have killed some one already. "He made no reply. She repeated this & he said, "No, I have killed a damned dog." That he put up this, took down a larger one, put some lead in his & started off saying, "If anyone inquires for me say I am gone to Beattys Ford."[15] He went however in an opposite direction & towards Reeds Canoe landing on Catawba River.

The State then introduced Mr. Reed[16] who swore that defendant stayed at his house Saturday and Saturday night as stated by his wife. That he had been drinking some. That he talked—became silent & moody, dropped his head down, remained with his head down sometime—raised up & said, "Damn him if he don't pay me my money I will cut his bowels out."

William Sherrill,[17] a State's witness, swore he knew defendant, & on the morning of the Sunday aforesaid he saw him running from the direction of the house of deceased towards Reeds Ferry over the river low grounds. That defendant saw witness, stopped & said, "If you tell any one you have seen me here I will kill you," & then started again towards Reeds Ferry in a run. He had a linen or flax coat on, on the left arm of which there was something looking like dirt.

A grass[18] or linen coat was produced & witness Lemly swore he found it in his yard on the Sunday aforesaid. His own coat was missing & he swore his coat was now on the prisoner at the bar. The left sleeve & the coat had bloody spots on it.

Albert Nance,[19] a State's witness, swore that he put the defendant across the ferry on the Sunday aforesaid about nine o'clock A.M. That he had a gun & said to him, "Tell Reed I will leave the gun or his gun where he can get it" & then started off in a run.

A knife was produced with a three or four inch blade which witness swore (one Sherrill)[20] that he exchanged to defendant on Saturday, as he was on his way to Reeds, defendant giving him a small worthless knife & saying he would reexchange back again.

Mr. Cline[21] the Sheriff of Catawba was then examined as a witness for the State who swore that while defendant was confined in the jail of his county he said "he" understood Jimmy Cornelius was dead; he was sorry for it—he had stabbed him with the knife which Waugh brought from Tennessee. This is the knife produced in court & is the same knife spoken of by Sherrill.

The State then introduced Mr. Waugh[22] who swore he resided in Tennessee 105 miles from Catawba County. That he saw defendant pass his store on May the 12th 1859. That he had a gun. Witness asked him, "Are you travelling?" Defendant said, "Yes." "Where from?" He said he came from below Statesville, North Carolina. Was going to Tennessee and passed on. Sometime after the stage & mail arrived & brought information of the supposed murder. Witness started off in pursuit of defendant & came in sight of him 28 miles distant from where witness first saw him. Defendant seemed uneasy—looked back at him—stepped from the road—stood with both hands on the gun & then broke & ran—then stopped & said he would shoot witness. Witness rushed on him—grappled with him—scuffled & threw defendant, held him down & called to a man who was with him to bring a rope & help tie him. A rope was brought. They tied him & let him get up. When tying him he said, "You need not tie me. What have I done? "Witness replied, "It is said you have killed a man. I am going to take you back to North Carolina." Defendant replied, "I cut Jimmy Cornelius bad but I did not know that he was dead." Witness took from him a knife which he handed to Sheriff Cline which looked like the knife exhibited in court. Defendant after he got up again asked, "Is Jimmy Cornelius dead?" Witness told him, "It is so reported." Defendant replied, "I am damned glad of it. He was a damned dog. It is hard to be killed for one damned dog. If I could kill one more I would die willingly." Defendant objected to all the declarations of defendant to Waugh. The objection was overruled.

There was no evidence that defendant carried with him any stick when he left Reeds house or brought back any with him when he returned.

The declarations admitted and defendant excepted. The witness further stated he brought defendant back to N. Carolina & delivered him to Mr. Cline Sheriff of Catawba County. The defendant then offered to show that on the morning of the next day after Waugh arrested him he made another confession in which he stated that he killed Cornelius in self defense. The State objected to the reception of this evidence. The objection was sustained by the court. The second confession ruled out & defendant excepted.

The Solicitor for the State insisted the defendant was the perpetrator & the crime murder. The defendant through his counsel insisted first the stabbing & other injuries were not inflicted by defendant & if inflicted by him it was manslaughter & not murder and asked the following instructions: first, if the prisoner was merely assaulting deceased with the stick as stated by the Corneliuses & in the excitement of the conflict the Negroes approached with the rail & this induced the defendant to use the knife, the slaying was manslaughter. Second, if there was no intention to kill until deceased called for Jim & defendant had reason to believe that Jim or Jim & others would come on him with violence, & in consequence thereof killed with the knife, it was manslaughter only. Third, if the Negroes were assisting or making violent demonstrations towards defendant when defendant stabbed with the knife, the killing was but manslaughter. Fourth, if the killing occurred as stated by Jesse Cornelius, it was manslaughter not murder.

The court declined to give the instructions in the form prayed but told the jury the defendant was indicted for murder & in order to convict him thereof the State must satisfy them beyond a rational doubt that the defendant killed deceased & that the killing was of malice express or implied. The court recited the evidence & told the jury that there was evidence introduced on the part of the State to show that defendant killed the deceased & that he did it with express malice and if they believed on the whole case that the defendant did kill deceased & the killing was of malice the defendant was guilty of murder and not of manslaughter as manslaughter and a killing of malice could not coexist. Every malicious killing was murder.

The counsel at this point enquired of the court if the killing would not be manslaughter on the testimony of Jesse Cornelius to which the court replied it would be murder upon his evidence if under the circumstances sworn to, defendant was striking deceased at the time when the Negro approached with the stick found on the premises, such stick being a deadly weapon. The court then instructed the jury if there was a sudden quarrel & conflict & defendant drew a knife & killed deceased and there was no preconceived malice it was not murder but was manslaughter.

Appendix C

Newspaper Accounts

Relating to Edward Isham

Western Democrat (Charlotte, North Carolina), May 10, 1859

STOP THE MURDERER!
The following information of a most unprovoked outrage in Catawba, was received on Sunday night last:

CATAWBA COUNTY, May 8th, 1859.
This morning a man by the name of Hardaway Bone attacked Mr. James Cornelius with a knife, inflicting several severe wounds upon different parts of his body, which are considered fatal. Bone has made his escape, crossing the Catawba river into Iredell county. He is originally from Georgia and worked for a good many years in the Lumpkin Gold Mines in that State. For a year or two past he has been living in Iredell county, near Statesville. He is about five feet nine or ten inches high with light hair and complexion, well-formed and rather good looking. Has mild eyes; the forehead very prominent immediately above the eyes, and then gradually receding. Speaks rather slowly but determined; generally keeps a knife in his hand when talking with any one or sitting alone, having his head slightly inclined one way or the other, and also keeps it in that position when talking. He is a Ditcher by trade. Drinks liquor freely at times, and is fond of gambling—proposing to bet on any thing or with any body, whether acquainted or not. He has been speaking of going to Gold Hill for a week or two.

A reward of $500 will be paid for his apprehension and confinement in any Jail in or out of the State. Bone has also one thumb cut off close to the hand, and uses the left instead of the right hand.

AUSTIN CORNELIUS.
We learn that the cause of the attack on Mr. Cornelius was a lawsuit. Bone went to the house of Mr. Cornelius on Sunday morning and demanded the amount of a debt which he claimed as due him; Cornelius told him that he could not then pay it, whereupon Bone struck him with a club and then stabbed him three times.

Western Democrat (Charlotte, North Carolina), May 10, 1859

Gaston Superior Court
There is but one lawyer living in Dallas, D. Schenck, Esq. We suppose this is an indication that the citizens have but little work for those who expound the law. We were gratified to hear our friends in Gaston speak of Mr. Schenck as a young gentleman of ability and high character, and as possessing an amiable and pleasant disposition which makes him a favorite with his acquaintances.

North Carolina Whig (Charlotte, North Carolina), May 10, 1859

Brutal Murder.
We learn that a most brutal murder was perpetrated in Catawba county, on Sunday morning last, by a man named Hardaway Bone on the body of James Cornelius. If we have been correctly informed the circumstances that led to this melancholy catastrophe are as follows: Mr. Cornelius had employed Bone to ditch for him, and after it was completed, his charge being high, Cornelius refused to pay it. Bone sued him and recovered before a magistrate $5 for 1¾ days' work. This was stayed by Cornelius. On Sunday morning, Bone came to Cornelius' house armed with a stick, and demanded his money, threatening at the same time that if he did not pay the money he would kill him. Cornelius told him that he did not have the money. Bone then commenced beating Cornelius with the stick, who called for his negroes. When they came, Bone drew his knife and flourished it at the women and a boy, which frightened them off—his negro man had left home. Bone then stabbed Cornelius in the side and back two or three times, and then made his escape. See advertisement in another column offering $500 reward for him.

North Carolina Whig (Charlotte, North Carolina), May 10, 1859

STOP THE MURDERER! $500 REWARD.

On Sunday Morning, the 8th of May, HARDAWAY BONE, without any provocation, attacked and fatally stabbed James Cornelius at his residence in Catawba County, N. C., 5 miles from Beatties' Ford. Bone immediately made his escape, crossing the Catawba River into Iredell county. For a year or two past he has been living near Statesville. He follows the business of ditching. He is about 27 years old, five feet 9 or 10 inches high, light hair and complexion, with mild blue eyes, the forehead very prominent; speaks slowly but determined, with his head slightly inclined one way or the other when talking—He drinks spirits freely at times and likes to gamble. The thumb on the right hand is off.

Bone was originally from Georgia, having worked in the Lumpkin Gold Mines of that State.—He is considered a very bad man. The above reward will be paid for his apprehension and confinement in any Jail in or out of the State.

AUSTIN CORNELIUS Charlotte, N. C. May 10, 1859.

Carolina Watchman (Salisbury, North Carolina), May 10, 1859

Stop the Murderer.—Hardaway Bone, fatally stabbed James Cornelius, at his residence in Catawba county, on Sunday morning last, and is endeavoring to escape. He weighs about 140 lbs., has blue eyes, speaks slowly but firmly. *His right thumb is gone,* and he may be known by that more easily than anything else. He is a ditcher. It is likely he will endeavor to pass by some other name. A reward of $500 is offered for his arrest and confinement. It is said he had no money when he left, and if it be true, he will most likely beat around in the country some days before he gets off. Look out for him.

Iredell Express (Statesville, North Carolina), May 13, 1859

Outrageous Assault—Probable Murder

On Sunday morning last, one Harlan Bone, who had been engaged by Mr. James Cornelius, residing in the edge of Catawba county, to cut some ditches, committed a murderous assault upon the person of Mr. Cornelius, by beating him with a club and cutting with a knife, in a manner so severe that it is believed death must ensue. Bone was engaged to work by the month, but having worked two days, went on Sunday morning to Mr. Cornelius, who is a bachelor and resides alone with only his negroes on the farm, and demanded a settlement. Mr. Cornelius asked him how much was his demand, Bone said eight dollars, Mr. C. replied that that was too much, but he was willing to pay what was right. Bone was armed with a club, knife and rifle, and with the former dealt a heavy blow which felled Mr. Cornelius to the floor, and repeated the licks a number of times and then drew his knife and with it inflicted sundry gashes and wounds in a savage manner. He then departed, and told some neighbors of Mr. C. what he had done, threatening to defend himself from arrest by using his rifle against whomsoever might attempt to take him. He was suffered by those who first saw him, after the bloody outrage to depart, and, so far as we know to the present time has succeeded in making his escape.

A reward of $500 is offered for the apprehension of Bone, which may be seen in our advertising columns, and many persons have gone in pursuit of him. We hope the rascal may be caught.

Iredell Express (Statesville, North Carolina), May 13, 1859

Murder! $500 REWARD!
On Sunday last in Catawba county, N.C., Harlan Bone committed an assault with intent to murder, by beating with a club and cutting with a knife, James Cornelius, from which wounds it is believed death must ensue.

Bone is about 5 feet 10 inches high, say 35 years old, weight about 150 pounds, has fair skin, light hair, grey eyes, face smoothe and rather boney, quick spoken, stands erect and has a bold look.—his right thumb is cut off at or near the joint. His clothing as well as recollected was a black cloth frock coat with velvet collar, much worn, a pair of black cashmere pants and a pair of white summer pants with red stripes, and black wool hat with broad band and tolerably high crown. He also had a rifle gun, which he might sell. A reward of $500 will be paid by the subscribers for the apprehension and delivery of said Bone to the Sheriff of Catawba county, so that the ends of justice might be subserved.

WILLIAM CORNELIUS   JESSE CORNELIUS   AUSTIN CORNELIUS
Catawba county, May 9th, 1859.

Western Democrat (Charlotte, North Carolina), May 24, 1859

ARRESTED.—It will be seen by the following that Bone, who attacked and stabbed Mr. Jas. F. Cornelius in Catawba county two weeks ago, has been arrested, and is now in Newton Jail.

CATAWBA COUNTY, May 19, 1859.
Mr. Yates—Dear Sir:—I have the pleasure of informing you that Mr. W. B. Waugh and Mr. A. B. Slimp of Johnston [Johnson] county, Tennessee, caught H. Bone in Carter county, Tenn., on Thursday evening last and brought him back to Newton and put him in jail to await his trial.

Mr. James Cornelius still lingers, but there is no hope of his recovery; only it is said while there is life there may be hope.

Respectfully yours,
A. CORNELIUS.

Iredell Express (Statesville, North Carolina), May 27, 1859

Bone the Murderer Caught.
Harlan Bone who committed an assault upon James Cornelius of Catawba county, with intent to kill, was pursued and captured in the edge of Tennessee, one day last week, and has been brought back and lodged in the jail at Newton. A reward of five hundred dollars was paid to the person that arrested Bone. Mr. Cornelius still survives but without the least prospect for recovery.

We have since learned that Mr. Cornelius died on Saturday last, the 21st instant.

Iredell Express (Statesville, North Carolina), June 1, 1860

Hung.
On Friday last, Hardaway Bone was hung at Dallas for the murder of James Cornelius in Catawba county. We learn he made no remarks on the gallows, but appeared unconcerned to the last.—*Charlotte Democrat.*

Notes

Preface

1. *Greensboro Patriot,* September 3, 1902.
2. David Schenck Notebook, David Schenck Papers, North Carolina Division of Archives and History, Raleigh.

Introduction

1. An older study dealing with the image of poor whites is Shields McIl-waine, *The Southern Poor White: From Lubberland to Tobacco Road* (Norman: University of Oklahoma Press, 1939). See also the pertinent comments in Victoria Bynum's "Mothers, Lovers, and Wives," chapter 6 in this volume.
2. J. E. Cairnes, in *The Slave Power* (1861), quoted in Frank L. Owsley, *Plain Folk of the Old South* (Baton Rouge: Louisiana State University Press, 1949), 4.
3. Owsley, *Plain Folk of the Old South;* Bill Cecil-Fronsman, *Common Whites: Class and Culture in Antebellum North Carolina* (Lexington: University Press of Kentucky, 1992); Steven Hahn, *The Roots of Southern Populism: Yeoman Farmers and the Transformation of the Georgia Upcountry, 1850–1890* (New York: Oxford University Press, 1983); J. William Harris, *Plain Folk and Gentry in a Slave Society: White Liberty and Black Slavery in Augusta's Hinterlands* (Middletown, Conn.: Wesleyan University Press, 1985); Bruce Collins, *White Society in the Antebellum South* (New York: Longman, 1985). Isham grew up and spent much of his adult life in the upcountry Georgia area that is the focus of Steven Hahn's book.
4. Isham's story does, however, correspond to much of the backcountry

southern culture as portrayed in Elliott J. Gorn, "'Gouge and Bite, Pull Hair and Scratch': The Social Significance of Fighting in the Southern Backcountry," *American Historical Review* 90 (1985): 18–43.

5. An excellent guide to the issues for historians, as well as an exemplary analysis, is Natalie Zemon Davis, *Fiction in the Archives: Pardon Tales and Their Tellers in Sixteenth-Century France* (Stanford: Stanford University Press, 1987).

6. This comment on "propertylessness" is made with the caveat that, near the end of his short life, Isham reported that he "bought 10 acres of ground." This purchase was probably made on credit and would not likely have been enough to support his new wife. He abandoned the property after his third wife died in childbirth.

7. Charles C. Bolton, *Poor Whites of the Antebellum South: Tenants and Laborers in Central North Carolina and Northeast Tennessee* (Durham, N.C.: Duke University Press, 1994).

8. On the household economy, see especially Hahn, *Roots of Southern Populism,* and Stephanie McCurry, *Masters of Small Worlds: Yeoman Households, Gender Relations, and the Political Culture of the Antebellum South Carolina Low Country* (New York: Oxford University Press, 1995).

9. The nature and importance of kinship ties in the antebellum South have been perhaps most clearly described in Robert Kenzer, *Kinship and Neighborhood in a Southern Community: Orange County, North Carolina, 1849–1881* (Knoxville: University of Tennessee Press, 1987).

10. Most notably in Victoria E. Bynum, *Unruly Women: The Politics of Social and Sexual Control in the Old South* (Chapel Hill: University of North Carolina Press, 1992).

11. Jonathan D. Spence, *The Search for Modern China* (New York: W. W. Norton, 1990), xix.

1: Autobiography of Edward Isham, Alias "Hardaway Bone"

1. If his age listed on the 1850 federal census for Carroll County, Georgia, is correct, Edward Isham was born in 1826 or 1827. The mortality schedule of the 1860 federal census for Gaston County, North Carolina, gave his age as thirty-two years.

2. Edward Isham, Sr., successfully drew a lot in the 1832 land lottery. He picked land lot no. 854, district 18, section 3, a plot of land located just

north of Carroll County. On the 1850 federal census for Carroll County, Edward Isham, Sr., is listed as a sixty-year-old landless miner. He lived with Cynda Elkins, aged thirty-five, and four Elkins children ranging in age from six months to ten years.

3. Pine Mountain was a short distance north of the future site of Villa Rica. Gold was discovered there in 1830.

4. A William Godard is listed on the 1847 tax list for Carroll County, Georgia. He owned no property.

5. The 1850 federal census for De Kalb County, Georgia, shows that Charles Icems was at the time an eighty-six-year-old farmer who owned land valued at $1,000 in the Buckhead District. He initially acquired land in this county during the 1832 land lottery. He also owned two slaves in 1850, according to the federal census.

6. Nancy Creek, in northern Fulton County, Georgia.

7. According to the 1850 federal census for Forsyth County, Georgia, Hardin Miller was a forty-six-year-old landless farmer living in the household of John and Mary Miller, who also owned no real property. John and Mary Miller were probably Hardin's parents and, therefore, Edward Isham's maternal grandparents.

8. Presumably Isham was working as part of the county's road crew.

9. Located on Peachtree Creek in present-day Atlanta.

10. Should be Cobb County, Georgia, the place where Howell's Mill was located.

11. Located in east central Alabama.

12. Like Isham, Jeff Chambers was probably an occasional resident of Carroll County, Georgia. Although he is not listed on the 1850 federal census for Carroll County, the 1853 tax list for that county has a Jeff Chambers, a man who owned no real property but $375 worth of personal property.

13. Allen Fletcher was convicted in Stewart County, Georgia, of manslaughter in 1834. He served almost all of a four-year sentence in the state penitentiary before he was pardoned in November 1837. At the time of his conviction, Fletcher was a twenty-nine-year-old farmer. Allen Fletcher is listed on the 1847 tax list for Carroll County, Georgia, as having no property.

14. This store was probably the one operated by Hansan Hargrove, who is listed on the 1853 tax list for Carroll County, Georgia, with no land but $1,800 worth of merchandise and $6,500 worth of money and solvent debts.

15. Presumably Cobb County, Georgia.

16. The Ishams of Macon County were likely related to this Hutchinson family by marriage. In 1845 John D. Isom, probably Isham's brother, married Susan Hutchinson in Tallapoosa County, Alabama.

17. The 1850 federal census for Walker County, Georgia, lists Mary Brown as the twenty-four-year-old wife of Hiram Brown, a landless mechanic.

18. The 1850 federal census for Walker County, Georgia, enumerates a James Fulcher. He was a sixty-three-year-old farmer who owned no real property.

19. The *Sam Markin* worked on the Tennessee River between Knoxville, Tennessee, and Decatur, Alabama, during the 1840s and was captained by a man named Rogers. The boat was owned by a group of men in Chattanooga who hoped to persuade the Western and Atlantic Railroad to locate the northern point of their line at Chattanooga. The boat's main function was to show that the Tennessee River was navigable, making it possible for a potentially large volume of commerce to pass through Chattanooga. See Donald Davidson, *The Old River: Frontier to Secession,* vol. 1 of *The Tennessee* (Knoxville: University of Tennessee Press, 1946).

20. The volunteers would have been returning in late 1847 or early 1848. Around the country, the Mexican War volunteers were often welcomed home by large, cheering crowds. Enthusiasm in Tennessee for the war rivaled that in any other southern state. At the war's beginning, 30,000 Tennesseans had responded to the call for 3,000 soldiers.

21. This Jake Floor may have been Jacob Flora, listed on the 1850 federal census for Hamilton County, Tennessee (the county in which Chattanooga is located), as a forty-one-year-old landless farmer.

22. One of the oldest mills in Georgia, located two miles from the town of Chickamauga. The mill was built by James Gordon in the 1830s.

23. Chuck-a-luck, a game played with two or three dice.

24. A federal road passed through this town, which is the county seat of present-day Catoosa County, Georgia.

25. The missing word here and for the blank below is probably "whore" or "bawdy." Because of his religious sensibilities, frequently evidenced in his diaries, David Schenck may have been reluctant to write the word down.

26. The 1850 federal census for Walker County, Georgia, lists a Mary A. Isam as the head of a household. She is forty years old, and the household also includes eight-year-old Mary S. and eleven-year-old William A.M.

27. The 1850 federal census for Walker County, Georgia, lists Hiram Brown as a twenty-two-year-old landless mechanic born in Tennessee. His wife Mary, aged twenty-four, was born in Alabama. Also living in the household was a six-month-old boy and Caroline Nelson, aged eighteen, most likely Hiram's sister.

28. Tunnel Hill was a major obstacle to the completion of the Western and Atlantic Railroad. The first train went through Tunnel Hill on October 30, 1849.

29. The 1850 federal census for Carroll County, Georgia, lists William Bivings as a thirty-year-old landless laborer born in North Carolina. Within the previous year, he had married twenty-five-year-old Melissa, Edward Isham's sister.

30. Located in Cobb County, Georgia.

31. The 1850 federal census for Cobb County, Georgia, lists John Everett as a thirty-eight-year-old farmer; he owned land valued at $255.

32. Located in western Fulton County, Georgia, at the upper headwaters of the Big, or Cedar, Creek.

33. Chattahoochee River.

34. Located in northern Georgia.

35. Probably Thursday Ann Murphy, who was mentioned in S. D. Crane's will, which was drafted in 1849 in Lumpkin County. In the will, Crane left Murphy "my bedstid and all my bed clothes," a bequest perhaps indicating that the two were lovers. If so, Crane might have been the man mentioned in the autobiography as "keeping" Murphy. No additional information about Murphy could be found in census or tax records.

36. Should be Dahlonega, located in Lumpkin County, Georgia.

37. Franklin is located in Macon County, Alabama.

38. The railroad.

39. A word has possibly been omitted.

40. The absence of Isham's right thumb was one of the physical characteristics listed in newspaper advertisements for his arrest after James Cornelius's killing. See appendix C.

41. Dick Fenley is listed on the 1852 tax list for Carroll County, Georgia, as having no property.

42. Rachel Webb is the woman listed as living with Edward Isham on the 1850 federal census for Carroll County, Georgia.

43. The 1850 federal census for Carroll County, Georgia, lists Elijah New as a twenty-three-year-old landless miner. New is listed on the census manuscript seven households away from Edward Isham.

44. The only Hendricks listed on the 1853 tax list for Carroll County, Georgia, is J. M. Hendricks, a man who owned no property.

45. The 1860 federal census for Hamilton County, Tennessee, lists a Mary Isham, aged fifty-four, as a domestic owning $250 worth of real property and $350 worth of personal property. Also living in the household were Nancy Oliver, age sixteen; Sarah Carson, age nineteen; and John Carson, age one.

46. The Hiwassee Railroad was chartered in 1850 and ran from Knoxville, Tennessee, to Cleveland, Tennessee.

47. Probably the Nashville and Chattanooga Railroad, completed to Chattanooga in the early 1850s.

48. Should be Johnson County, Arkansas, located in northwest Arkansas.

49. Completed just before the outbreak of the Mexican War in 1846, Fort Smith in the fifteen years before the Civil War served as a key communications center, military headquarters, and supply post for the southwest frontier. Administrators at the fort also supervised Indian matters west of Arkansas.

50. Probably Opelika, Alabama, the county seat of present-day Lee County.

51. Gilmer County, located in north Georgia.

52. Originally a Cherokee town, during Isham's life Ducktown was a Tennessee mining town, located near the point where the borders of Tennessee, Georgia, and North Carolina meet.

53. This railroad ran through north Georgia.

54. Probably the Tuckasegee River in northeast Tennessee.

55. The 1850 federal census for Blount County, Tennessee, lists a group of free blacks with the last name of Fagg. Isham's "Fax" may have been a member of one of these families.

56. Located in southwest Burke County, Brindletown was the center of one of North Carolina's gold-mining regions.

57. Morganton was the county seat for Burke County.

58. Statesville was the county seat for Iredell County.

59. The Western North Carolina Railroad reached Statesville in 1858.

60. James Lasley appears as a thirty-five-year-old laborer in the 1850 federal census for Iredell County.

61. Living with James Lasley [Lesley] in 1850 (no wife is listed) was fourteen-year-old Amanda. Neither individual appears in the 1860 federal census.

62. Perhaps Isham is referring to Charles A. Carlton, agent for the State Bank of North Carolina, who lived in Statesville. According to the 1860 federal census for Iredell County, Carlton owned $2,000 in real estate and $5,100 in personal property. No record of a land transaction between Carlton and Isham could be found.

63. On election day, August 5, 1858, Democratic candidate John W. Ellis handily defeated his Whig opponent. Isham's fight with Clarke, who is not readily identifiable in census reports, resulted in the assault and battery case *State v. H. Bone,* August term 1858, Iredell County Court of Pleas and Quarter Sessions Trial Docket, North Carolina Division of Archives and History, Raleigh, North Carolina. The indictment, issued to Lincoln County where Isham fled, was dropped after Isham's arrest for the May 1859 killing of James Cornelius.

64. A twenty-three-year-old farmer named Eli Beaver, with real estate valued at $80, lived near James Lasley in 1850, according to the 1850 federal census. There is no record in this instance of legal action against Isham.

65. Taylorsville was settled in 1847 and was the county seat for Alexander County.

66. Lincoln County was the home of David Schenck.

67. The 1850 federal census for Catawba County shows James Cornelius as a farmer, age forty and a bachelor, who owned real estate valued at $2,580 and possessed three slaves, all female. In 1859 he was taxed $18.76 for 236 acres of land valued at $3,540 and four slaves. See the Catawba County List of Taxables, 1857–68, North Carolina Division of Archives and History, Raleigh.

68. No record of Isham's suit could be found. Compare with Thomas Beaty's testimony at Isham's trial (appendix B).

69. The twenty-six-year-old Dr. J. J. Mott owned $6,000 of real estate and $8,400 of personal property, according to the 1860 federal census, making him and James Cornelius's brother, Austin, two of the most affluent residents in the Sherrill's Ford neighborhood of southeastern Catawba County. Dr. Mott later attended the mortally wounded James Cornelius but failed to appear at Isham's trial. See trial transcript for further details (appendix B).

70. Isham was staying at the Catawba County home of William and Susan Reed or Reid (both of whom later testified against Isham at his murder trial), although for how long a period of time is unclear, as newspaper advertisements for his arrest state that he lived near Statesville, in adjoining Iredell County. Isham's infant was called Margaret Bone, and she lived

in the Reed household for at least the next twenty years. In the 1880 federal census for Iredell County she was listed as Margaret F. Boone, aged twenty-two, and was described as a "boarder" in the home of James Reid, William's oldest son. Her father's place of birth was given as Georgia. Perhaps her status in the household and the knowledge of her father's origin indicate that Margaret was never considered an intimate member of the family that had cared for her after Edward Isham's execution. She appears neither in later census reports nor in North Carolina marriage or death records.

71. Lincoln County farmer Washington Sherrill owned $3,500 of real estate and $3,550 of personal property in 1860. Sherrill, aged forty-eight, and his forty-six-year-old wife, Mattie, had eight children. Sherrill testified against Isham at his murder trial.

72. James Cornelius's property lay in the southeastern corner of Catawba County near where Mountain Creek joined the Catawba River. The property is now covered by Lake Norman. Austin Cornelius, his brother, was his nearest neighbor, according to the 1860 federal census.

73. Presumably Isham wanted to cross the Catawba River eastward to the Iredell County side.

74. Beginning at this point, Schenck highlighted with indentation and ditto marks the section of Isham's narrative concerning the death of Cornelius.

75. May 8, 1859.

76. One of James Cornelius's neighbors, according to the 1860 federal census, was the farmer Mary Little, whose son, James Little, owned a twenty-seven-year-old male slave in 1860. James Little's personal property, which also included a young female and an infant male slave, was valued at $4,800. Mary Little held an older female slave and owned personal property valued at $550 and real estate at $1,200.

77. This parenthetical element is the one point in the narrative where Schenck's voice is clearly evident.

78. William J. Sherrill was listed in the 1860 federal census as a twenty-six-year-old farm laborer, living in the Catawba County household of the fifty-eight-year-old Sarah Sherrill, who had a farm that was valued at $5,000 and personal property worth $8,200.

79. Beatties Ford crossed the Catawba River from Lincoln to Mecklenburg Counties. The site is now under Lake Norman.

80. Iredell County farmer Daniel Fink, aged fifty-four, and his wife

Elizabeth, aged fifty, owned $4,500 worth of real estate and $400 worth of personal property in 1860, according to the 1860 federal census.

81. This individual is perhaps the Charlie Carlton from whom Isham obtained land when he first came to North Carolina.

82. Named for Daniel Boone, Boone is the county seat of present-day Watauga County, North Carolina.

83. Isham had come to Carter County, Tennessee, at the northeastern end of Tennessee. According to Waugh's trial testimony, Isham must have traveled nearly a hundred miles in the four days after his assault on Cornelius.

84. William K. Waugh of Johnson County, Tennessee, was a forty-eight-year-old merchant in 1860. Married to Julia and the father of three children, Waugh owned real estate valued at $1,000 and personal property valued at $2,000.

85. Newton, incorporated in 1855, is the present-day county seat of Catawba County, North Carolina.

86. This penciled note was added in Schenck's handwriting.

2: Edward Isham and Poor White Labor in the Old South

An earlier draft of this essay was presented in November 1993 at the annual meeting of the Southern Historical Association. I thank Bradley G. Bond, Scott P. Culclasure, J. William Harris, and David K. Kleit for their comments on various versions of this essay.

1. Salisbury (N.C.) *Carolina Watchman,* May 10, 1859; Charlotte (N.C.) *Western Democrat,* May 10, 1859.

2. This figure of 100,000 is a conservative estimate. According to J. D. B. Debow's *Compendium of the Seventh Census* (Washington, D.C.: A. O. P. Nicholson, 1854), 302,607 individuals in the South were classified as either laborers or farm laborers. Many of these people, however, were younger sons living with their parents, although it is impossible to know exactly how many fell into this category, since local census enumerators recorded information in a variety of different ways. For example, a 250-household sample of the 1850 federal census for Davidson County, North Carolina, reveals that 69 percent of laborers in that county were actually younger sons living with their parents, while a 250-household sample of the 1850 federal census for Pontotoc County, Mississippi, shows

that only 31 percent of laborers counted there were younger sons living with their parents. In Pontotoc County, the enumerator labeled most of these younger sons "farmers." My low estimate of 100,000 is based on the assumption that in all counties as many as two-thirds of those listed on the census as laborers or farm laborers may actually have been younger sons living with their parents. Many adult women, of course, also worked for wages, but determining their numbers from aggregate census records is virtually impossible, since enumerators frequently did not list a specific occupation for women on the census schedules.

3. Charles C. Bolton, *Poor Whites of the Antebellum South: Tenants and Laborers in Central North Carolina and Northeast Mississippi* (Durham: Duke University Press, 1994), chapters 2 and 5; Ralph Mann, "Mountains, Land, and Kin Networks: Burkes Garden, Virginia, in the 1840s and 1850s," *Journal of Southern History* 58 (August 1992): 423–25; Randolph B. Campbell, "Planters and Plain Folk: Harrison County, Texas, as a Test Case, 1850–1860," *Journal of Southern History* 40 (August 1974): 369–98; Gavin Wright, "'Economic Democracy' and the Concentration of Agricultural Wealth in the Cotton South, 1850–1860," *Agricultural History* 44 (January 1970): 63–93; James C. Bonner, "Profile of a Late Antebellum Community," *American Historical Review* 49 (July 1944): 663–80.

4. A number of recent works have increased our knowledge about the world of antebellum white nonslaveholders: Stephanie McCurry, *Masters of Small Worlds: Yeoman Households, Gender Relations, and the Political Culture of the Antebellum South Carolina Low Country* (New York: Oxford University Press, 1995); Bolton, *Poor Whites of the Antebellum South;* Bill Cecil-Fronsman, *Common Whites: Class and Culture in Antebellum North Carolina* (Lexington: University Press of Kentucky, 1992); Victoria E. Bynum, *Unruly Women: The Politics of Social and Sexual Control in the Old South* (Chapel Hill: University of North Carolina Press, 1992); Lacy K. Ford, *Origins of Southern Radicalism: The South Carolina Upcountry, 1800–1860* (New York: Oxford University Press, 1988); J. William Harris, *Plain Folk and Gentry in a Slave Society: White Liberty and Black Slavery in Augusta's Hinterlands* (Middletown, Conn.: Wesleyan University Press, 1985); and Steven Hahn, *The Roots of Southern Populism: Yeoman Farmers and the Transformation of the Georgia Upcountry, 1850–1890* (New York: Oxford University Press, 1983), among others. Despite this recent scholarly attention, the poorest of the Old South's nonslaveholders, landless whites, remain the most elusive.

5. Gilbert E. Govan and James W. Livingood, *The Chattanooga Country, 1540 –1951: From Tomahawks to TVA* (New York: E. P. Dutton, 1952), chapter 8; Autobiography of Edward Isham.

6. Autobiography of Edward Isham.

7. Autobiography of Edward Isham; Statesville (N.C.) *Iredell Express,* May 13, 1859. The Western North Carolina Railroad reached Statesville in Iredell County on October 1, 1858, and construction continued westward through the county until it was halted by the Civil War. See Homer M. Keever, *Iredell: Piedmont County* (Statesville, N.C.: Brady Printing, 1976), 219.

8. Journal of work by Moses E. D. Pike in Hugh W. Johnson Papers, Duke Manuscript Collection (DMC), Perkins Library, Duke University, Durham, North Carolina; Colleen Morse Elliott and Louise Armstrong Moxley, eds., *The Tennessee Civil War Veterans Questionnaires,* 5 vols. (Easley, S.C.: Southern Historical Press, 1985), 2:537, 4:1764. Additional examples are located throughout the five volumes of questionnaires.

9. Account of John Poss, George B. Hudson Store and Farm Account Book, in Mrs. Don G. Aiken Collection, Georgia Department of Archives and History, Atlanta (GDAH); 1850 federal census for Gwinnett County, Georgia, schedule 1 (population); 1850 federal census for De Kalb County, Georgia, schedule 1; 1860 federal census for Cobb County, Georgia, schedule 1.

10. 1850 and 1860 federal censuses for Lincoln County, North Carolina, schedule 1; 1850 federal census for Gaston County, North Carolina, schedule 1. The census enumerator for Lincoln County in 1860 gave not only the state but also the county of birth for each individual. In 1860 the county had seventy-two households headed by landless laborers or miners. Forty-eight of these had been born in Lincoln County, twenty-one in other North Carolina counties, and three in locations outside of North Carolina. Many of the Lincoln County natives, like Jonathan Anthony, resided not in Lincoln County but in neighboring counties — such as Gaston — in 1850. For further evidence of intracounty and regional mobility among white laborers, see Bolton, *Poor Whites of the Antebellum South,* 33 –34, 52 –53.

11. For a discussion of farm labor in the Midwest, see Paul W. Gates, *Landlords and Tenants on the Prairie Frontier* (Ithaca, N.Y.: Cornell University Press, 1973); and David E. Schob, *Hired Hands and Plowboys: Farm Labor in the Midwest, 1815 – 60* (Urbana: University of Illinois Press, 1975). For details on how slavery exerted a downward pressure on the

wages of white southern laborers, see Bolton, *Poor Whites of the Antebellum South,* 17–18.

12. Elliott and Moxley, eds., *The Tennessee Civil War Veterans Questionnaires,* 1:262.

13. Autobiography of Edward Isham; David Williams, *The Georgia Gold Rush: Twenty-niners, Cherokees, and Gold Fever* (Columbia: University of South Carolina Press, 1993); Bolton, *Poor Whites of the Antebellum South,* 35–36. While Carroll County, Georgia, was somewhat peripheral to the primary gold-mining country of the state farther north, gold mining was clearly a major economic activity in Edward Isham's Pinetown.

14. Account with John Fowler, in Account Book, Mary G. Franklin Papers, DMC.

15. Autobiography of Edward Isham; 1850 federal census for Carroll County, Georgia, schedule 1, households no. 1131 and 1138.

16. Autobiography of Edward Isham; Williams, *The Georgia Gold Rush,* 117–18.

17. Charlotte (N.C.) *Western Democrat,* May 10, 1859; Brent David Glass, "King Midas and Old Rip: The Gold Mining District of North Carolina" (Ph.D. diss., University of North Carolina, Chapel Hill, 1980), esp. chap. 2. *DeBow's Review* 5 (1848): 93, describes the iron ore located in Lincoln County. The 1860 federal census for Lincoln County, North Carolina, schedule 1, lists a number of landless miners in the county, but since the county had no schedule 5 (manufacturing) in 1850, it seems likely that the county had no corporate mines.

18. Autobiography of Edward Isham; 1850 federal census for Macon County, Alabama, schedule 5.

19. Autobiography of Edward Isham; Account of D. C. Rutledge, George B. Hudson Store and Farm Account Book, GDAH; 1850 federal census for Gwinnett County, Georgia, schedules 1, 2, and 4 (agriculture).

20. Charles B. Dew's *Bond of Iron: Master and Slave at Buffalo Forge* (New York: W. W. Norton, 1994) vividly shows that employers in a slave society generally preferred slave labor over free.

21. John Wilkes to his father, May 31, 1856, July 24, 1856, and August 3, 1856, all in Wilkes Family Papers, DMC.

22. Autobiography of Edward Isham.

23. H. Scott to his nephew, May 9, 1855, John Mebane Allen Letters, Southern Historical Collection, University of North Carolina Library, Chapel Hill.

24. Autobiography of Edward Isham. The autobiography claims that Isham asked Cornelius for seven dollars, but an account of the dispute between the two men in the North Carolina *Iredell Express,* May 13, 1859, states that Isham requested eight dollars as payment for two days' work. Court records claim that Isham asked for "$7.87/100 for 1 & ¾ days work." See Case 7858, Supreme Court Original Cases, North Carolina Division of Archives and History (NCDAH). See appendix B for the complete text of this case. The more typical wage of one dollar a day for white ditchers can be seen in Account of William W. Duck, 1856, George B. Hudson Store and Farm Account Book, GDAH. The lives of the landless population in a nearby part of Iredell County can occasionally be glimpsed in Paul D. Escott, ed., *North Carolina Yeoman: The Diary of Basil Armstrong Thomasson, 1853–1862* (Athens: University of Georgia Press, 1996).

25. Carlton H. Rogers, *Incidents of Travel in the Southern States and Cuba* (New York: R. Craighead, 1862), 260–64; James W. Overcash to J. S. Overcash, May 14, 1860, and May 20, 1860, and James W. Overcash to Joseph Overcash, June 1, 1860, all in Joseph Overcash Papers, DMC. Only eleven days separate Overcash's last North Carolina letter to his brother and his first letter from Panola County, Mississippi, to his father. Later that summer, the 1860 federal census enumerator recorded that James Overcash was living back in Rowan County as a landless laborer in the household of a brickmason in the area.

26. Mann, "Mountain, Land, and Kin Networks," 428–32, shows that landless families in Tazewell County, Virginia, often found jobs working for wealthier kin in their homes or in surrounding communities.

27. Autobiography of Edward Isham; 1850 federal censuses for De Kalb and Forsyth Counties, schedule 1.

28. 1850 and 1860 federal censuses for Carroll County, Georgia, schedules 1 and 4; 1860 federal census for De Kalb County, Georgia, schedules 1 and 4. Only four of the thirty household heads who lived in the dwellings surrounding that of Edward Isham could be located in the 1860 federal census for Carroll County; the family composition of all four remained essentially unchanged between the two census years except for children added to or leaving the household. Five additional household heads were located in the 1860 census records for nearby Georgia counties; again, all showed no or only relatively minor changes in the membership of their households between 1850 and 1860. A sample of 250 house-

holds from the 1850 federal census for Davidson County, North Carolina, also reveals that adult white laborers in that county generally lived as families, not as isolated individuals.

29. C. J. Cowles to Thornton Profit, April 20, 1861, Calvin J. Cowles Papers, NCDAH.

30. Accounts of William W. Duck and Elizabeth Bradbury, George B. Hudson Store and Farm Account Book, GDAH. Additional examples of the work done by the spouses and children of landless laborers can be located throughout the five volumes of *The Tennessee Civil War Veterans Questionnaires*.

3: A Stereoscopic View of the Frontier: George Swain, Edward Isham, and the Resettlement of the Cherokee Country

I gratefully acknowledge the support of the National Endowment for the Humanities. This essay underwent significant revision made possible by a 1994–95 dissertation grant from the National Endowment for the Humanities.

1. John Mack Faragher, *Sugar Creek: Life on the Illinois Prairie* (New Haven: Yale University Press, 1986).

2. See Richard White, *"It's Your Misfortune and None of My Own": A New History of the American West* (Norman: University of Oklahoma Press, 1991); and Charles C. Bolton, *Poor Whites of the Antebellum South: Tenants and Laborers in Central North Carolina and Northeast Mississippi* (Durham: Duke University Press, 1994), esp. chap. 4: "Poverty Moves West: The Migration of Poor Whites to the Old Southwest," 66–83.

3. George Swain's frequent letters to his brother, often written to explain why he needed more money, provide detailed reports on his activities for over twenty years. All citations to letters either to or from David Swain are from the David Lowry Swain Papers, North Carolina Division of Archives and History, Raleigh.

4. As an adult, he said he was born August 30, 1792. See George Swain to David Swain, August 15, 1852, and August 30, 1858. The federal census of 1850 identifies him as fifty-nine years old, and the census of 1860 records his age as seventy-two. While still living in North Carolina, George Swain suffered injuries he believed contributed to his difficulties as an adult in Georgia: "At about 18 years old I was near getting killed by a horse & so badly hurt that neither my mind nor bodily faculties have ever been

the same since." See George Swain to David Swain, undated. See also George Swain to David Swain, March 6, 1842, and March 11, 1843.

On George Swain's family, see Carolyn Andrews Daniel, "David Lowry Swain, 1801–1835" (Ph.D. diss., University of North Carolina, Chapel Hill, 1954), esp. 1–11. Originally from the North, George Swain, Sr., arrived in South Carolina in 1785 and subsequently moved on to Georgia. He "attained considerable local prominence while in Georgia. He became justice of the peace, a member of the legislature, and a delegate to the constitutional convention of 1795." Daniel, "David Lowry Swain," 5. The Swain family moved to Buncombe County, North Carolina, in 1796.

5. John C. Inscoe, *Mountain Masters, Slavery, and the Sectional Crisis in Western North Carolina* (Knoxville: University of Tennessee Press), 19. It was not uncommon for mountain slaveholders to pursue a wide variety of activities. See Inscoe, *Mountain Masters*, 59–76.

6. George Swain to David Swain, undated.

7. 1830 federal census for Jackson County, Georgia. This was the county in which Edward Isham was born in about 1827.

8. George Swain to David Swain, December 6, 1839. By the spring of 1841, 300 acres of land had been cleared on this site. See George Swain to David Swain, March 29, 1841.

9. George Swain to David Swain, December 6, 1839.

10. Although David Swain considered buying formerly Cherokee lands in North Carolina, he balked at the high prices produced by the September 1838 North Carolina auction of Cherokee lands. Instead, he bought some lands in Cherokee Georgia and provided financial support for his brother's efforts. Patience, the widowed sister of George and David, had fewer resources than her brothers did. She attempted to establish an occupant claim on land in Alabama that had recently belonged to the Indians and had not yet been redistributed to American owners. When this effort failed, she and her family joined George Swain's household. See George Swain to David Swain, August 13, 1838, and June 25, 1841.

11. George Swain to David Swain, August 6, 1839.

12. By far the most important source for Edward Isham's life is the Autobiography of Edward Isham in the David Schenck Notebook, David Schenck Papers, North Carolina Division of Archives and History, Raleigh. See also Scott P. Culclasure, "'I Have Killed a Damned Dog,'" chapter 4 in this volume. I thank Charles Bolton and Scott Culclasure for sharing with me their research concerning Edward Isham. Scott Culclasure's typescript of the Isham autobiography has been particularly helpful.

13. The Isham family lived in Pinetown, also known as Pine Mountain Town, just north of Villa Rica. Gold mining began in this area around 1830. "Edward Isom," Sr., entered the 1832 Cherokee land lottery, and he is recorded as a resident of Carroll County. In the lottery, he won a lot from among the Cherokee lands believed to have gold (lot no. 854 in district 18, section 3). See S. Emmett Lucas, *The 1832 Gold Lottery of Georgia: Containing a List of the Fortunate Drawers in Said Lottery* (Easley, S.C.: Southern Historical Press, 1976), 263.

14. Carroll County was formed primarily of lands taken from the Creek Indians during the 1820s. After the Creeks were pushed out, the county's northern border became disputed territory between Georgia and the Cherokee Nation. In an effort to increase the pressure upon the Cherokees to accept removal to lands west of the Mississippi River, Georgia claimed a significant amount of Cherokee land under the dubious premise that it was really Creek land that had been acquired by Georgia through treaties with the Creeks. James C. Bonner, *Georgia's Last Frontier: The Development of Carroll County* (Athens: University of Georgia Press, 1971), 20, provides a succinct explanation of the dispute and its compromise resolution.

15. Isham later recalled: "No preacher could ever live or preach in Pine town, one lived there once and they tore down his fences and run him off, there never was any school there." See Autobiography of Edward Isham.

16. Autobiography of Edward Isham.

17. The culture of backcountry fighting is perceptively analyzed in Elliott J. Gorn, "'Gouge and Bite, Pull Hair and Scratch': The Social Significance of Fighting in the Southern Backcountry," *American Historical Review* 90 (February 1985): 18–43.

18. Isham mined gold within the Cherokee country in Forsyth, Cobb, and Lumpkin Counties in Georgia. Also within the Cherokee country, he gambled and probably mined copper at Ducktown in Polk County, Tennessee. In addition, he worked as a gold miner just south of the Cherokee country in De Kalb County and, of course, in Carroll County, Georgia.

19. The amount owed him is his own estimate. See George Swain to David Swain, October 23, 1841.

20. Under the circumstances, the resulting auctions were certain to produce a disappointing return.

21. Beginning in 1839, David Swain had difficulty providing the funds George requested. In a particularly dramatic example from 1839, George without asking committed his brother to a $1,600 debt, due immediately,

and David took months scrambling for better terms and the capital to meet them. By the end of 1842, David Swain had effectively loaned his brother at least several thousand dollars. The total amount is unclear, in part because some of the money sent from David Swain to George Swain was intended to purchase property for David. See, for example, George Swain to David Swain, August 13, 1838; April 4, 1840; March 6, December 2, 1842. The 1860 federal census reports that David Swain had $1,000 in real property and $75,000 in personal property.

22. In December 1839, George reported difficulty collecting debts owed to him and an increasing scarcity of money in the area. Yet while now "hard run" for money, George continued to buy land both for himself and for David. See George Swain to David Swain, December 6, 1839. By the end of 1840 he had begun to understand the true crisis: "I assure you it is the most alarming time to be in debt I have ever seen & unfortunately for me I am at this juncture more deeply in debt than I ever was before & yet holding a considerable quantity of surplus land that is doing me no good without any chance to sell for the pressure of the times." See George Swain to David Swain, December 20, 1840. See also George Swain to David Swain, June 9, 1841.

23. George Swain to David Swain, December 20, 1840. George would regret this intensely in the years that followed. The price included $5,000 to be paid immediately.

24. M. C. Long to David Swain, December 14, 1845.

25. George Swain to David Swain, December 28, 1845, and May 6, 1846.

26. George Swain's extensive plans for several mills are described in George Swain to David Swain, July 4, 1844. See also George Swain to David Swain, April 19, September 28, 1845; December 12, 1846; and Turner Trippe to David Swain, January 21, 1846.

27. George and David's father would also have objected to the distillery had he still been alive, for "he remained through life a strict Presbyterian, . . . and was strongly opposed to the use of alcohol." See Daniel, "David Lowry Swain," 7. George Swain began running his stills by the start of 1843, but he abandoned the project in 1846 after having invested over $500 in the endeavor. See George Swain to David Swain, December 6, 1841; January 20, March 6, November 27, 1842; March 11, 1843; July 22, September 28, 1845; July 1, 1846.

28. George Swain was willing at least to consider anything, whatever its moral implications. When he was forced to sell his own slaves, he hit upon

the idea of becoming a slave trader himself. Even more than his distillery business, slave trading would have undermined his brother's support, and he did not pursue it. See George Swain to David Swain, February 11, 1844. George Swain lamented the splitting up of slave families and his loss of Swain "family" slaves, but he apparently saw no contradiction in his own interest in the slave trade.

29. George Swain's daughter described the problem to David Swain: "Most of the families living on that place are there because they could get no home elsewhere, Who going there in debt have contributed much toward his present distresses." George recognized the problem, but was, in his daughter's view, "too merciful in his disposition to refuse a family which he thinks suffering a home, and more he will hinder their plunder from being sold, by paying out for it the money which he so much needs & which rightly employed might pay many of his debts." See M. C. Long to David Swain, December 14, 1845.

30. George Coleman to David Swain, January 22, 1849. Coleman asked for what he called an independent view from a Colonel Woods. Woods concurred with Coleman's assessment that the farm was poorly managed and had the potential for sizable profits if better run. See Woods to David Swain, February 7, 1849.

31. Swain noted: "Besides all the rest, in 1827 I lost my wife & since that time the business of my house affairs has been entrusted into the hands of every body or any body I could catch up until in my house I have very little or nothing left." See George Swain to David Swain, undated (perhaps late 1840s).

32. See Gorn, 20. Isham's life fits fairly well within the culture of backcountry brawling as portrayed by Elliot Gorn. Nonetheless, it remains hard to comprehend the sheer frequency and ferocity with which Isham resorted to violence.

33. Bolton, *Poor Whites of the Antebellum South*.

34. Autobiography of Edward Isham.

35. Autobiography of Edward Isham.

36. Autobiography of Edward Isham. During the 1850s, the railroad gave him the means of rapid escape he often needed.

37. Autobiography of Edward Isham.

38. Autobiography of Edward Isham.

39. Autobiography of Edward Isham.

40. Autobiography of Edward Isham.

41. Autobiography of Edward Isham.

42. Autobiography of Edward Isham.

43. Autobiography of Edward Isham.

44. The property was immediately resold for $10,000. Unlike George Swain, the new owner had sufficient resources to exploit its potential, and he quickly moved a substantial force of slaves to the farm to build it into a plantation.

45. David Swain to George Swain, copied excerpt, August 10, 1849.

46. George Swain to David Swain, December 7, 1849.

47. George Coleman to David Swain, September 7, 1849; and George Swain to David Swain, May 4, 1847.

48. David Swain repeatedly offered George the opportunity to live on this land over the years, but George usually had a scheme of his own that he preferred over farming his brother's land. See George Swain to David Swain, July 15, 1855.

49. George Swain to David Swain, June 30, August 15, 1852; January 9, 1853; and January 2, 27, May 6, 1854. The inaccessible nature of George's mountain lands contrasted sharply with the lands David had offered for his use. David Swain's Murray County land was on a river that went directly to a nearby railroad depot.

50. Swain also tried teaching school, but he found this work "quite too confining for me." See George Swain to David Swain, August 15, 1852. See also George Swain to David Swain, October 10, 1852. A sudden move to Alabama in 1857 to try stock raising may have been an attempt to avoid court action against him for debts in Georgia. See George Swain to David Swain, February 20, March 21, 1857.

51. George Swain to David Swain, April 16, May 8, 1853.

52. George Swain to David Swain, April 16, June 26, 1853; August 6, November 20, 1854; January 27, July 17, August 5, October 9, 1855.

53. George Swain to David Swain, October 8, November 14, 1853.

54. Eventually George came to regard the property as his own, although David never transferred ownership to him or even intended to do so. See C. W. Long to David Swain, February 5, 1867.

55. Unsigned letter to David Swain, August 26, 1860. George Swain confirmed some of this portrait himself: "I am shifting about from port to pillow & [have] no certain place to stay & being thus situated I cannot enjoy myself nor neither can I content myself or get anything like justice for what I do." See George Swain to David Swain, November 28, 1861.

In 1867, George Swain's son-in-law wrote David Swain what David himself must have long since concluded, that George had for at least ten years been "incapable of managing any business." He had made a practice of providing George with clothing and small amounts of money for immediate needs, but "to furnish him money for any other purpose I saw was entirely useless, as he would be swindled out of it immediately." See C. W. Long to David Swain, February 5, 1867.

56. These events are discussed in Autobiography of Edward Isham. They have been described more fully, using additional sources, in Culclasure, "'I Have Killed a Damned Dog,'" chapter 4 in this volume.

57. Culclasure, "'I Have Killed a Damned Dog,'" chapter 4 in this volume. Isham may have chosen not to mention whatever assistance he received, but his course of action suggests otherwise. Isham did get a gun from an acquaintance, but it is unclear whether he stole it or it was a voluntary loan.

58. Isham's limited, recently formed ties in the area were insufficient to inspire a petition campaign for his pardon. See Scott P. Culclasure, "Edward Isham and Criminal Justice for the Poor White in Antebellum North Carolina," chapter 5 in this volume.

59. Culclasure, "'I Have Killed a Damned Dog,'" chapter 4 in this volume.

4: "I Have Killed a Damned Dog": Murder by a Poor White in the Antebellum South

This article, here modified slightly, originally appeared in the *North Carolina Historical Review* 70 (January 1993): 14–39.

1. Edward Isham's case can be followed in *State v. Hardaway Bone,* fall term 1859, Catawba County Superior Court Minutes, and fall term 1859, Gaston County Superior Court Minutes, North Carolina Division of Archives and History, Raleigh (NCDAH). The North Carolina Supreme Court designation is *State v. Hardaway Bone, North Carolina Reports* 52 (1859): 121. The trial transcript, complete with copies of the relevant superior court minutes, is in Case 7858, Supreme Court Original Cases, 1800–1909, NCDAH. The most complete newspaper accounts of the murder are in the *Iredell Express* (Statesville), May 13, May 27, 1859, and June 1, 1860; and in the *Western Democrat* (Charlotte), May 10, May 24, May 31, and November 1, 1859.

2. "Fall Circuit, 1859," 409, Diary of David Schenck, David Schenck Books, Southern Historical Collection, University of North Carolina Li-

brary, Chapel Hill. David Schenck's invaluable and largely untapped diaries, books, and papers held in the Southern Historical Collection run to nineteen volumes and cover most of the years of his life (1835–1902). Isham's autobiography, however, is contained in the David Schenck Notebook, David Schenck Papers, NCDAH. All quotations of Isham are from the Isham autobiography, unless otherwise noted.

3. Early in this century, historians Paul H. Buck and A. N. J. Den Hollander examined the political role and the reputation of poor whites in two widely cited but woefully outdated essays. See Paul H. Buck, "The Poor Whites of the Ante-Bellum South," *American Historical Review* 31 (October 1925): 41–54, and A. N. J. Den Hollander, "The Tradition of 'Poor Whites,'" in *Culture in the South,* ed. W. T. Couch (Chapel Hill: University of North Carolina Press, 1934), 403–31. Important contemporary observers include Daniel R. Hundley, *Social Relations in Our Southern States* (New York: Henry B. Price, 1860), and Frederick Law Olmsted, *A Journey in the Back Country* (New York: Mason Brothers, 1860). Steven Hahn has analyzed census returns (including those from Carroll County, Georgia, Isham's home) to determine the degree of antebellum tenancy and what tenancy signified; see his *The Roots of Southern Populism: Yeoman Farmers and the Transformation of the Georgia Upcountry, 1850–1890* (New York: Oxford University Press, 1983). A work that makes extensive use of petitions in gubernatorial and legislative papers is Bill Cecil-Fronsman, *Common Whites: Class and Culture in Antebellum North Carolina* (Lexington: University Press of Kentucky, 1992). For the use of court records by another historian who recognizes the value of Edward Isham's autobiography, see Charles C. Bolton, *Poor Whites of the Antebellum South: Tenants and Laborers in Central North Carolina and Northeast Mississippi* (Durham: Duke University Press, 1994). Calling for greater attention to poor whites is the review of a variety of recent works on the nonelite by Michael Fellman, "Getting Right with the Poor White," *Canadian Review of American Studies* 18 (Winter 1987): 527–39. My article will show that the role of poor whites in the antebellum South has recently received greater attention from historians.

4. I am indebted to Bertram Wyatt-Brown for suggesting that Isham embodies his concept of shamelessness, which he elaborates in Wyatt-Brown, *Southern Honor: Ethics and Behavior in the Old South* (New York: Oxford University Press, 1982), 398–99.

5. Frank Lawrence Owsley, *Plain Folk of the Old South* (Baton Rouge: Louisiana State University Press, 1949), 36. Owsley helped to shift atten-

tion away from poor whites to the larger number of all southern nonland-holders, concluding that most of the latter group found a reasonable degree of economic security through migratory occupations like cattle herding. The status of poor whites continued to be ignored as Owsley minimized their existence and as historians debated the validity of the statistical analyses of landholding patterns employed by Owsley. Until a consensus develops on what to call the group—the confusion reflects uncertainty about how to define antebellum poverty as well as an understandable desire to avoid pejoratives—there will continue to be a plethora of descriptive terms. One point is clear: those described as "poor whites" are only part of a larger group variously labeled "plain folk," "common whites," or "yeomen." That poor whites require a many-faceted definition is well demonstrated in Edward Magdol and Jon L. Wakelyn, *The Southern Common People: Studies in Nineteenth-Century Social History* (Westport, Conn.: Greenwood Press, 1980), although few historians have taken up the challenge of studying the various groups of poor whites.

6. William Gilmore Simms, *Guy Rivers: A Tale of Georgia,* rev. ed. (Chicago: Donohue, Henneberry, 1890). The novel is actually set to the northeast of Carroll County in the area between the branching of the Chattahoochee and Chestatee Rivers (an area Isham would later know when he visited an uncle and dug for gold in Forsyth County). Simms described the novel as "a tale of Georgia—a tale of the miners—of a frontier and wild people, and the events are precisely such as may occur among a people & in a region of that character." Simms to James Lawson, December 29, 1833, *The Letters of William Gilmore Simms,* ed. Mary C. Simms Oliphant et al. (Columbia: University of South Carolina Press, 1952). A sturdy local history of Carroll County is James C. Bonner, *Georgia's Last Frontier: The Development of Carroll County* (Athens: University of Georgia Press, 1971).

7. For a description of the violence that attended the gold rush of the late 1820s and early 1830s on the lands of the Creek and Cherokee Indians, see George R. Gilmer, *Sketches of Some of the First Settlers of Upper Georgia* (Americus, Ga.: Americus Book, 1926), 282–344. That violence marked the lives of miners in North Carolina (where Isham did not work in mining) is shown in Brent D. Glass, "The Miner's World: Life and Labor at Gold Hill," *North Carolina Historical Review* 62 (October 1985): 439. Carroll County was some distance from the center of gold mining in the Dahlonega Gold Belt to the northeast, and Isham's youth meant that he had missed most of the boom. Still, the area around the county's Villa Rica, renowned for the purity of its gold, continued to attract those im-

poverished hopefuls who believed that gold "can be had, to the satisfaction of avarice itself by a little labour." This statement, made by a Georgian "twenty-niner," is quoted in David Williams, *The Georgia Gold Rush: Twenty-niners, Cherokees, and Gold Fever* (Columbia: University of South Carolina Press, 1993), 28.

8. Schenck Diary, 417; *Iredell Express,* May 13, 1859, and June 1, 1860; Bolton, *Poor Whites,* 1–10.

9. Two complementary works that deal with violence as part of southern notions of honor are Wyatt-Brown, *Southern Honor,* and Edward L. Ayers, *Vengeance and Justice: Crime and Punishment in the Nineteenth-Century American South* (New York: Oxford University Press, 1984).

10. The year of Isham's birth is inferred from the federal manuscript censuses for 1840 and 1850, in which both Isham and his father appear. In addition, the mortality schedule of the census for Gaston County in 1860 lists Isham's age at the time of his death as thirty-two. See 1840 federal census for Carroll County, Georgia, population schedule; 1850 federal census for Carroll County, Georgia, population schedule; and 1860 federal census for Gaston County, North Carolina, mortality schedule.

11. 1840 federal census for De Kalb County, Georgia, population schedule.

12. Simms, *Guy Rivers,* 14.

13. Simms, *Guy Rivers,* 280. Observations about the southerner's fear of a passionate individual operating within the frontier environment of minimal restraints owe much to Dickson Bruce's skillful use of antebellum literature in *Violence and Culture in the Antebellum South* (Austin: University of Texas Press, 1979), 218–21, and the worthy article on Simms's fiction by Simon Vauthier, "Of Time and the South: The Fiction of William Gilmore Simms," *Southern Literary Journal* 5 (Fall 1972): 20–25. Several deadly themes common to the lives of Isham and many other poor whites received humorous attention in antebellum literature. See the satirical account of "Samuel Hele, Esq.," describing a father's tutelage of his son's villainy in Joseph G. Baldwin, *The Flush Times of Alabama and Mississippi: A Series of Sketches* (New York: Appleton, 1853), 295–302. To give an impression of the treachery of the rascally Captain Simon Suggs, author Johnson Jones Hooper asked his readers to imagine the effect of spending much of a lifetime in Carroll County, "in the 'sovereignty' of Georgia, where, from 'time immemorial,' the chief occupation of the inhabitants has been to steal horses." That Captain Suggs learned many of the gambling and fighting skills possessed by Isham is apparent in Johnson

Jones Hooper, *Adventures of Captain Simon Suggs, Late of the Tallapoosa Volunteers,* introd. Manly Wade Wellman (1845; reprint, Chapel Hill: University of North Carolina Press, 1969), 8–10.

14. For the view that southerners were pessimists who believed that passion led to violence and that violence, in turn, was "an essential fact of human life somehow built in," see Bruce, *Violence and Culture,* 7.

15. Southern child-rearing practices are described in Wyatt-Brown, *Southern Honor,* 117–48. "Plain-folk" violence perpetuated by family upbringing is treated in Bruce, *Violence and Culture,* 95–97.

16. 1850 federal census for Carroll County, Georgia, population and agriculture schedules. For similar observations and a tidy, more chronological summary of Isham's life, see Bolton, *Poor Whites,* chap. 1. For Bolton, the South's failure to minimize the economic stratification of its white population greatly heightened internal tensions at the very time the region was preparing to fight against the perceived external threat of the North.

17. The effects of evangelicalism on rural antebellum behaviors are considered in Ayers, *Vengeance and Justice,* 118–25.

18. Frederick Law Olmsted met an Alabama iron miner who sometimes "took up bee-huntin' for a spell," making money by collecting wild honey. The miner confided to an incredulous but attentive Olmsted his secret for avoiding bee stings: carry in the hand three leaves, each of a different tree, and "never a bee would dare to sting you." The encounter is described in Frederick Law Olmsted, *The Cotton Kingdom: A Traveller's Observations on Cotton and Slavery in the American Slave States,* ed. Arthur Schlesinger (New York: Alfred A. Knopf, 1953), 385.

19. Solomon Smith, *Theatrical Management in the West and South for Thirty Years* (New York: Harper and Brothers, 1868), 111–13, commented on the dangers of sitting opposite a professional river gambler.

20. Isham offered several examples of fights that he undertook simply as contests of prowess. In that sense, he fulfilled one of the most constant of the poor white stereotypes. As examples of the literary treatment of fighting among humbler classes of whites, see Augustus Baldwin Longstreet, "The Fight," in *Georgia Scenes: Characters, Incidents, etc., in the First Half-Century of the Republic* (New York: Harper and Brothers, 1835), or Harden E. Taliaferro, "Fighting," in *Fisher's River (North Carolina) Scenes and Characters* (New York: Harper and Brothers, 1859). Although he considered the "Southern Bully" most often a "loafering ex-overseer," D. R. Hundley provided a description that could fit Isham well in *Social Relations,* 239–41. An excellent overview of fighting as part of "an in-

tensely communal yet fiercely competitive way of life" in the rural South is found in Elliott J. Gorn, " 'Gouge and Bite, Pull Hair and Scratch': The Social Significance of Fighting in the Southern Backcountry," *American Historical Review* 90 (February 1985): 18–43.

21. Eugene D. Genovese, *Roll, Jordan, Roll: The World the Slaves Made* (New York: Pantheon Books, 1974), 23.

22. Hahn, *Roots of Southern Populism*, 30–31. Frederick Law Olmsted noted that owners and overseers of large plantations felt "habitual irritation" toward poor whites from a belief that this group encouraged laziness among slaves. Given the fact that Isham does not fit easily into the group of "shiftless" farmers, Olmsted unintentionally illustrates the necessity of defining clearly the poor whites. See Olmsted, *Journey in the Back Country*, 449. Kenneth M. Stampp cited the generally accepted rule of plantation management of not allowing slaves to "associate with 'mean white men' who might be disposed to make them dissatisfied," in *The Peculiar Institution: Slavery in the Ante-Bellum South* (New York: Alfred A. Knopf, 1956), 149.

23. That class antagonism existed in the antebellum South to a greater degree than was earlier thought is evident in a fascinating article by Fred A. Bailey, "Tennessee's Antebellum Society from the Bottom Up," *Southern Studies* 22 (Fall 1983): 260–73. Bailey reports that nearly half of the Civil War veterans who were classified as poor "believed that economic opportunities did not exist for them prior to 1861." Bailey's use of Tennessee Civil War veterans' questionnaires illustrates how the voices of the poor can be heard through the historian's use of nontraditional sources.

24. Wyatt-Brown suggests that women confronted not only the hostile actions of men but also the formidable institution of law and, a factor he believes often goes unrecognized, an inner acceptance of their status that was reinforced by the fear of disgrace. See Wyatt-Brown, *Southern Honor*, 246–47. That even elite southern women, however cognizant they might have been of the restrictions imposed upon them by gender conventions, were unlikely to be interested in either "protofeminism" or "protoabolitionism" is an important theme in Elizabeth Fox-Genovese, *Within the Plantation Household: Black and White Women of the Old South* (Chapel Hill: University of North Carolina Press, 1988). Fox-Genovese argues that southern women's history should "challenge us to recognize class and race as central, rather than incidental, to women's identities and behavior—to their sense of themselves as women" (39).

25. In *Southern Honor*, 222, Wyatt-Brown concludes that the eco-

nomic and social factors facing someone like Isham "made family inter-twinings both necessary and very chaotic." D. R. Hundley believed that poor whites rarely possessed the "energy and self-reliance" to move indi-vidually into newer regions of the Southwest; rather, they emigrated "by whole neighborhoods," which might help to explain the preservation of kinships across large geographical areas. See Hundley, *Social Relations,* 271. Mary Elizabeth Stovall has quoted from the diary of a northern schoolteacher who moved to Mississippi and caustically noted the physical deformities that resulted from inbreeding among families of poor whites. While prejudice often characterizes observations of poor white degener-acy, such accounts illustrate the degree to which intermarriage existed, for a variety of reasons, among all classes of white southerners. The diary of schoolteacher Horace Justis is quoted in Mary Elizabeth Stovall, "White Families in the Central South, 1850–1880" (Ph.D. diss., University of Chicago, 1983), 59.

26. Twice in this portion of Isham's autobiography Schenck left a blank space before the word "house" to describe places where Isham gambled, quarreled, and fought. Given that he often exhibited piety in his diary, one can easily imagine Schenck's omitting any distasteful word that Isham might have used. On another occasion Isham told of fighting with Irish boatmen along the Tennessee River "about some lewd women."

27. *Western Democrat,* May 10, 1859.

28. *State v. H. Bone,* August term 1858, Iredell County Court of Pleas and Quarter Sessions Trial Docket, NCDAH. A bill of indictment was brought on October 26, 1858, and issued to Lincoln County on Janu-ary 28, 1859. The case was discontinued nolle prosequi in the May 1859 term, by which time Isham was under arrest for the murder of Cornelius.

29. Catawba County List of Taxables, 1857–68, NCDAH; 1860 fed-eral census for Catawba County, North Carolina, population, slave, and agriculture schedules.

30. *Iredell Express,* May 13, 1859.

31. Thomas Beaty, who was present at the magistrate's hearing, said that Isham claimed to have ditched for one and three-quarters days for a wage of $7.87. Presumably, the Dr. Motte to whom Isham had pawned his gun was the physician who attended James Cornelius. All testimony is taken from the transcript for *State v. Hardaway Bone,* Supreme Court Original Case 7858, NCDAH.

32. *Western Democrat,* May 10, 1859; *Iredell Express,* May 13, 1859; *Carolina Watchman* (Salisbury), May 10, 1859; *North Carolina Whig*

(Charlotte), May 10, 1859. Austin Cornelius, with surviving brothers Jesse and William, aided area newspapers in creating this detailed impression of Isham. Isham was said to be penniless at the time of the assault. Historian Jack Williams has observed how newspapers in South Carolina luridly reported crimes and searched for odd behaviors in criminals. See Jack Kenny Williams, *Vogues in Villainy: Crime and Retribution in Ante-Bellum South Carolina* (Columbia: University of South Carolina Press, 1959), 27–35. Wyatt-Brown has written of criminals in the antebellum legal justice system, "How gratifying it was that there should be so close a resemblance between shamelessness of character and the outward appearance of evil." See Wyatt-Brown, *Southern Honor*, 398.

33. Isham did not testify in his defense at the trial, although he described his actions in detail to David Schenck.

34. The transcript of the will is in the Catawba County Superior Court Minutes, spring term 1860, NCDAH. When the will was presented to the Court of Pleas and Quarter Sessions in July 1859, several of James Cornelius's siblings entered a caveat whose exact nature is unclear. See July term 1859, Minutes of the Catawba County Court of Pleas and Quarter Sessions, NCDAH.

35. Keeping track of the witnesses' names recorded by Schenck, Henry Cline (the clerk of the Catawba County Superior Court), and John G. Lewis (the Gaston County Superior Court clerk who prepared the trial transcript for the North Carolina Supreme Court) can be challenging, especially when federal census reports do not provide corroboration. Lemly's name (alternately spelled "Lemley"), for example, appears as "Lesley" in the notes that Schenck wrote during the trial, which raises the possibility that the witness was related to Isham's wife Mandy.

36. Perhaps this individual was the same Charlie Carson (or Carlton) who sold Isham the ten acres of land he farmed in Iredell County.

37. *Western Democrat,* May 24, 1859; *Iredell Express,* May 27, 1859; *Asheville News,* June 2, 1859.

38. *Iredell Express,* May 10, 1859; "Fall Circuit, 1859" and "New Year, 1860," Schenck Diary.

39. "Fall Circuit, 1859," Schenck Diary; fall term 1859, Catawba County Superior Court Minutes, and fall term 1859, Gaston County Superior Court Minutes, both in NCDAH.

40. 1860 federal census for Gaston County, North Carolina, population schedule; Ayers, *Vengeance and Justice,* 23. Comparing the more vigorous prosecution of people for assaults, riots, and brawls, kinds of vio-

lence often associated with lower classes, with those guilty of dueling, Michael Hindus has asserted that "the double standard in South Carolina justice was not limited to blacks." See Michael Stephen Hindus, *Prison and Plantation: Crime, Justice, and Authority in Massachusetts and South Carolina, 1767–1878* (Chapel Hill: University of North Carolina Press, 1980), 252. Wyatt-Brown plays down the significance of class-conscious justice, but he does believe that deviants who challenged the social order "had to be rendered powerless." See Wyatt-Brown, *Southern Honor,* 369–70.

41. The *Revised Code of North Carolina, 1855* provided capital punishment for manslaughter only upon the second offense. See Guion Griffis Johnson, *Ante-Bellum North Carolina: A Social History* (Chapel Hill: University of North Carolina Press, 1937), 652–54. Helping Schenck with the defense was Captain R. F. Hoke, presumably Robert F. Hoke (1820–88), Lincolnton lawyer, legislator, and Confederate officer. "Fall Circuit, 1859," Schenck Diary, gives no indication of Hoke's role in the defense.

42. Details of the challenging of jurors, testimony given in court, and the judge's rulings and instructions to the jury come from *State v. Hardaway Bone,* Supreme Court Original Case 7858, NCDAH. Additional evidence in the Schenck Papers, NCDAH, consists of two documents that relate to Isham's murder trial. One is a fragment listing the names of challenged jurors Pegram and Rutledge. Along with summaries of their declarations are marks that appear to record the number of counsel's juror challenges. The top row has twenty-two marks beside the abbreviation "Defdt," one less than the number of peremptory challenges allowed in a capital case by the *Revised Code of North Carolina, 1855,* c. 35. The words "challenged for cause" appear beside two marks, with "stood aside" written beside two more, suggesting that Pegram and Rutledge were the only jurors challenged for cause by the defendant. No clue explains the peremptory challenges. The paper is torn and some of the writing is missing, unlike the second item, in which Schenck summarized the testimony given in the trial and an earlier court case to which he referred in preparing his manslaughter argument.

43. Dr. J. J. Mott, the twenty-six-year-old physician who attended James Cornelius, failed to appear at the trial, and the doctor who testified in his absence offered inconclusive evidence. Thomas Beaty stated that Mott had complained of rheumatism on the Saturday before the trial. Mott was fined eighty dollars for failing to appear unless he explained his ab-

sence to the justice of the peace. That judgment is appended to the summary of Isham's trial in fall term 1859, Gaston County Superior Court Minutes, Docket, NCDAH.

44. "Fall Circuit, 1859," Schenck Diary.

45. *State v. Hardaway Bone, North Carolina Reports* 52 (1859): 121; spring term 1860, Gaston County Superior Court Minutes, NCDAH.

46. *Iredell Express,* June 1, 1860; William L. Sherrill, *Annals of Lincoln County, North Carolina* (Charlotte: Observer Publishing House, 1937), 167–68. Isham's name appeared in the census of 1860 only in the mortality schedule for Gaston County. The entry confirms his age as thirty-two years, specifies that he was widowed, and lists his occupation as "Ditcher." See the 1860 federal census for Gaston County, North Carolina, mortality schedule.

47. July term 1859, Minutes of the Catawba County Court of Pleas and Quarter Sessions; fall term 1859, spring term 1860, and fall term 1860, Catawba County Superior Court Minutes, all in NCDAH; *Catawba County Cemeteries,* 7 vols. (Hickory, N.C.: Catawba County Genealogical Society, 1986–91), 1:66–69. The headstones were moved to the Rehobeth Church Cemetery at Terrell, N.C.

48. "Fall Circuit, 1859," Schenck Diary.

49. The life of lawyer, state legislator, and Confederate congressman William Lander (1819–68) is sketched in Sherrill, *Annals of Lincoln County,* 197–200. Schenck, whose career included a superior court judgeship, a bitter Reconstruction campaign for election to the state supreme court, leadership in the Ku Klux Klan, and creation of the Guilford Battleground Company, has not received the biography he deserves.

50. English historian E. P. Thompson has described the "sense of double vision" that comes from examining a culture in which the surface appearance of "consensus, deference, accommodation" is suddenly and surprisingly punctured by violent abuse rising "from an anonymous and obscure level." The thoughts in the last two paragraphs owe much to his essay "The Crime of Anonymity," in *Albion's Fatal Tree: Crime and Society in Eighteenth-Century England,* ed. Douglas Hay et al. (New York: Pantheon Books, 1975), 304–8. Less convincing is the belief by Bruce Collins that "aberrant" behavior "can hardly claim to reveal the fundamental dynamics of a society in which such phenomena were atypical." Isham's life, while not typical, arguably illustrates in dramatic fashion many of the tensions inherent in the "fundamental dynamics" of southern society. Never-

theless, for a useful synthesis that emphasizes the shared values which the author believes minimized class distinctions, see Collins, *White Society in the Antebellum South* (New York: Longman, 1985), 144 (quoted).

5: Edward Isham and Criminal Justice for the Poor White in Antebellum North Carolina

An earlier version of this essay was presented in November 1993 at the annual meeting of the Southern Historical Association. The author is indebted to Charles C. Bolton, David H. Kleit, and J. William Harris for their comments. The essay, here modified slightly, originally appeared in *Journal of Southern Legal History* 3 (1994): 71–96.

1. Bertram Wyatt-Brown relates how Mississippi attorney Henry S. Foote destroyed a sixty-page narrative given him for publication by convicted murderer Alonzo Phelps out of fear that Phelps's evident delight in his wrongdoing would corrupt public morals. See Wyatt-Brown, *Southern Honor: Ethics and Behavior in the Old South* (New York: Oxford University Press, 1982), 36–37.

2. For an older interpretation of southern violence as fostered by the insecurity of life on what remained in many ways a frontier, see John Hope Franklin, *The Militant South, 1800–1861* (Cambridge, Mass.: Harvard University Press, 1956). In *Violence and Culture in the Antebellum South* (Austin: University of Texas Press, 1979), Dickson D. Bruce, Jr., stresses that violence was part of a gloomy southern view of how personal relationships functioned. The interplay of violence and conceptions of honor and a recognition of the values of courtroom testimony are important themes in the imaginative work of Wyatt-Brown, *Southern Honor.* In *Vengeance and Justice: Crime and Punishment in the Nineteenth-Century South* (New York: Oxford University Press, 1984), Edward L. Ayers argues that a culture of honor, cutting against evangelical Christianity and the rule of law, lent the South its distinctive tendency toward violence. The connections between violence, community expectations, and the criminal justice system are explored by Michael S. Hindus in *Prison and Plantation: Crime, Justice, and Authority in Massachusetts and South Carolina, 1767–1878* (Chapel Hill: University of North Carolina Press, 1980). For an opinion on the limitations inherent in the study of criminal behavior, see Bruce Collins, *White Society in the Antebellum South* (New York: Longman, 1985), 144. For a more detailed discussion of the relationship between these

sources and Isham, see Scott P. Culclasure, "'I Have Killed a Damned Dog,'" chapter 4 in this volume.

3. Bill Cecil-Fronsman, *Common Whites: Class and Culture in Antebellum North Carolina* (Lexington: University Press of Kentucky, 1992). Cecil-Fronsman inadvertently illustrates the difficulty of identifying the humbler classes of southern whites with the term "common whites." By including 75 to 80 percent of the white population in this category (his estimate), he renders the term nearly useless, thereby obscuring whatever tensions might have existed between social groups.

4. On the difficulties of prosecuting violent crimes in southern courts, see Ayers, *Vengeance and Justice*, 112–15.

5. See, for example, "*The State vs. Parker Perry,*" *North Carolina Standard* (Raleigh), April 20, 1853.

6. The North Carolina Division of Archives and History (NCDAH) in Raleigh maintains the heading "Crime and Punishment" in the Governors' Papers' card file index that provides citations to both the Governors' Papers (GP) and Governors' Letter Books (GLB). The index, however, ends in 1858. Considering the small number of cases available for this study, oversights and erroneous citations found in the card file, while few, added another obstacle that could be corrected only by perusing the original records. The Governors' Papers generally represent incoming mail sorted by month and year. Many but by no means all of the received memorials and petitions were copied by the governors' secretaries in the Letter Books along with any gubernatorial response. The original papers reveal a wide variety of handwriting samples and writing styles, tempting but not overly reliable indicators of social standing.

7. Nathan Capan to Thomas Bragg, November 20, 1855, vol. 139, GP; Bragg to Capan, December 4, 1855, GLB, 43:339.

8. See, for example, David S. Reid, "Message to the General Assembly," November 20, 1854, GLB, 41:286.

9. In addition to *State v. Alvin Preslar* (1856 Union County Superior Court Minutes; murder), which was petitioned to the governor, the Superior Court Minutes of Union County list two cases that were not: *State v. John Preslar* (1853 Union County Superior Court Minutes; manslaughter) and *State v. Lemmond* (1857 Union County Superior Court Minutes; rendered nolle prosequi, 1858 Union County Superior Court Minutes), NCDAH. In addition to *State v. Arnold* (1850 Columbus County Superior Court Minutes; murder), which was petitioned to the governor, the Superior Court Minutes of Columbus County show six manslaughter

convictions that were not: *State v. Jacobs* (1850 Columbus County Superior Court Minutes); *State v. Fields* (1855 Columbus County Superior Court Minutes); *State v. Thompson* (1855 Columbus County Superior Court Minutes); *State v. Boswell* (1856 Columbus County Superior Court Minutes); *State v. Kelly* (1857 Columbus County Superior Court Minutes); *State v. Mitchell* (1860 Columbus County Superior Court Minutes), NCDAH. In addition, the murder conviction in *State v. Rouse* (1858 Columbus County Superior Court Minutes) resulted in the defendant's being ordered to the North Carolina Asylum for the Insane in Raleigh. All documents located in NCDAH.

10. Governor David S. Reid (1851–54) treated cases brought before him as follows: manslaughter convictions pardoned: *State v. Durham* (1852 Henderson County Superior Court Minutes; GLB, 40:339); *State v. Barnham* (1852 Duplin County Superior Court Minutes; GLB, 40: 388); manslaughter convictions not pardoned: *State v. Joseph Starns* (1852 Union County Superior Court Minutes; no response in vol. 40, GLB, to petitions and counterpetitions dated May 17, 24, and June 25, 1852, vol. 130, GP); *State v. Barnhill* (1854 Bladen County Superior Court Minutes; GLB, 41:263); *State v. Keith* (1854 Wake County Superior Court Minutes; no response in vol. 41, GLB, to petitions dated October 21 and November 11, 1854, vol. 136, GP); murder convictions pardoned: *State v. Collins* (1848 McDowell County Superior Court Minutes; GLB, 40:62); *State v. Arnold* (1850 Columbus County Superior Court Minutes; GLB, 40:310); *State v. Sasser* (1854 Green County Superior Court Minutes; GLB, 41:289); and murder convictions not pardoned: *State v. Perry* (1853 Wake County Superior Court Minutes; GLB, 41: 140); *State v. Baker* (1854 Cumberland County Superior Court Minutes; GLB, 41:292). All documents located in NCDAH.

Governor Thomas Bragg (1855–59) treated cases brought before him as follows: manslaughter convictions pardoned: *State v. Adams* (1854 Pitt County Superior Court Minutes; GLB, 43:44); *State v. Sharp* (1855 Mecklenberg County Superior Court Minutes; GLB, 43:373); manslaughter convictions not pardoned: *State v. Keith* (1854 Franklin County Superior Court Minutes; GLB, 43:141); *State v. Wyse* (1855 Craven County Superior Court Minutes; GLB, 43:194); *State v. Edwards* (1857 Nash County Superior Court Minutes; GLB, 44:225); murder convictions pardoned: none found; and murder convictions not pardoned: *State v. Williams* (1855 Person County Superior Court Minutes; GLB, 43:359); *State v. Johnson* (1855 Guilford County Superior Court Minutes; GLB,

43:461); *State v. Samuel* (1855 Rockingham County Superior Court Minutes; GLB, 43:483); *State v. Johnson* (1855 Sampson County Superior Court Minutes; GLB, 43:632); *State v. McDonald* (1856 Bladen County Superior Court Minutes; GLB, 44:123). All documents located in NCDAH.

No cases were found for the brief tenure of Governor Warren Winslow (1854–55).

11. Reid's stand on suffrage is outlined in William S. Powell, *North Carolina Through Four Centuries* (Chapel Hill: University of North Carolina Press, 1989), 301–2.

12. GLB, 41:218–21.

13. Governor John W. Ellis (1859–61) treated cases brought before him as follows: manslaughter convictions pardoned: none found; manslaughter convictions not pardoned: none found; murder convictions pardoned: *State v. Neville* (1859 Halifax County Superior Court Minutes; GLB, 45:141); *State v. Simmonds* (1858 New Hanover County Superior Court Minutes; GLB, 45:149); *State v. West* (1859 Burke County Superior Court Minutes; GLB, 45:151); *State v. Hogue* (1859 Wake County Superior Court Minutes; GLB, 45:168); and murder convictions not pardoned: *State v. Starling* (1859 Wayne County Superior Court Minutes; GLB, 45:120). All documents located in NCDAH.

14. R. M. Saunders to Bragg, November 27, 1858, vol. 145, GP. Judge Saunders did not place this figure within the context of the state's growth in population during that period.

15. *Eighth Census of the United States, 1860: Statistics* (Washington, D.C.: Government Printing Office, 1866), 27.

16. Edward Isham had at least this much to his credit: if his own account is to be believed, he never committed violence against any of the nearly one dozen women he mentions in his autobiography. Women, however, often played a role in his disputes. In one incident, Isham entered into "a difficulty" with Betsy Wedding in Pinetown, Georgia, perhaps because he had been "too intimate" with a free black woman, but the ensuing "feud" was with Warner Lyons, who "was keeping" Betsy at his grocery. Even so, none of the criminal charges dealt in any apparent way with women. See the Autobiography of Edward Isham, David Schenck Notebook, David Schenck Papers, NCDAH. For a less sanguine view, see Victoria E. Bynum, "Mothers, Lovers, and Wives," chapter 6 in this volume.

17. The cases involving women cover a range of issues. Achiles Durham, a farmer with $1,000 of property, drunkenly beat his wife to death

(1852 Henderson County Superior Court Minutes), while Samuel Parker Perry, another farmer of some substance, killed his wife by striking her with an ax and throwing her down a well (1853 Wake County Superior Court Minutes). Henry Barnhill, who according to the 1850 census was illiterate, killed a man who had quarreled with Barnhill's wife (1854 Bladen County Superior Court Minutes). Reuben F. Samuel used a wooden mallet to murder a man who he believed was engaged in ongoing adultery with his wife. Deciding whether Samuel had grounds for his belief confounded both Chief Justice Thomas Ruffin and Governor Bragg (1854 Rockingham County Superior Court Minutes). James and D. C. Sharp were accused of murdering their brother because he had married a woman whom he had kept as a mistress (1855 Mecklenberg County Superior Court Minutes). Elias Neville murdered a man after Neville's wife accused him of attempting to rape her (1859 Halifax County Superior Court Minutes). The circumstances that led John Starling to kill Sally Cotton, who apparently was a widow close to sixty years of age in 1859, are unclear (1859 Wayne County Superior Court Minutes). All documents located in NCDAH. On Durham's wealth, see the 1850 federal census for Rutherford County, North Carolina, population schedule. On Perry's wealth, see 1850 federal census for Wake County, North Carolina. On Sally Cotton's status, see 1850 federal census for Wayne County, North Carolina.

18. The supreme court decision contains many details of the crime. *State v. Preslar,* 48 N.C. 421 (1856); December 15, 20, and 22, 1856, vol. 141, GP; GLB, 43:639, 642–45, 651; 1850 federal census for Union County, North Carolina.

19. *State v. Preslar,* 421–26.

20. *State v. Preslar,* 421.

21. *State v. Preslar,* 421.

22. *State v. Preslar,* 428.

23. *State v. Preslar* (1856 Union County Superior Court Minutes); December 15, 1856, vol. 141, GP.

24. Lander to Bragg, December 20, 1856, GLB, 43:652–53. No one had much good to say about Alvin Preslar. There was "none in the county more honest, more amiable or more respected" than Preslar's family and friends, observed Samuel H. Walkup, who had nothing to say about Preslar himself. See December 15, 1856, vol. 141, GP.

25. GLB, 43:651–52. In *Unruly Women: The Politics of Social and Sexual Control in the Old South* (Chapel Hill: University of North Carolina Press, 1992), 86, Victoria E. Bynum cites this case as illustrating "the lim-

its of paternalism in protecting southern wives." Details taken from pardon petitions for this case add nuance: the questionable medical evidence provided by a doctor widely believed to have been defrauding the defendant of his property, the obstreperousness of a Preslar relative who was somehow impaneled on the jury in the first trial, and the solicitor's opinion that the community was convinced of Preslar's culpability. Governor Bragg occasionally granted brief reprieves to prisoners who petitioners argued were unprepared to die, but little in his handling of such cases suggests a willingness to prevent execution. None of these considerations, however, detracts from Bynum's assertion that drunkenness as a mitigating factor was gendered, a point she demonstrates again in her gloss of a manslaughter conviction that appears in an accompanying note. The Henderson County Superior Court ordered Achiles Durham, who was convicted of killing his ill wife by hitting her with his fists while he was drunk, branded and imprisoned for six months (*State v. Durham*, 1852 Henderson County Superior Court Minutes). Several of the jurors believed that Durham deserved a pardon because he was intoxicated when he struck his wife and could therefore be said not to have intended to kill her. According to one petitioner, by the time he received Governor Reid's pardon, Durham had sat in an unheated jail for ten months (May 1852, vol. 130, GP). Nonetheless, if the roles of husband and wife—aggressor and victim—had been reversed, "social norms" would have been "defied." See Bynum, *Unruly Women,* 82–86, 178, n. 95.

26. In vol. 130, GP, the petition supporting Starns is dated May 1852; the counterpetition is dated May 24, 1852. See also the petitions of May 24 and June 25, 1852, both opposing executive clemency. Since Governor Reid's letter book contains no response, the branding and sentence of six months' imprisonment presumably stood. In a letter regarding an unrelated case, Reid described his habit of not replying to all applications for executive clemency. See November 8, 1852, vol. 41, GLB. Samuel H. Walkup was an active man when it came to petitions; he signed the one dated May 1852, opposing a pardon for Starns and the one dated December 15, 1856, defending Alvin Preslar. See vol. 141, GP.

27. The importance of local autonomy in the process of determining justice is emphasized in Wyatt-Brown, *Southern Honor,* 365–66.

28. Edward Isham enjoyed a very different status: members of the Georgia communities in which he resided seemed so cowed by him that they approached him only en masse. At his uncle's residence in De Kalb County, Georgia, he said that "everybody was afraid of me and no officer

would attempt to take me." Later, residing in the same county, Isham found his house surrounded at night "by about 30 men and the bailiff," who took him prisoner. See the Autobiography of Edward Isham.

29. *State v. Thomason,* 46 N.C. 274 (1854); October 23, 1854, vol. 136, GP; and GLB, 41:257–58.

30. 1850 federal census for Brunswick County, North Carolina.

31. October 23, 1854, vol. 136, GP.

32. GLB, 41:258.

33. October 3 and November 1856, vol. 141, GP.

34. November 1856, vol. 141, GP; *Greensboro Patriot,* September 23, 1856.

35. November 1856, vol. 141, GP.

36. Wyatt-Brown downplays social class conflict in favor of the concept of honor vindicated or abused. See Wyatt-Brown, *Southern Honor,* 320. Carolyn J. Powell uses this concept to explain the prosecution, conviction, and execution of Iredell County resident John Hoover, who in 1839 brutally murdered his slave Mira. It was one thing to destroy one's own slave property, Powell concludes, but quite another to dishonor the community in the process; such a breach of norms would not pass without sanction. See Carolyn J. Powell, "In Remembrance of Mira: Reflections on the Death of a Slave Woman," in *Discovering the Women in Slavery: Emancipating Perspectives on the American Past,* ed. Patricia Morton (Athens: University of Georgia Press, 1996), 47–60.

37. October 15, 1852, vol. 131, GP. Additional documents in this large collection of petitions include August 23, October 6, 16, 17, 20, 27, November 1, 3, 1852, vol. 131, GP; GLB, 40:395–96.

38. The details are from a summary of the trial testimony prepared for Governor Reid by Boyd's lawyers. See Patrick H. Winston, Alexander Little, and George C. Mendenhall to Reid, November 1, 1852, vol. 131, GP.

39. "Statement of Martin J. Pickett," August 23, 1852, vol. 131, GP.

40. P. M. Powell to Reid, October 15, 1852, vol. 131, GP.

41. October 16, 21, and 27, 1852, vol. 131, GP.

42. Medley's letter offers a curious mixture of practiced handwriting and weak spelling. J. Medley to Reid, October 17, 1852, vol. 131, GP.

43. GLB, 40:396.

44. Referring to South Carolina, Michael S. Hindus observes that "the criminal justice system was a malleable adjunct to the other, traditional forms of authority that felt free to manipulate the legal system for personal ends, depriving it of the force of legitimacy." See Hindus, *Prison and Plan-*

tation, 86. Wyatt-Brown asserts that law was applied in accordance with community consensus. See Wyatt-Brown, *Southern Honor*, 364.

6: Mothers, Lovers, and Wives: Images of Poor White Women in Edward Isham's Autobiography

1. Autobiography of Edward Isham, David Schenck Notebook, David Schenck Papers, North Carolina Division of Archives and History, Raleigh. Census records suggest that Mary Brown died between 1860 and 1870. I have not ascertained her maiden name but suspect that it was Hutchinson or perhaps Hatch. Edward identified Mandy Hatch as Mary's sister (Autobiography of Edward Isham), but "Hatch" may have been Schenck's abbreviation for Hutchinson, since Edward also identified Mandy as the sister-in-law of his brother John, who married Susan Hutchinson in 1845. (Thanks to Charles Bolton for information about this marriage.) Mary Brown appeared in the 1850 federal census for Walker County, Georgia, as the twenty-four-year-old mate of Hiram J. Brown. The household included six-month-old Alfred Brown. In the 1860 federal census for Hamilton County, Tennessee, Mary was listed as the thirty-two-year-old mate of Hiram J. Brown. Their household then included four children: Alfred, age eleven; Vandera, age eight; William, age five; and John, age two. In 1870, the household included only Hiram, Vandera, and a new mate, twenty-five-year-old Martha. Also included was five-year-old Octavia O. Parks, perhaps a child of Martha's from an earlier marriage. The absence of the two youngest Brown children suggests that they, like Mary, had died.

2. Autobiography of Edward Isham. I have been unable to locate either John Isham (Edward's brother) or Peter Windley (Mary's first husband) in the federal manuscript census of 1850 for Macon County, Alabama. John Isham appears to have died; his probable widow, Susan Isham, age twenty-six, lived next door to his mother, Mary Isham, in 1860 in Chattanooga (see note 57). See the 1850 federal census for Hamilton County, Tennessee.

3. Autobiography of Edward Isham.

4. David H. Kleit, "A Stereoscopic View of the Frontier," chapter 3 in the present volume; Charles C. Bolton, *Poor Whites of the Antebellum South: Tenants and Laborers in Central North Carolina and Northeast Mississippi* (Durham: Duke University Press, 1994), 66–83; Elliott J.

Gorn, "'Gouge and Bite, Pull Hair and Scratch': The Social Significance of Fighting in the Southern Backcountry," *American Historical Review* 90 (February 1985): 35.

5. For descriptions of drinking, gambling, and fighting among southern men as aspects of "primal honor," see Bertram Wyatt-Brown, *Southern Honor: Ethics and Behavior in the Old South* (New York: Oxford University Press, 1982), 41–44. For a discussion of backcountry violence, honor, and manhood, see Gorn, "'Gouge and Bite, Pull Hair and Scratch.'"

6. The physical description of Edward Isham is from Scott P. Culclasure, "'I Have Killed a Damned Dog,'" chapter 4 in this volume. On the advantages for a criminal who possessed a "handsome, manly countenance," see Wyatt-Brown, *Southern Honor*, 398.

7. Autobiography of Edward Isham; Gorn, "'Gouge and Bite, Pull Hair and Scratch,'" 41. The literature on the "plain," or "common," people of the Old South continues to grow. More recent works include Stephanie McCurry, *Masters of Small Worlds: Yeoman Households, Gender Relations, and the Political Culture of the Antebellum South Carolina Low Country* (New York: Oxford University Press, 1995); Bolton, *Poor Whites of the Antebellum South;* Bill Cecil-Fronsman, *Common Whites: Class and Culture in Antebellum North Carolina* (Lexington: University Press of Kentucky, 1992); Fred Arthur Bailey, *Class and Tennessee's Confederate Generation* (Chapel Hill: University of North Carolina Press, 1987); J. William Harris, *Plain Folk and Gentry in a Slave Society: White Liberty and Black Slavery in Augusta's Hinterlands* (Hanover, N.H.: University Press of New England, 1985); and Steven H. Hahn, *Roots of Southern Populism: Yeoman Farmers and the Transformation of the Georgia Upcountry, 1850–1890* (New York: Oxford University Press, 1983).

8. This is not to say that Isham told lies to his attorney, though he may have. As Elliott Gorn argues in "'Gouge and Bite, Pull Hair and Scratch,'" "more than realism or fantasy alone, fight legends stretched the imagination by blending both" (33).

9. Gorn, "'Gouge and Bite, Pull Hair and Scratch,'" 32; Carroll Smith-Rosenberg, "Davy Crockett as Trickster: Pornography, Liminality, and Symbolic Inversion in Victorian America," in her *Disorderly Conduct: Visions of Gender in Victorian America* (New York: Alfred A. Knopf, 1985), 93, 102–3.

10. Smith-Rosenberg, "Davy Crockett as Trickster," 103–4.

11. Peter D. Swaim, Esq., to Benjamin P. Elliot, February 22, 1841,

Benjamin P. Elliot Papers, Duke Manuscript Collection, Perkins Library, Duke University, Durham, North Carolina.

12. Swaim to Elliot, August 29, 1843, Benjamin P. Elliot Papers.

13. Swaim to Elliot, August 29, 1843, Benjamin P. Elliot Papers.

14. Swaim to Elliot, August 29, 1843, Benjamin P. Elliot Papers. Swaim's conscious or unconscious use of the phrase "impalements of war" rather than "implements of war" underscores the extent to which his mind was on rough sex rather than battlefields.

15. Culclasure, "'I Have Killed a Damned Dog,'" chapter 4 in this volume. On "disorderly houses," see Victoria E. Bynum, *Unruly Women: The Politics of Social and Sexual Control in the Old South* (Chapel Hill: University of North Carolina Press, 1992), 93.

16. On the dangers and possible consequences of kinlessness and shamelessness, see Wyatt-Brown, *Southern Honor,* 62, 398–400. On the importance of class distinctions between Edward Isham and James Cornelius, his victim, see Culclasure, "'I Have Killed a Damned Dog,'" chapter 4 in this volume.

17. Autobiography of Edward Isham.

18. Autobiography of Edward Isham. The many "grocery stores" mentioned by Isham surely doubled as taverns. See Stephanie McCurry, "The Politics of Yeoman Households in South Carolina," 34, in *Divided Houses: Gender and the Civil War,* ed. Catherine Clinton and Nina Silber (New York: Oxford University Press, 1992).

19. Quoted in Cecil-Fronsman, *Common Whites,* 142.

20. Bynum, *Unruly Women,* 70–73; Wyatt-Brown, *Southern Honor,* 281–82.

21. *Richmond Observer,* Richmond, Va., April 6, 1857; *Orange Recorder,* Orange County, N.C., June 1, 1859.

22. Scott P. Culclasure, "Edward Isham and Criminal Justice for the Poor White in Antebellum North Carolina," chapter 5 in this volume; Bynum, *Unruly Women,* 70–71, 82–86, 109.

23. William Ransom Hogan and Edwin Adams Davis, eds., *William Johnson's Natchez: The Ante-Bellum Diary of a Free Negro* (1951; reprint, Baton Rouge: Louisiana State University Press, 1993), 93, 133, 137, 146.

24. Hogan and Davis, eds., *William Johnson's Natchez,* 93, 133, 137, 146.

25. Hogan and Davis, eds., *William Johnson's Natchez,* 182–83, 568.

26. Autobiography of Edward Isham.

27. Autobiography of Edward Isham.

28. Autobiography of Edward Isham.

29. Autobiography of Edward Isham.

30. Autobiography of Edward Isham.

31. Autobiography of Edward Isham. From the time the younger Mary took up with Edward—except for the brief period in which Mary Isham lived in Chattanooga, Tennessee, and Mary Brown lived in Ringgold, Georgia—until their deaths, the two women lived near one another. By 1850, Edward had moved his mother back to Ringgold. She may be the forty-year-old "Mary A. Isam" who headed a household that included Mary S., age eight, and William A. M., age eleven (1850 federal census for Walker County, Georgia). By 1860, both women lived near one another in Chattanooga (1860 federal census for Hamilton County, Tennessee). This reinforces the probability (see notes 1 and 57) that they were related not only through Edward but by the marriage of Mary Isham's son, John, to Susan Hutchinson, who was probably a sister to Mary Brown.

32. For varying perspectives on the construction of gender relations in the antebellum southern patriarchy, see McCurry, *Masters of Small Worlds;* Bynum, *Unruly Women;* Joan E. Cashin, *A Family Venture: Men and Women on the Southern Frontier* (Baltimore: Johns Hopkins University Press, 1991); Elizabeth Fox-Genovese, *Within the Plantation Household: Black and White Women in the Old South* (Chapel Hill: University of North Carolina Press, 1988); Jean Friedman, *The Enclosed Garden: Women and Community in the Evangelical South, 1830–1900* (Chapel Hill: University of North Carolina Press, 1985); Suzanne Lebsock, *The Free Women of Petersburg: Status and Culture in a Southern Town, 1784–1860* (New York: W. W. Norton, 1984); Wyatt-Brown, *Southern Honor;* Catherine Clinton, *The Plantation Mistress: Woman's World in the Old South* (New York: Pantheon Books, 1982); Anne Firor Scott, *The Southern Lady: From Pedestal to Politics, 1830–1930* (Chicago: University of Chicago Press, 1970); and Anne Firor Scott, "Women's Perspective on the Patriarchy in the 1850s," *Journal of American History* 61 (June 1974): 52–64.

33. Wyatt-Brown, *Southern Honor,* 93.

34. Geoffrey Chaucer, *The Legend of Good Women,* translated and with an introduction by Ann McMillan (Houston: Rice University Press, 1987), 101, 105.

35. 1850 federal census for Walker County, Georgia. The fact that Hiram J. Brown was born in Tennessee suggests that Mary Brown first met him while living in Chattanooga.

36. Gorn, "'Gouge and Bite, Pull Hair and Scratch,'" 36. The phrase "make her a living" is from Chester Sullivan, *Sullivan's Hollow* (Jackson: University Press of Mississippi, 1978), 56.

37. Autobiography of Edward Isham.

38. In 1850, sixty-year-old Edward Isham, Sr., and thirty-five-year-old Cynda Elkins lived together in Pinetown with five children who ranged in age from six months to ten years. It would appear that at least some of Elkins's children were from a previous relationship or marriage. The 1840 census (which lists only household heads by name) lists no woman within her age range living in the household of Edward, Sr., but does list a white female whose age range conforms with that of Mary Isham. Autobiography of Edward Isham; 1840 and 1850 federal censuses for Carroll County, Georgia.

39. The Mary A. "Isam" who lived in Ringgold in 1850 was reported as forty years old (1850 federal census for Walker County, Georgia). In 1860, Mary "Isham," who by then had moved back to Chattanooga, was reported as fifty-four years old (1860 federal census for Hamilton County, Tennessee). The 1850 census gave the age of Edward Isham, Jr., as twenty-four; at the time of his execution, it was reported as thirty-two. He must therefore have been born between 1826 and 1828. He stated that he had three brothers, John, James, and William (Autobiography of Edward Isham). The members of his father's household who were enumerated by age and gender in the 1840 federal manuscript census included one male between ages thirty and forty (Edward, Sr.), one male between ages ten and fifteen (probably Edward, Jr.), one male under age five (probably William), one female between ages thirty and forty (Mary Isham), one between ages fifteen and twenty (probably Melissa, who married William Bivens and was twenty-five years old in 1850), and two between ages ten and fifteen (names unknown). John and James had apparently moved out of the household by 1840 (1840 federal census for Carroll County, Georgia).

40. Autobiography of Edward Isham; 1850 federal census for Walker County, Georgia; 1860 and 1870 federal censuses for Hamilton County, Tennessee.

41. Mary Brown's age was reported as twenty-four in 1850 (1850 federal census for Walker County, Georgia), and as thirty-two in 1860 (1860 federal census for Hamilton County, Tennessee).

42. Autobiography of Edward Isham.

43. Autobiography of Edward Isham.

44. Autobiography of Edward Isham. As was typical, Edward offered

no explanation as to when or why his mother moved back to Chattanooga. Whether she moved there alone or with others is uncertain. In 1860, her household included Nancy Oliver, age sixteen; Sarah Carson, age nineteen; and John Carson, age one. I have not determined whether these people were kinfolk or merely boarders. I found no Mary Isham reported in the U.S. Federal Manuscript Censuses for either Chattanooga, Tennessee, Ringgold, Georgia, or Carroll County, Georgia, in 1870 or 1880, and I presume that she had died by then.

45. Autobiography of Edward Isham.

46. Autobiography of Edward Isham. The woman Edward called Caroline Brown was probably Caroline Nelson, age eighteen, who lived with Hiram and Mary Brown in 1850. See the 1850 federal census for Walker County, Georgia.

47. Autobiography of Edward Isham.

48. Autobiography of Edward Isham.

49. Autobiography of Edward Isham.

50. Autobiography of Edward Isham.

51. Autobiography of Edward Isham.

52. Autobiography of Edward Isham; Chaucer, *Legend of Good Women,* 99.

53. Autobiography of Edward Isham.

54. Autobiography of Edward Isham. The 1850 federal census for Iredell County listed James "Lasley," age thirty-five, as a laborer living with apparently his five children: W.P., age twenty; Amanda (Mandy), age fourteen; Elizabeth, age twelve; James, age nine; and Jane L., age seven.

55. Autobiography of Edward Isham.

56. In 1860, the federal census enumerator recorded that Mary Isham owned real estate worth $250 and personal property worth $350. See the 1860 federal census for Hamilton County, Tennessee.

57. In 1860, Susan Isham's age was reported as twenty-six, while her son George was reported as fourteen, making her twelve years old at the time of his birth. The 1880 census repeated this age span. By then George Isham, age thirty-six, headed his own household; Susan, age forty-eight and identified as his mother, lived with him (1860 and 1880 federal censuses for Hamilton County, Tennessee). Mary Isham's son John married a Susan Hutchinson in 1845 and appears to have died before 1850. The Alabama birthplaces listed for Susan Isham's four youngest children suggest that she is John's widow. That would also make her the sister of Mandy Hatch (Hutchinson?) and, by extension, Mary Brown (see note 1).

58. 1860 and 1870 federal censuses for Hamilton County, Tennessee. Both censuses reported Hiram J. Brown as owning property valued at $300.

59. The 1860 federal census for Catawba County, North Carolina, listed Margaret Bone, age one, as living with William and Susan Reed. By 1870, the Reeds had moved to Iredell County where Margaret F., age eleven, continued to live with them. By 1880, she was listed as Margaret F. Boone, age twenty-two, a "boarder" in the household of the Reeds' oldest son, James H. Reed. My thanks to Scott Culclasure for providing me this information.

7: The Worlds of Nineteenth-Century Condemned Men

1. For other treatments of Isham's life and times, see Scott P. Culclasure, "'I Have Killed a Damned Dog,'" chapter 4 in this volume; and Charles C. Bolton, *Poor Whites of the Antebellum South: Tenants and Laborers in Central North Carolina and Northeast Mississippi* (Durham: Duke University Press, 1994), chap. 1.

2. Autobiography of Edward Isham.

3. Dickson D. Bruce, Jr., *Violence and Culture in the Antebellum South* (Austin: University of Texas Press, 1979), 96–97, notes white lower-class fathers' concern that their sons defend themselves.

4. Autobiography of Edward Isham. For a detailed description of life in the mining camps, see David Williams, *The Georgia Gold Rush: Twenty-niners, Cherokees, and Gold Fever* (Columbia: University of South Carolina Press, 1993), chaps. 5–6.

5. For a general treatment, see Malcolm J. Rohrbough, *The Trans-Appalachian Frontier: People, Societies, Institutions, 1776–1850* (New York: Oxford University Press, 1978).

6. Steven Hahn, *The Roots of Southern Populism: Yeoman Farmers and the Transformation of the Georgia Upcountry, 1850–1890* (New York: Oxford University Press, 1983); Bolton, *Poor Whites*. See also John C. Inscoe, *Mountain Masters, Slavery, and the Sectional Crisis in Western North Carolina* (Knoxville: University of Tennessee Press, 1989).

7. Bruce, *Violence and Culture*, 91, 93–94; Elliott J. Gorn, "'Gouge and Bite, Pull Hair and Scratch': The Social Significance of Fighting in the Southern Backcountry," *American Historical Review* 90 (February 1985): 18–43.

8. Autobiography of Edward Isham.

9. In addition to Gorn, "'Gouge and Bite,'" see Bruce, *Violence and Culture*, esp. chaps. 1 and 4; Edward L. Ayers, *Vengeance and Justice: Crime and Punishment in the Nineteenth-Century American South* (New York: Oxford University Press, 1983), chap. 1; and Bertram Wyatt-Brown, *Southern Honor: Ethics and Behavior in the Old South* (Oxford: Oxford University Press, 1982).

10. Autobiography of Edward Isham.

11. Autobiography of Edward Isham.

12. Autobiography of Edward Isham. Bruce, *Violence and Culture*, 94–95, describes such frontier families as functional units rather than fonts of emotional sustenance.

13. Lawrence M. Friedman, *Crime and Punishment in American History* (New York: Basic Books, 1993), 10. See also Louis P. Masur, *Rites of Execution: Capital Punishment and the Transformation of American Culture, 1776–1865* (New York: Oxford University Press, 1989).

14. During the late nineteenth century, reformers persuaded public officials to conduct executions behind penitentiary walls to shield refined sensibilities from the spectacle of public hangings. But from the late eighteenth century through Isham's time, citizens turned out in throngs to witness public hangings, often for the "pleasure and gratification," as one observer of an 1817 execution noted, "of seeing a wretched malefactor sent, with violence and ignominy, into eternity." "A large proportion of the multitude," noted the observer, "were females." Few commentaries better reflect the dynamic tension between moral outrage and voyeuristic fascination that animated viewers of these proceedings. See *Life & Confession of John Tuhi, (A Youth of 17 Years), Who Was Executed at Utica, (N.Y.) on Friday, July 25th, 1817, for the Murder of his Brother Joseph Tuhi* (N.p. [1817]), 11. For an intriguing analysis of the relationship between humanitarian reform and the popular fascination with sensational crime, as well as the developing equation between pain and pornography, see Karen Halttunen, "Humanitarianism and the Pornography of Pain in Anglo-American Culture," *American Historical Review* 100 (April 1995): 303–34. For a pioneering examination of the political-economic context of crime and punishment in eighteenth-century England, see Peter Linebaugh, *The London Hanged: Crime and Civil Society in the Eighteenth Century* (Cambridge: Cambridge University Press, 1992).

15. Culclasure, "'I Have Killed a Damned Dog,'" chapter 4 in this volume.

16. Contrast Schenck's apparent indifference to Isham's spiritual state with the concern expressed by the compilers of two early nineteenth-century confessions: Peter Stout, *The Last Speech, Confession, and Dying Words of Peter Stout . . .* (Morristown, N.J., 1803); and especially *A Full and Particular Narrative of the Life, Character and Conduct of John Banks, A Native of Nieuport, in Austrian Flanders . . .* (New York: n.p., 1807).

17. Autobiography of Edward Isham.

18. T. R. Gray, *The Confession, Trial and Execution of Nat Turner, The Negro Insurrectionist; also, a List of Persons Murdered in the Insurrection in Southampton County, Virginia, on the 21st and 22nd of August, 1831, with Introductory Remarks* (Petersburg, Va.: John B. Ege, 1831), 3–6, 4 (quoted passages). See also Kenneth S. Greenberg, ed., *The Confessions of Nat Turner and Related Documents* (Boston: Bedford Books of St. Martin's Press, 1996), 8–9.

19. H. A. Rockafield, *The Manheim Tragedy: A Complete History of the Double Murder of Mrs. Garber & Mrs. Ream: With the Only Authentic Life and Confession of Alexander Anderson. Together with a Correct Account of the Arrest, Trial . . . and Execution of Anderson and Henry Richards, his Accomplice* (Lancaster, Pa.: Printed at the Evening Express Office, 1858). "Authentic" is italicized in the original.

20. Halttunen, "Humanitarianism and the Pornography of Pain," 328–30.

21. For a sense of the puzzlement and frustration that compilers experienced when they encountered an unrepentant condemned man, see *The Genuine Declaration and Confession of William Morris, Alias Joseph Martin, Who Was Executed at Baltimore, on Friday the 22d of April, 1808. For the Murder of George Workner* (Philadelphia: n.p., [1808]).

22. For the testimony of condemned men regarding their turbulent early years, see: Rockafield, *Manheim Tragedy*, 27–31; Charles Cunningham, *The Dying Confession of Charles Cunningham . . .* (York, Pa.: Mc-Clellan, 1804), 3; William Gross, *The Last Words and Dying Confession of Wm. Gross Who Was Executed on the 7th of February, 1823, for the Murder of Kesiah Stow, in the City of Philadelphia. Being that which Was Given by Wm. Gross to Mr. Roberts, while under Sentence of Death, Containing his Full Confession and Experience while in Prison* (Philadelphia: Printed and Published for the Purchasers, [1823]), 3; *The Confession of John Battus, A Mulatto . . . Executed . . . for the Crimes of a Most Cruel Rape and Murder on the Body of Salome Talbott . . .* (N.p., [1804?]), 3–5; and *Life & Con-*

fession of John Tuhi, (A Youth of 17 Years), Who Was Executed at Utica, (N.Y.) on Friday, July 25th, 1817, for the Murder of his Brother Joseph Tuhi (N.p. [1817]), 3.

23. Thomas David Carr, *Life and Confession of Thomas D. Carr: Who Was Hung at St. Clairsville, Ohio, Thursday, March 24, 1870, for the Murder of Louisa C. Fox* (St. Clairsville, Ohio: J. H. Heaton, 1870), 3. Cunningham, *Dying Confession,* 4. Alexander Anderson credited canal boatmen with impressing their felonious ways, particularly the propensity to theft, upon him. See Rockafield, *Manheim Tragedy,* 28. For an insightful study of the lives (and the often vicious habits) of nineteenth-century canal diggers, see Peter Way, *Common Labour: Workers and the Digging of North American Canals, 1780–1860* (Cambridge: Cambridge University Press, 1993), esp. chap. 6.

24. Autobiography of Edward Isham.

25. Carr, *Life and Confession,* 3.

26. Cunningham, *Dying Confession,* 7.

27. Stout, *The Last Speech,* 6.

28. More than any other historian of early America, Alfred F. Young has explored the social and political dimensions, with their frequently violent manifestations, of working-class identity. See, for instance, his "George Robert Twelves Hewes (1742–1840): A Boston Shoemaker and the Memory of the American Revolution," *William and Mary Quarterly,* 3d ser., vol. 38 (October 1981): 561–623. See also Way, *Common Labour,* chaps. 6–8.

29. Gross, *Last Words and Dying Confession,* 4–6, 9–10. See also Christine Stansell, *City of Women: Sex and Class in New York 1789–1860* (New York: Alfred A. Knopf, 1986), esp. chaps. 4, 9.

30. Alexander Anderson describes these in Rockafield, *Manheim Tragedy,* 29–36.

31. Autobiography of Edward Isham.

32. Autobiography of Edward Isham.

33. Autobiography of Edward Isham.

34. Autobiography of Edward Isham.

35. Autobiography of Edward Isham.

36. Autobiography of Edward Isham.

37. Autobiography of Edward Isham.

38. Autobiography of Edward Isham.

39. For a contemporary overview of this variety, see Frederick Law

Olmsted, *The Cotton Kingdom: A Traveler's Observations on Cotton and Slavery in the American Slave States,* ed. Arthur M. Schlesinger, Sr., introd. Lawrence N. Powell (1861; reprint, New York: Modern Library, 1984), chap. 12.

40. Autobiography of Edward Isham.

41. Autobiography of Edward Isham.

42. See Wyatt-Brown, *Southern Honor,* esp. chap. 13, for a general treatment but one that tends to slight honor among the lower classes. See also Bruce, *Violence and Culture,* esp. chap. 4, "Violence in Plain-Folk Society."

43. Autobiography of Edward Isham.

44. Autobiography of Edward Isham.

45. Carr, *Life and Confession,* 5. Disputes over wages figured in recollections of other condemned men. See, for instance, Gross, *Last Words and Dying Confession,* 3.

46. See Victoria E. Bynum's "Mothers, Lovers, and Wives," chapter 6 in this volume. For recent studies of antebellum southern women, see Victoria E. Bynum, *Unruly Women: The Politics of Social and Sexual Control in the Old South* (Chapel Hill: University of North Carolina Press, 1992); Stephanie McCurry, *Masters of Small Worlds: Yeoman Households, Gender Relations, and the Political Culture of the Antebellum South Carolina Low Country* (New York: Oxford University Press, 1995); and Elizabeth Fox-Genovese, *Within the Plantation Household: Black and White Women of the Old South* (Chapel Hill: University of North Carolina Press, 1988).

47. Autobiography of Edward Isham.

48. Autobiography of Edward Isham.

49. Autobiography of Edward Isham.

50. Autobiography of Edward Isham.

51. Autobiography of Edward Isham.

52. Autobiography of Edward Isham.

53. Autobiography of Edward Isham.

54. Autobiography of Edward Isham.

55. Autobiography of Edward Isham.

56. Rockafield, *Manheim Tragedy,* 29–36.

57. Gross, *Last Words and Dying Confession,* 6–7, 9–10.

58. *Confession and Repentance of Lieutenant R. Smith, Who is Now under Sentence of Death for the Murder of Captain John Carson . . .* (Phila-

delphia: n.p., 1816), 6. See also *Account of the Execution of Lieutenant R. Smith for the Murder of Capt. J. Carson . . .* (Philadelphia: n.p., 1816) for the extenuating circumstances of the killing.

59. See Ira Berlin, *Slaves Without Masters: The Free Negro in the Antebellum South* (New York: Pantheon, 1974), 265–66, for other evidence of interracial sexual relationships.

60. Autobiography of Edward Isham.

61. Autobiography of Edward Isham.

62. Autobiography of Edward Isham.

63. Autobiography of Edward Isham.

64. Autobiography of Edward Isham. For an account of an antebellum slave who captained lumber flatboats on the Mississippi and its tributaries and numbered white and black men in his crews, see John Hebron Moore, "Simon Gray, Riverman: A Slave Who Was Almost Free," *Mississippi Valley Historical Review* 49 (December 1962): 472–84. The best general survey of free African Americans in the antebellum South remains Berlin, *Slaves Without Masters;* see esp. 44, 260–66, for evidence of interracial fraternization.

65. The premier student of the leveling of racial distinctions among southern evangelical sects during the early nineteenth century is John B. Boles. See his "Evangelical Protestantism in the Old South: From Religious Dissent to Cultural Dominance," in *Religion in the South,* ed. Charles Reagan Wilson (Jackson: University Press of Mississippi, 1985), esp. 28–29; and *Black Southerners, 1619–1869* (Louisville: University Press of Kentucky, 1983), esp. 156–62. See also Dickson J. Bruce, Jr., *And They All Sang Hallelujah: Plain-Folk Camp-Meeting Religion, 1800–1845* (Knoxville: University of Tennessee Press, 1974); and Donald G. Mathews, *Slavery and Methodism: A Chapter in American Morality, 1780–1845* (Princeton: Princeton University Press, 1965), chap. 3, and *Religion in the Old South* (Chicago: University of Chicago Press, 1977).

66. Gray, *Confession, Trial and Execution of Nat Turner,* 11.

67. On the fears regarding illicit trafficking with slaves, see Daniel R. Hundley, *Social Relations in Our Southern States,* ed. William J. Cooper, Jr. (1860; reprint, Baton Rouge: Louisiana State University Press, 1979), 226, 228–30; Joseph P. Reidy, *From Slavery to Agrarian Capitalism in the Cotton Plantation South: Central Georgia, 1800–1880* (Chapel Hill: University of North Carolina Press, 1992), chaps. 2–4; John Campbell, "As 'A Kind of Freeman?' Slaves' Market-Related Activities in the South Carolina

Up Country, 1800–1860," in *Cultivation and Culture: Labor and the Shaping of Slave Life in the Americas,* ed. Ira Berlin and Philip D. Morgan (Charlottesville: University Press of Virginia, 1993); and McCurry, *Masters of Small Worlds,* 116–21.

68. An especially insightful survey of such possibilities appears in John Hebron Moore, *The Emergence of the Cotton Kingdom in the Old Southwest: Mississippi, 1770–1860* (Baton Rouge: Louisiana State University Press, 1988), chap. 11. See also Richard C. Wade, *Slavery in the Cities: The South, 1820–1860* (New York: Oxford University Press, 1964).

69. See Hahn, *Roots of Southern Populism,* chaps. 1–2. Olmsted, *Cotton Kingdom,* 348–49, notes the importance of peddlers in acquainting slaves with a world beyond their masters' ken. Peddlers also figure in slaves' attempts to escape; see the advertisement for Gid in the *North Carolina Standard* (Raleigh) for June 30, 1836, printed in Freddie L. Parker, ed., *Stealing a Little Freedom: Advertisements for Slave Runaways in North Carolina, 1791–1840* (New York: Garland Publishing, 1994), 858–59.

70. Hundley, *Our Southern States,* 194.

71. Inscoe, *Mountain Masters,* 72–79, 88–89, 100. See also Williams, *Georgia Gold Rush,* 84–88.

72. It is striking that Isham provided the names of all his wives and consorts except for the "free girl." See Autobiography of Edward Isham. On perceptions of racial superiority among yeomen, see Hahn, *Roots of Southern Populism;* McCurry, *Masters of Small Worlds;* and Bolton, *Poor Whites.* For a stunning evocation of a particularly significant retreat into racial privilege in a more recent context, see James Goodman, *Stories of Scottsboro* (New York: Pantheon, 1994), chap. 3, esp. 21–22.

73. Rockafield, *Manheim Tragedy,* 40; Cunningham, *Dying Confession,* 13.

74. *Full and Particular Narrative,* quoted statements at 15, 6, 19, respectively.

75. Gray, *Confession, Trial and Execution of Nat Turner,* 22.

76. *The Genuine Declaration and Confession of William Morris, Alias Joseph Martin, Who Was Executed at Baltimore, on Friday the 22d of April, 1808. For the Murder of George Workner* (Philadelphia: n.p., [1808]), 7, 8, 11.

77. Gorn, "'Gouge and Bite,'" 24, 27–33, notes the importance of boasting in the personal interactions among men on the frontier.

78. Autobiography of Edward Isham.

79. Autobiography of Edward Isham.

80. Autobiography of Edward Isham.

81. Autobiography of Edward Isham. On "The Southern Bully," see Hundley, *Our Southern States,* chap. 6.

82. Autobiography of Edward Isham.

Appendix B: Superior Court Judge Robert R. Heath's Statement of the Case *State v. Hardaway Bone*

1. Robert R. Heath had received his master of arts degree from the University of North Carolina in May 1859, the time of James Cornelius's murder. President James Buchanan delivered the commencement address.

2. October 26, 1859.

3. Winchester Pegram was called for the petit jury. At the time of the 1860 federal census for Gaston County, he was a sixty-one-year-old farmer whose holdings included $4,425 of real estate and $10,600 of personal property.

4. Alexander Rutledge was called for the petit jury. He had moved to Stokes County by 1860 where, according to the federal census, he was a landless farmer who owned personal property valued at $300.

5. At age twenty-one, Henry Cornelius was the oldest of nine children listed by the 1860 federal census in the family of James's brother Austin and Austin's wife, Ann.

6. Austin Cornelius's holdings in Catawba County included real estate valued at $14,000 and personal property valued at $18,000. In 1860, at forty-nine years of age, he and his wife Ann, aged forty-four, were the parents of nine children, the youngest of whom was two years old. According to the agricultural schedule of the federal census, Cornelius produced 2,000 bushels of corn and 430 bushels of wheat during 1859 on a farm with 300 acres of improved land. Cornelius's operation was made possible by the labor of sixteen slaves (some of whom may previously have belonged to his deceased brother).

7. William Lander (1817–68) was a lawyer in Lincolnton, North Carolina, who later served as a member of the North Carolina General Assembly. After his election to the congress of the Confederacy, his seat in the North Carolina legislature was taken by David Schenck, also a native of Lincolnton, who had become Lander's law partner in 1860.

8. According to Isham's account, Jim, a slave belonging to Little, "came running with a rail in his hand" upon hearing Cornelius's cry for help. After he stabbed Cornelius, Isham was ready to throw a rock at Jim but stopped when he saw him being restrained by "the negro women." Ironically, none of the slaves who had seen the slaying could testify against a white person, even one as detested as Isham.

9. Thomas Beaty was a fifty-eight-year-old farmer who owned $4,000 of real estate and $12,200 of personal property, according to the 1860 federal census for Catawba County. He and his thirty-six-year-old wife Elizabeth had one child.

10. No mention of Isham's suit has been found in county court records; the case was probably tried before a local justice of the peace.

11. Jesse Cornelius of neighboring Iredell County owned $12,000 of real estate and $8,200 of personal property, according to the 1860 federal census. A fifty-five-year-old farmer, he and his forty-seven-year-old wife Margaret had six children.

12. Dr. Moore is not readily identifiable in census reports. The physician who attended the dying James Cornelius, neighbor J. J. Mott of Catawba County failed to appear at the trial, perhaps, as Thomas Beaty suggested in a statement appearing in the docket included in the Gaston County Superior Court minutes, because he was suffering from rheumatism. Nevertheless, Mott was fined by the court for failing to obey its summons, unless he came to explain his absence.

13. Thomas Lemly (or Lernly) is not readily identifiable in federal census reports.

14. Susan Reed (Reid) was the forty-six-year-old wife of Catawba County farmer William Reed (see note 16 below).

15. Beatties Ford.

16. William H. Reed (Reid), aged forty-seven, owned $200 of personal property, according to the 1860 federal census for Catawba County. The census for 1850 described Reed as a house carpenter. By 1870, the family, including Margaret F. Bone, had moved to Iredell County. William, Susan, and their eldest son, James H. Reed—with whom Margaret was living at the time of the 1880 federal census for Iredell County—were all illiterate.

17. William J. Sherrill of Catawba County.

18. A fine, light cloth resembling linen.

19. Albert Nance was living in Gaston County in 1860 where, as a twenty-two-year-old farmer, he owned no real property and $711 of personal property.

20. Washington Sherrill of Lincoln County, North Carolina.

21. Besides serving as sheriff, Jonas Cline was a farmer owning $4,000 of real estate and $7,775 of personal property, according to the 1860 federal census for Catawba County.

22. William K. Waugh of Johnson County, Tennessee.

Contributors

Charles C. Bolton is associate professor of history, director of the Center for Oral History and Cultural Heritage at the University of Southern Mississippi, and author of *Poor Whites of the Antebellum South: Tenants and Laborers in Central North Carolina and Northeast Mississippi* (1994).

Victoria E. Bynum is associate professor of history at Southwest Texas State University. She is the author of *Unruly Women: The Politics of Social and Sexual Control in the Old South* (1992); "Misshapen Identity: Memory, Folklore, and the Legend of Rachel Knight," in *Discovering the Women in Slavery*, edited by Patricia Morton (1996); "'White Negroes' in Segregated Mississippi: Miscegenation, Racial Identity, and the Law," *Journal of Southern History* (forthcoming); and *Mississippi's Longest Civil War: Memory, Community, and the "Free State of Jones"* (forthcoming).

Scott P. Culclasure earned his Ph.D. in curriculum and teaching at the University of North Carolina at Greensboro. He is coordinator of the International Baccalaureate at High Point Central High School, High Point, North Carolina (Guilford County Schools). He received the National Endowment for the Humanities/Reader's Digest Teacher-Scholar Award for 1991–92. Currently he is preparing his dissertation, "The Past As Liberation from History," for publication.

J. William Harris is associate professor and chairman of the Department of History at the University of New Hampshire. He is the author of *Plain Folk and Gentry in a Slave Society: White Liberty and Black Slavery in Augusta's Hinterlands* (1985) and editor of *Society and Culture in the Slave South* (1992).

David H. Kleit is a graduate student in the Department of History at Duke University. He is writing a dissertation about Cherokee Removal and the American resettlement of the lands taken from the Cherokees.

Joseph P. Reidy is professor of history at Howard University. He is the author of *From Slavery to Agrarian Capitalism in the Cotton Plantation South: Central Georgia, 1800–1880* (1992) and, with others, of *Freedom: A Documentary History of Emancipation, 1861–1867*, 4 vols. (1982–1993); *Free at Last: A Documentary History of Slavery, Freedom, and the Civil War* (1992); and *Slaves No More: Three Essays on Emancipation and the Civil War* (1992).

Index